The Evolution

of Spanish

The Evolution of Spanish

THIRD EDITION

by

TOM LATHROP

Juan de la Cuesta
Newark, Delaware

(302) 453–8695
Fax: (302) 453–8601

MANUFACTURED IN THE UNITED STATES OF AMERICA

ISBN: 0–936388–58–7

Contents

To the Memory of

BILLIE MAY TUNE

who died in a motorcycle
acccident in 1950
while returning to Los Angeles
from near Palm Springs.
She was about 20 years old,
a friendly, pretty young woman.

Preface to the Third Edition

WHEN I BEGAN TO STUDY the evolution of the Spanish language thirty *or so* years ago, I would have liked to find a concise historical grammar written in English and designed for the novice. I looked for but couldn't find such a volume. Later, as a professor of the same subject, I wanted that type of book for my students, but still none could be found. It was then that I decided to prepare this volume myself.

When you became interested in the Spanish language, chances are you didn't come equipped with a knowledge of Classical Latin. For this reason, the book's first chapter deals with the major features of that language, especially with those which are important to the development of Spanish. At the same time it describes the workings of Vulgar Latin—the spoken language of the masses. It was, after all, this spoken, simplified version of Latin, and not the Classical variety, which gave rise to the Romance Languages.

The second chapter deals with historical phonetics—the evolution of sounds—from Latin to Spanish. It assumes that you don't know the definitions or mechanics of the various processes that cause phonetic change, and each new feature or technical term is defined as it arises. Several examples illustrate each point, and these examples are clearly set off.

The third and final chapter deals with historical morphology—the development of nouns, adjectives, verbs, and so on—from Latin to Spanish, again with what I hope are good explanations and sufficient examples.

The difficult part about putting this book together was in deciding what to commit to print, and what to pass over in silence; what to explain in detail, what to simplify, and what to mention merely in passing. It is obvious that since language is the most complex invention of man, the development of a language must of necessity be an extraordinarily complicated subject, worthy of a series of volumes; this short manual cannot, therefore, answer—or even ask—every question. Its purpose is only to introduce you—a novice historical grammarian—to some of the facts and problems of the development of Spanish and to prepare you for a detailed study of the masterworks of Spanish historical grammar.

Since the object of the book is to describe the development of standard modern Spanish, it would be inappropriate to complicate and confuse issues by discussing dialectal developments. These have been mentioned on just a few occasions, and then only in passing. On the other hand, it seems both appropriate and useful to discuss Old Spanish developments when they contrast with or shed light on modern forms.

Likewise, since the goal of historical grammar is to trace the evolution of a language, this book focuses attention virtually exclusively on "traditional" developments, and excludes almost entirely "learned borrowings," since the latter, by definition, do not contribute to the understanding of the evolution of the language. A "traditional" word is one that has been in constant use (and therefore in constant evolution) from the days when Latin was spoken until the present. On the other hand, a "learned borrowing" is a word which has been taken in relatively recent times from Classical Latin vocabulary and integrated into the modern idiom with just a change or two to conform to current spelling and pronunciation. Frequently, both a "traditional" development and a "learned borrowing" deriving from the same Latin word exist in modern Spanish. For example, the traditional development of Latin *artículum* is *artejo* 'finger joint [= *articulation* point]' through a regular series of phonetic changes. The same Latin word has also given the learned *artículo* merely through the substitution of –o for the Latin –um. You should not be distressed, then, to find *artejo* listed as the only development of *artículum* (§§9, 77, 98, 102, 142), while no mention is made of the learned *artículo*.

Although Latin forms the foundation of Spanish, other languages, notably Arabic, Germanic, and French have contributed considerably to Spanish vocabulary. There are some standard volumes on the subject as well. Some good sources in English are W. J. Entwistle's *The Spanish Language* and R. K. Spaulding's *How Spanish Grew*; in Spanish, Rafael Lapesa's monumental *Historia de la lengua española* is the standard text.

If you are interested in more details about the topic of this book, consult Paul Lloyd's *From Latin to Spanish* (Philadelphia: American Philosophical Society, 1987–) and Ralph Penny's *A History of the Spanish Language* (Cambridge: Cambridge University Press, 1991).

A new feature of this third edition is the inclusion of much more information about the quality of Classical vowels and the timbre of Vulgar Latin vowels, as well as their stress. This is done particularly in the first chapter.

*   *   *

I would like to thank various people for their encouragement or helpful comments at various stages of the production of the work. Those people who read the typescript in its entirety include: Gerhard Probst of the Free University of Berlin, who was especially helpful in matters of Classical Latin culture; Richard Abraham of the University of Miami, whose kind words were greatly appreciated; Richard Kinkade of the University of Arizona, who read the work in an earlier version, and whose critique helped to shape this final format; and Martha Shopmyer, who, while she was my student, offered comments from the undergraduate's point of view. When the Latin chapter was being written, Marie Helmer, a Classicist and researcher who works in Madrid, answered numerous queries about Classical Latin morphology. When the chapter was finished it was read by my classical uncle, Richard O. Hale, professor emeritus at the University of North Dakota, and by Howard Marblestone of Lafayette College. Fredrick Agard, late of Cornell University, offered a valuable critique about a variant of the present chapter about Latin. The final two chapters were critiqued by Frede Jensen of the University of Colorado, my mentor in Romance Philology. I should also like to thank Samuel G. Armistead of the University of California, Davis, whose courses at UCLA gave me a foundation in Hispanic historical linguistics.

I also am grateful for comments given to me after the first edition of this book was published, either in reviews or in letters from colleagues. The published reviews include Paul A. Gaeng (*South Atlantic Review*, 48 [1983], 91–94), Ronald M. Barasch

(*Modern Language Journal*, 65 [1981], 446–47), Steven Dworkin (*La Corónica*, 10 [1981], 86–88), John M. Lipski (*Hispania*, 65 [1982], 318–19), Ralph Penny (*Bulletin of Hispanic Studies*, 59 [1982], 318–19), Nancy Joe Dyer (*Hispanic Review*, 51 [1983], 455–57), Juana Muñoz Liceras (*Revista canadiense de estudios hispánicos*, 9 [1985]), and Melvyn C. Resnick (*Journal of Hispanic Philology*, 7 [1982], 57–59). I owe a particular debt of gratitude to Steven Lee Hartman of Southern Illinois University for letting me see an advance copy of his review for *Romance Philology* (which appeared in 40 [1987], 525–29), and for additional comments sent to me in a letter. The second edition was reviewed in *Hispania* 72 (1989), 157–58, by William Patterson.

After they used the book in class, Joseph R. Jones of the University of Kentucky and Daniel Eisenberg of Florida State University gave me a number of useful suggestions. David Gies of the University of Virginia made additional valuable comments and corrections, and Thomas Suits of the University of Connecticut gave me some insights into the Latin content of the book. I also thank Gerald Culley of the University of Delaware who also answered my queries about Latin. I must confess that I did not take all of the suggestions made by my friends and colleagues listed above, and I am responsible for any lingering infelicities in the text.

I am grateful to Francisco Rico of the Real Academia Española, who considered this book valuable enough to include in his collection *Letras e Ideas*. In that series it bears the REALLY DRY title *Curso de gramática histórica española* (Barcelona: Ariel, 1984; second edition, 1989, first reprinting 1992, second reprinting 1995). The revisions, corrections, and bibliography (now updated) for the Spanish edition have been incorporated in this edition. It is a rare distinction for a foreign author to publish a book on this topic in Spain—I was the first, followed by Paul Lloyd and Ralph Penny. The Spanish edition was reviewed by Manuel Seco, of the Real Academia de la Lengua, *ABC Sábado Cultural*, (September 22, 1984), p. C–xv, by Steven Lee Hartman, *Romance Philology*, 40 (1987), 526–29, and by Barbara A. Lafford, *Hispania* 68 (1985), 330–31.

I have gone over the book many times and have marked the typographical errors that I have seen and that were pointed out to me. Some of my students used gallies of the second edition as a textbook, and they listed the misprints that they saw. These students, whom I thank here, include Robert MacPherson, Amy M. Jones, Derek Courson, Beth Worrilow (all Americans), and Manuel del Cerro, Eduardo Burrieza, Johanna González, and Estela García (all Spaniards). I also thank David Toccafondi of the University of Pennsylvania who is in large part responsible for reformatting the book from photocomposition to electronic typesetting. If you see anything that still needs fixing, please don't hesitate to communicate (lathrop@udel.edu or fax 800-784-4935).

I am indebted to the Del Amo Foundation of Los Angeles, whose research grant allowed me to prepare the first edition of this book in Madrid—much of it was done in the Casa de Velázquez's wonderful library. I also thank Hal Barnell who did the cover. It is a delight to work with Hal, who develops vague ideas into terrific visual concepts. Finally, I thank my wife, Connie, who read the entire project as it was being written, and whose expertise in matters of Romance historical grammar kept a great number of *bêtises* from leaving the family.

T.L.

Newark, Delaware
December, 1995

Phonetic Symbols and Diacritical Marks

Vowels

[i] as in Spanish *sí*
[ɪ] as in English *bit*
[e] as in Spanish *quepo*
[ɛ] as in Spanish *sentar*
[a] as in Spanish *hablo*
[ɔ] as is Spanish *flor*

[o] as is Spanish *cómo*
[ʊ] as is English *look*
[u] as is Spanish *lugar*
[y] as in Spanish *siento*
[w] as in Spanish *bueno*

A subscript hook under a vowel means that is it open. A subscript dot under a vowel means that it is close.

i̦ = [i]
i̧ = [ɪ]
ȩ = [e]
ȩ = [ɛ]

ǫ = [ɔ]
ọ = [o]
u̧ = [ʊ]
u̧ = [u]

Consonants

[p] as in Spanish *pierna*
[t] as in Spanish *tomar*
[k] as in Spanish *casa*
[b] as in Spanish *hambre*
[d] as in Spanish *andar*
[g] as in Spanish *tengo*
[β] as in Spanish *haber*
[đ] as in Spanish *bledo*
[ɣ] as in Spanish *hago*
[f] as in Spanish *favor*

[θ] as in Spanish *cinco* (Spain)
[s] as in Spanish *sed*
[z] as in English *zebra*
[ʃ] as in English *ship*
[ʒ] as in English *leisure*
[č] as in Spanish *chico*
[ǯ] as in English *jump*
[x] as in Spanish *ajo*
[ɫ] as in Spanish *calle* (Spain)
[ŋ] as in Spanish *tengo*

1
The Heritage of Vulgar Latin

§1. At the same time educated Romans were speaking and writing according to the rules of the Classical Latin language (*sermo urbanus*), the largely uneducated populace—foot soldiers, merchants, and laborers—were speaking (and writing, if they could) a less complex version of the language which we know as Vulgar Latin (*sermo vulgaris*).[1]

When Rome fell towards the end of the fourth century A.D., the educated ruling class disappeared, and with it the educated spoken and written language, Classical Latin, also faded away. But Vulgar Latin, spoken by the masses in the huge area between Lusitania and Dacia (modern Portugal and Romania), was easily able to survive the fall of the distant capital, and the disappearance of the Classical tongue—spoken by a very small portion of the Empire's population—went largely unnoticed by the ordinary people. It was therefore Vulgar Latin and not Classical Latin, which was to evolve day by day, century by century, into the Romance Languages.

Vulgar Latin differed from Classical Latin on all linguistic levels. Its vowels were quite distinct from Classical vowels, and its consonants showed certain variations as well. Vulgar Latin nouns and verbs were more simply organized than, or differed from, their Classical equivalents, and because of these differences, a number of changes had to take place in Vulgar Latin syntax. In its vocabulary, Vulgar Latin preferred emphatic, expressive, and diminutive words,

---

[1] Vulgar Latin is traditionally divided into Western and Eastern halves. Eastern Vulgar Latin gave rise to the Eastern Romance Languages (Italian and Rumanian), and Western Vulgar Latin gave rise to the Western Romance Languages (French, Spanish, Portuguese and Catalan).

and as a result, many of the less forceful and less picturesque
Classical words were not continued. Finally, Vulgar Latin readily
assimilated foreign words of diverse origin into its vocabulary,
unlike Classical Latin which accepted only a few, and those were
mostly from Greek.

But if Vulgar Latin was the spoken language of largely illiterate
speakers who spent their lives in lower military ranks, in market-
places, or at construction sites, how can we have any notion of what
their spoken language was like? Surprisingly, there is quite a bit of
information which survives in a number of written sources, but
mostly in bits and pieces.

You might think that the least likely place to look for data
concerning Vulgar Latin would be in the works of Classical authors,
yet there are a few good sources. In the comedies of Plautus (ca.
254–184 B.C.) some of the characters are modeled after "the man in
the street," and when they speak, we glimpse Vulgar Latin. The first
century satirist, Petronius, in his famous *Cena Trimalchionis*
'Trimalchio's Feast' describes a colorful banquet attended by the
lower classes of society, and in the characters' bawdy language we
can see traits of Vulgar Latin.

Turning to the works of untrained writers, you would naturally
expect to see the authors' speech habits reflected in their work, and
such was indeed the case. A good example of this is the *Peregrinatio
ad loca sancta* 'Pilgrimage to Holy Places' a description of the
travels of a nun to the Holy Land in the early centuries of our era.
The author's Latin prose anticipates some of the structures that the
Romance Languages would adopt and discards some that would be
later rejected by the Romance Languages.

There were a few treatises written by specialists who were qualified in their fields, but not so well qualified in the Classical idiom,
and from these we can also find information about Vulgar speech.
Mulomedicina Chironis was a manual written by the fourth century
veterinarian Chiro, in which he explains how to recognize and cure
a number of afflictions that might befall a mule. A cook of the same
period named Apicius wrote a cookbook, *De re coquinaria*, which

has both linguistic and culinary interest.[2] During the earlier Augustan period (43 B.C. to 13 A.D.) there lived a master architect named Vitruvius who wrote a treatise called *De architectura*,[3] ten short books on virtually every aspect of Roman architecture and city planning. Although he said that the architect had to be knowledgeable in many different fields, grammar was not necessarily one of them: "Non architectus potest esse grammaticus" 'It is not an architect who can be a grammarian'.

An extraordinarily rich source of Vulgar Latin is found among various types of inscriptions. In 79 A.D. Vesuvius erupted and its lava sealed the towns of Pompeii and Herculaneum. But through this terrible natural disaster a great linguistic service was rendered, because over five thousand precious and ordinarily quite perishable graffiti were preserved on almost every wall at Pompeii. Proclamations, humorous sayings, curses, shopping lists, campaign notices, and the customary coarse phrases were scrawled everywhere. These inscriptions were largely scribbled by the populace, and they provide a rich harvest of facts about Vulgar Latin. Another type of inscription is epitaphs found on gravestones (which were frequently carved by a semi–literate relative of the deceased).

Finally, the *defixionum tabellæ* 'execration tablets' contained a rather special type of Vulgar Latin inscription. Curses designed to bring misfortune to one's enemy or rival were carved onto lead tablets, and were then placed in graves or thrown into wells where they could there attract the attention of the dark forces.

Medieval word lists, called glossaries, are yet another valuable (although late) source of information about Vulgar Latin. The *Glossary of Reichenau* (named after the monastery where the document used to be kept) is the most important one for the Romance Languages. The purpose of this list was to explain some three thousand words of the Latin Vulgate Bible[4] which were no longer

---

[2] It is available in English published as a Dover paperback.

[3] Also available in English as a Dover paperback.

[4] The Vulgate is the Latin Bible prepared in about the year 400 A.D. by St. Jerome. It had been used throughout the Catholic world for a thousand years when it became the official Bible of the Catholic church at the Council of Trent in 1546. It is still available, and is now undergoing a

understood by eighth century readers. The archaic words of the Latin biblical text were glossed (that is, they were translated) in the margins with "contemporary" (eighth century) Vulgar Latin equivalents.

The most precious Vulgar Latin document is the famous *Appendix Probi*, a list of 227 "correct" Classical Latin forms followed by the "incorrect" Vulgar Latin forms (SAY THIS... NOT THIS... [*auriculas non oriclas*]). It was prepared by a Roman schoolteacher whose mission was to improve the pronunciation and declension skills of his students. However, for modern scholars, this anonymous schoolteacher has left a great wealth of facts about the *lingua franca* of the day. The list of words eventually came to be bound with a manuscript written by the first century grammarian, Probus; thus the list came to be known as the *Appendix Probi* 'Probus' Appendix'. You will see examples from the above sources throughout this chapter.

Many times a Vulgar Latin word that philologists would have liked to have found simply does not exist in any known source. In cases such as these, philologists have been able, through a critical comparison of forms taken from the old and modern Romance dialects, to reconstruct what a missing Vulgar Latin form *must have* been. When these reconstructed forms are cited, they are usually preceded by an asterisk to show that the form is hypothetical, or not as yet attested. Many forms which had formerly been "starred" (i.e., reconstructed), have actually been found in later manuscript discoveries, exactly as postulated.[5]

The Vulgar Latin Vocalic System

§2. In Classical Latin there were ten vowels; five were long

---

thorough revision.

[5] In this elementary introduction to the development of the language, I felt that making a differentiation between the hypothetical and the attested forms was of little pedagogical use to the novice historical grammarian, and for this reason no asterisks precede any Latin forms in this book. As your philological skills and inquisitiveness grow, you may consult more detailed volumes which will distinguish the unattested forms. Hypothetical *Spanish* words *are* preceded by an asterisk.

(nowadays marked with ⁻ called "macron") and five were sh (marked with ˘ called "breve," pronounced [brɛv]).⁶ The difference in the length of vowels was crucial to the meaning of words, as these examples clearly show: *légit* (with long *e*) meant '[someone] read' while *légit* (with short *e*) meant '[someone] reads'. The noun *ōs* (with long *o*) meant 'mouth' while *ŏs* (with short *o*) meant 'bone'. Vowel length affected unstressed as well as stressed vowels: *frúctūs* (with long unstressed final vowel) meant 'fruits' while *frúctŭs* meant 'a fruit'.

§3. In Vulgar Latin, however, vowels were not distinguished by length but by TIMBRE. A Classical long vowel became a Vulgar Latin CLOSE vowel⁷ and a Classical short vowel became a Vulgar Latin OPEN vowel.

The notion of close and open vowels can be easily grasped: when you articulate a close *e* [e] (as in Sp. *quepo*) your mouth is physically more closed than when you articulate an open *e* [ɛ] (as in Sp. *quién*). Similarly, when you articulate a close *o* [o] (as in Sp. *cosa*), your mouth is more closed than when you articulate the open *o* [ɔ] (as in Sp. *favor*).

The VOWEL TRIANGLE⁸ graphically illustrates the arrangement of open and close vowels: While you are pronouncing the sound [i], you cannot put your finger into your mouth since the [i] is articulated too close to your top teeth. When you say [a], your tongue is at its

---

⁶ Classical Latin authors used no macrons nor breves. These diacritical marks are a convenience for the modern reader. Usually only the macron is used nowadays, and this book follows the norm; but when the breve is useful for pedagogical purposes, it, too, has been included. In a number of sections, mostly dealing with problems of stress, accent marks have also been included.

⁷ Vowels are *close* not *closed*. "Close" is pronounced like *closed*, but without the *–d*.

⁸ The 'vowel triangle' is very useful for pedagogical purposes, but points of articulation do not correspond *exactly* to the outline given in the figure, as all phoneticians recognize. For more details about points of articulation, the reader can consult Harry Deferrari's *The Phonology of Italian, Spanish and French* (Washington: 1954), and standard phonetics manuals.

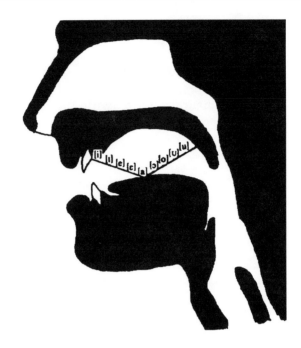

lowest level, giving doctors a nice view of your tonsils. When you produce the [u] sound, the front part of your mouth will be vacant, while your tongue is arched at the back of your mouth. These three points of reference give you an idea of the workings of the vowel triangle.

[i], [ɪ], [e], and [ɛ] are called FRONT VOWELS since they are articulated in the front of the mouth; [a] is called a CENTRAL VOWEL; and, finally, [ɔ], [o], [ʊ], and [u] are called BACK VOWELS. Similarly, [i] and [u] are called HIGH VOWELS while [e], [ɛ], [o], and [ɔ] are called MID–VOWELS.

If an *e* changes to an *i*, or if an *o* changes to a *u*, they are said to BE RAISED, or INFLECTED, since their points of articulation move higher on the vowel triangle. In §§7ab and 17b there are examples of raised vowels.

At the top of the next page are examples of how these nine vowels sound. Notice your tongue position as you produce these vowels:

[i] as in Spanish *sí*
[ɪ] as in English b*i*t
[e] as in Spanish *quepo*
[ɛ] as in Spanish *sentar*
[a] as in Spanish *hablo*
[ɔ] as is Spanish *flor*
[o] as is Spanish *cómo*
[ʊ] as is English l*oo*k
[u] as is Spanish l*u*gar

§4. What follows, then, are the differences between the vocalic systems of Classical and Vulgar Latin.[9] The nine vowels of the vowel triangle represent the *initial* Western Vulgar Latin version of the ten Classical vowels, but this stage was short lived since two sets of neighboring vowels were to simplify.[10] The open *i* [ɪ] merged with the close *e* [e], and the open *u* [ʊ] merged with the close *o* [o]. The chart below shows this double change:

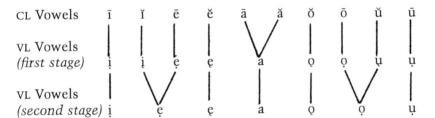

---

[9] Vulgar and Classical Latin were spoken during the same historical period, so they were variants of the *same* language (showing the types of differences we see nowadays between the speech of educated versus illiterate people).

[10] It is important to show both levels of Vulgar Latin vowels here because most inscriptions were *written* using the vowels given in the *first* stage of development, yet when the language was spoken, speakers undoubtedly pronounced according to the *second* stage. Bear this disconcerting inconsistency in mind when looking at the Vulgar Latin examples in this book, most of which derive from inscriptions.

CL lītem > VL lị̄te (Sp. *lid*)
CL vĭces > VL vẹces (Sp. *veces*)
CL sētam > VL sẹta (Sp. *seda*)
CL pĕdem > VL pẹde (Sp. *pie*)
CL pătrem > VL patre (Sp. *padre*)
CL prātum > VL pratu (Sp. *prado*)
CL nŏvem > VL nọve (Sp. *nueve*)
CL flōrem > VL flọre (Sp. *flor*)
CL bŭccam > VL bụcca (Sp. *boca*)
CL mūrum > VL mụru (Sp. *muro*)

§5. The three Classical Latin diphthongs (æ, œ, *au*) showed some divergence in Vulgar Latin. The first two (æ and œ) always simplified (æ > ẹ and œ > ẹ):

CL cæcum > VL cẹcu (Sp. *ciego*)
CL cælum > VL cẹlu (Sp. *cielo*)
CL fœdam > VL fẹdu (Sp. *feo*)

However, the diphthong *au* sometimes simplified to *o* in Vulgar Latin, and sometimes it did not:

CL *au*riculas > VL oriclas (Sp. *orejas*)
CL c*au*sam > VL c*au*sa (Sp. *cosa*)

The first example above is from the *Appendix Probi*: *auriculas non oriclas*.

   a. A few more comments need to be made about the *au*. In Vulgar Latin, if an unstressed *au* was followed by a syllable containing a *u*, the *au* regularly lost its [w] element and simplified to [a]:

CL *au*scultare > VL *a*scultare (Sp. *escuchar*)
CL *au*gustum > VL *a*gustu (Sp. *agosto*)
CL *au*gurium > VL *a*guriu (Sp. *agüero*)

The Spanish *escuchar* shows a CHANGE IN PREFIX (§157a) which accounts for its initial *e*.

   b. An *au* was created in Vulgar Latin by the loss of –*i* in the third person singular ending of the perfect active indicative (equivalent to the Spanish preterite) of the first conjugation verbs (§58a): CL *laudávit* > VL *laudáut* (Sp. *loó*), CL *cantávit* > VL *cantáut* (Sp. *cantó*). This phenomenon is unusual because it is one of the rare cases when a final Classical Latin vowel was not retained in Vulgar Latin.

§6. There was one case of a vowel appearing in Vulgar Latin where there had been none in Classical Latin. An *i–*, later to become *e–* in Western Romance through normal phonetic evolution, began to appear at the beginning of a word that began with *s* + consonant. The earliest known example dates from 79 A.D. in Pompeii: CL *Smyrma* > VL *Ismurna*—it was the name of a local prostitute scribbled on the outside of a brothel. There are many other attested examples from other parts of the Roman Empire showing more common words: CL *schŏla* > VL *iscola* (Sp. *escuela*), CL *státuam* > VL *istatua* (Sp. *estatua*), CL *scríptam* > VL *iscríta* (Sp. *escrita*).

Why did this change come about? The reason is that in all other cases where there was an *s* + consonant in Latin, the *s* ended the preceding syllable: *pás–tor* 'shepherd', *aus–cul–tá–re* 'to listen' *do–més–ti–cus* 'domestic'. The addition of the *i–* (called a PROTHETIC vowel by philologists) was initiated in order to regularize the sound system, allowing the *s* to end a syllable, as it usually did when a consonant followed. Vulgar Latin speakers often could not tolerate seeming irregularities, and they endeavored to "correct" them, as in this case.

§7a. In Classical Latin, when an *e* was in HIATUS [*hi! ate´ us*] with another vowel (that is, when an *e* was in contact with another vowel), each vowel counted as a separate syllable: *ví–ne–a* (Sp. *viña*) had three syllables, as did *lán–ce–a* (Sp. *lanza*) and *cá–ve–a* 'cage'. In Vulgar Latin, these *e*'s turned into the SEMI–VOWEL[11] [y] and the result of the process was that the words lost a syllable as the

---

[11] A PURE VOWEL is a sound produced with tongue and mouth in a stationary position; a SEMI–VOWEL is produced with the organs of speech moving; these semi–vowels are often called GLIDES—a very descriptive term, since your tongue does glide from one vowel position to another when producing a semi–vowel.

semi–vowel merged with the following vowel to form a single syllable: VL *vínia* [ví–nya], *láncia* [lán–tsa], *cávia* [ká–vya]. The three examples cited above are from the *Appendix Probi*:

> vinea non vinia
> lancea non lancia
> cavea non cavia

One also sees at Pompeii the two syllable *ábiat* [á–byat] for the three syllable *hábeat* [á–be–at].

The creation of the semi–vowel [y], which is known as YOD [yád] (after the Hebrew vowel of the same name), was to bring about far–reaching changes in both the Spanish vocalic and consonantal systems. In the history of Spanish, *yods* developed from a number of sources—this one was the earliest.

b. If a stressed *e* or *i* was in hiatus, one of two things happened. In a short word, the stressed vowel was raised, as in these attested examples:

> CL mĕa > VL mía
> CL vĭa > VL vía

Ordinarily, of course, the CL stressed *ĕ* becomes *ę* in Vulgar Latin, and not *i*, and the CL *i* becomes Vulgar Latin *ę*.

c. In longer words, the stress moved to the more open of the vowels. This phenomenon produced a *yod* as the stress changed place:

> CL mŭlíerem > VL muliére (Sp. *mujer*)
> CL lĭntéolum 'handkerchief' > VL lintiólu (Sp. *lenzuelo* 'tarpaulin for carrying straw')
> CL paríetem > VL pariéte > paréte (Sp. *pared*)

In the last example, the *yod* of *parete* seems to have been swallowed up in the course of its development by the *r*, giving the attested VL *parete*.

§8. In hiatus, like vowels contracted:

> CL librariĭ 'copiers' > VL librári
> CL lignáriĭ 'carpenters' > VL lignári
> CL mŏrtŭus (Sp. *muerto*) > VL mǫrtus
> CL ingĕnŭus 'natural' > VL ingęnus
> CL cárdŭus 'thistle' > VL cárdus

The fourth century grammarian Charisius commented: "Carduus trium syllabarum est" 'Cardus is of three syllables,' thus emphasizing that *cardus* (with only two syllables), "incorrect" in the Classical language, must have been the form in current use in his own time.

§9. Finally, a characteristic of the Western Vulgar Latin vocalic system that was to have a great effect on the development of Spanish consonants was that the unstressed vowels in the middle of words began to fall. This falling of vowels is known as SYNCOPE (*sing´ cuppy*); there are a number of examples of this feature in the *Appendix Probi*:

> speculum non speclum (Sp. *espejo*)
> masculus non masclus (Sp. *macho*)
> vetulus non veclus (Sp. *viejo*)
> articulus non articlus (Sp. *artejo*)
> oculus non oclus (Sp. *ojo*)

a. As the vowel fell, its absence sometimes created consonant clusters that had been unknown in the middle of Latin words, such as –scl– and –cl–. As Vulgar Latin developed, it had to cope with the new consonant clusters as well as it could—the Spanish results indicate that the clusters passed through a number of stages. The fall of the vowel in CL *vĕtulus* "should have" given VL vętlus, but since the –tl– cluster was so foreign to Latin, it quickly changed to the –cl– cluster, which was fast becoming common.

b. Many times after syncope, the resulting consonant cluster was one that had already existed in Classical Latin and it offered no phonetic complications:

CL áridus 'arid' > VL árdus
CL sólidus (Sp. *sueldo*) > VL sóldus
CL vǐridis (Sp. *verde*) > VL vi̯rdis
CL pǒsitus (Sp. *puesto*) > VL póstus

The Vulgar Latin Consonantal System

§10. A development which was to have far–reaching effect on Vulgar Latin grammar was the universal loss of final –m on words longer than one syllable; this phenomenon dates from the third century B.C. Here are some examples from the *Appendix Probi*:

> pridem non pride 'some time ago'
> olim non oli 'formerly'
> idem non ide 'the same'
> numquam non nunqua (Sp. *nunca*)

Just how the loss of final –m affected Vulgar Latin grammar will be seen in §24.

In monosyllabic words, the final –m generally was preserved throughout Vulgar Latin: CL *quěm* > VL *quem* (Sp. *quien*), CL *cǔm* > VL *cu̯m* (Sp. *con*), CL *tam* > VL *tam* (Sp. *tan*), CL *rěm* > VL *re̯m* (OSp. *ren* 'thing').

§11a. Another phonetic feature of Western Vulgar Latin was the change of *p*, *t*, and the *k* sound to *b*, *d*, and *g* when between vowels (that is, in INTERVOCALIC position) or when between a vowel and *r*. This process, known as VOICING, is illustrated in these examples attested in inscriptions:

> CL trǐticum > VL tri̯dicu (Sp. *trigo*)
> CL inmūtávit > VL inmu̯dávit '[someone] changed'
> CL pūtorem > VL pu̯dore (Sp. *pudor*)
> CL lěpra > VL lébra 'leprosy'
> CL frǐcāre > VL fregáre (Sp. *fregar*)
> CL mícat > VL mi̯gat '[someone] trembles'

b. If *p*, *t*, and *k* became *b*, *d* and *g* in Vulgar Latin, the question must arise just what happened to Classical Latin *b*, *d*, and *g* between vowels? Although the *b* remained strong, as time passed, Classical *d* and *g* tended to fall; in fact, even in Vulgar Latin the intervocalic *g* had changed to a *yod* and had already begun to fall, especially before *i*:

> CL mágĭster > VL maester 'teacher'
> CL rēgína > VL reína (Sp. *reina*)
> CL mágis > VL máis (Sp. *más*)
> CL vīgĭnti > VL vi̦i̦nti (Sp. *veinte*)
> CL trīgĭnta > VL tri̦i̦nta (Sp. *treinta*)

§12. The Classical Latin *v* was originally a semi–vowel pronounced [w]; *vīvō* 'I live' was pronounced [wíwo] and *vīnum* was pronounced [wínum]. Among other proofs, this fact is borne out by Greek transliterations of Latin words (that is, the way Greeks wrote Latin words they heard using Greek characters). The name of the Roman Emperor NERVA (32–98 A.D.) was transliterated Νέρουας [néruas]. The man's name VALERIUS was transliterated Οὐαλέριος [ualérios], and the volcano VESUVIUS was Οὐεσούιον [uεsúion]. After the first century of our era, however, we find the Classical *v* transliterated with a beta [β = b]: *Nerva* > Νέρβας [nérbas], *Vesuvius* > βέσβιον [bésbion].

In Vulgar Latin, it was this [b] that became the standard pronunciation for both Vulgar Latin *b* and *v*, thus causing the one to be hopelessly confused with the other in spelling. Our Roman schoolteacher tried to correct this confusion in the *Appendix Probi*:

> baclus non vaclus 'cane'
> vapulo non baplo 'I am beaten'
> plebes non plevis 'plebeian class'

Additional examples are found in inscriptions intended to be in Classical Latin, carved by people who were only semi–literate: CL *ūnĭvérsis* > VL *unibérsis*, CL *cīvitátis* > VL *cibitátis* 'of a city', CL *vīxit* > VL *bíxit* '[someone] lived'.

§13. In Classical Latin, the *c* was pronounced [k] before all vowels. Our modern notion that the Classical *c* was pronounced [č] before *e* and *i* derives from the way it came to be pronounced, through normal phonetic development, at the time of the Carolingian Renaissance (ca. 800 A.D.), when vigorous efforts were made to restore Classical Latin as a *lingua franca*; this late pronunciation has been with us ever since.

There is a number of proofs, however, which clearly show that the Classical *c* was pronounced [k]. In the Logudurese dialect of Sardinian, recognized as the phonetically least developed of any Romance dialect, the [k] has been preserved before *e* and *i*: CL *cérvum* 'deer' > Log. *kẹrbu*; CL *céram* 'wax' > Log. *kẹra*; Late Latin *cĭrcáre* 'to go across' > Log. *kịrcáre*; CL *cǽlum* 'sky' > Log. *kẹlu*.

Some Classical Latin words were borrowed by Old Germanic during the time of the Roman Empire, and modern German still preserves the ancient [k]: CL *cellárium* 'cellar' > Germ. *Keller*; CL *ceráseam* > Germ. *Kirsch* 'cherry'; CL *Cǽsar* > Germ. *Kaiser*.

The Romans conquered the Iberian Peninsula in about 200 B.C., and, from the earliest days, Latin loanwords went into Basque, the pre–Roman language of the northern part of the peninsula. CL *pácem* 'peace' > Basque *báke* was one of the early loanwords; the [k] is still preserved.

In Vulgar Latin, the *c* remained [k] before a central or back vowel, but before a front vowel it PALATALIZED (that is, it came to be pronounced against the roof of the mouth, the PALATE) and then became the sound [ts]. The evolution seems to have been this: *cĕntu* [kéntu] > [kyéntu] > [tyéntu] > [tséntu].

a. As the third and fourth stages of the above series indicate, *t* + *yod* also developed to the sound [ts] in Vulgar Latin. There are inscriptions from the third century with spelling errors because of the confusion between *ti* and *ci*, which were both pronounced the same: *terminaciones* for *terminationes*, *definiciones* for *definitiones*, and *terciae* for *tertiæ*. A Vulgar Latin word which passed into Germanic, probably in the fifth century A.D., also confirms the [ts] pronunciation. Germ. *Zins* [tsins] from CL *cénsus* 'census'.

b. The *qu* cluster, which had been pronounced [kw] in all cases in Classical Latin, simplified to [k] before all vowels (except *a*) in Vulgar Latin:

CL sĕquī [sékwi] > VL sęqui̧re [sɛkíre] (Sp. *seguir*)
CL quĕm [kwɛm] > VL quęm [kɛm] (Sp. *quien*)
CL quiētum [kwiétum] > VL quętu [kétu] 'quiet'
CL quŏmodo [kwómodo] > VL cǫmodo [kómodo] (Sp. *como*)

When did [kw] simplify to [k]? It must have been only after the Latin [k] had changed to [ts] before *e* and *i*, otherwise the Spanish result of the first two examples would have been the non–existent *secir and *cen.

There is one example, however, where *qu* before *i did* become [ts]. CL *quīnque* [kwíŋkwe] gave VL *cinque* [tsíŋke] (Sp. *cinco*) through the loss of the first *u* by DISSIMILATION (§149). That is, since speakers of a language sometimes do not tolerate two like sounds in the same word (and this is certainly true in the case of Spanish speakers), one of the sounds may be changed in some way, or even eliminated, as it is here, where *kw – kw* changed to *k – kw*, early enough for the first *k* to evolve to [ts].

c. Before *a*, the [kw] usually remained intact: CL *quando* [kwándo] > VL [kwándo] (Sp. *cuando*).

§14. The *h* sound had disappeared very early, before Classical Latin had become a literary language, although the *h* remained in Classical Latin spelling. In Vulgar Latin, since no *h* was pronounced, none was written. At Pompeii, *abiat* was written for *habeat* (Sp. *haya* has a restored h-), *anc* for *hanc* 'this', *omo* for *hŏmo* 'man', *ora* for *hōra* (Sp. *hora*, again with a restored h). The *Appendix Probi* gives this orthographic admonition:

> hostiæ non ostiae 'victims'
> adhuc non aduc 'until now'

§15. In Vulgar Latin, a number of consonant clusters simplified. Here are some attested examples:

a. *ns > s*

> ansa non asa (Sp. *asa*) [*Appendix Probi*]
> mensa non mesa (Sp. *mesa*) [*Appendix Probi*]

CL consideráte > VL cosideráte 'consider'
CL mónstrat > VL móstrat (Sp. muestra)
CL Rōmanénses > VL Romanéses 'Romans'
CL spónsæ > VL ispóse 'spouse'

Since –ns– simplified quite early to –s–, old and modern Spanish words with –ns– are borrowings directly from Classical Latin; *defensa, inmensa, pensar, recompensa, cansar* and *ansia* are examples of these.

 b. *ps > ss*

CL ípse > VL isse (Sp. ese)
CL ípsam > VL issa (Sp. esa)
CL scrípsit > VL scrisset '[someone] wrote'

 c. *pt > tt*

CL sĕptem > VL sétte (Sp. siete)

 d. *rs > ss*

CL dŏrsum > VL dossu 'back'
CL ŭrsum > VL ussu (Sp. *oso*)
CL sŭrsum > VL susu (OSp. *suso*)
CL pĕrsóna > VL pessóna 'person'

Sp. *persona* is a learned borrowing.

 e. *nct > nt*

CL cínctus > VL cintus 'cinched'
CL dēfŭnctus > VL defuntus 'dead'
CL sánctum > VL sántu (Sp. santo)

 f. *mn > nn*

CL alŭmnus > VL alunnus 'student'

CL dámnum > VL dánnu (Sp. daño)

Sp. *alumno* is obviously a learned word.

    g. *gr* > *r*

        CL íntĕgrum > VL intéru (§17c) (Sp. *entero*)
        CL pĭgrítia > VL pirítia (Sp. *pereza*)

Vulgar Latin Stress

§16. To understand Vulgar Latin stress patterns, you need to know about Classical Latin stress. If a Classical Latin word had only one syllable, it was stressed on that syllable:

        mḗl (Sp. *miel*)
        ṓs 'mouth'
        nŏ́x 'night'
        mū́s 'mouse'

A word that is stressed on the last syllable (= ULTIMA) is called OXYTONIC. In Classical Latin there are no oxytonic words except for the monosyllabics.

If a word has two syllables, it is stressed on the first:

        ĕ́mo 'I buy'
        cănis 'dog'
        ĕ́rrăt 'he wanders'
        hṓra (Sp. *hora*)

Philologists use PAROXYTONIC to mean "stressed on the next–to–last syllable" (= PENULT). A great percentage of Classical Latin words are paroxytonic.

If a word has more than two syllables in it, it can be paroxytonic or PROPAROXYTONIC, that is, "stressed three syllables from the end" (= ANTEPENULT) according to this simple rule: if the next–to–last syllable contains a long vowel, the word is paroxytonic; if it contains a short vowel, the word is proparoxytonic:

Paroxytonic Stress	*Proparoxytonic Stress*
natū́ra 'nature'	sátĭra 'satire,
servī́le (Sp. *servil*)	fácĭlis (Sp. *fácil*)
convḗnit 'he met'	cónvĕnit 'he meets'
extrḗmus 'extreme'	lī́bĕri 'children'

There is one variation of this rule. A short syllable is considered long for purposes of stress if a consonant ends the syllable. Classicists call the syllable LONG BY POSITION in this circumstance, as these examples show:

extĕ́rnus (ex–tĕ́r–nus) 'foreign'
invĭ́ctus (in–vĭ́c–tus) 'unconquered'
contĭ́ngit (con–tĭ́n–git) 'it borders on'
tempĕ́stas (tem–pĕ́s–tas) 'storm'

§17. The general rule is that the Classical Latin stressed vowel remained as the Vulgar Latin stressed vowel, even if there was syncope: CL vĭ́ridis > VL vĭ́rdis, CL ŏ́culus > VL ŏ́clus.
     a. There were, however, three cases where the stress did change place in Vulgar Latin. The first instance has already been seen in the section dealing with hiatus (§7c): CL paríetem > VL pariéte, CL lintéolum > VL lintiólum.
     b. The second stress change affected a number of verbs with prefixes. Before showing this change in stress, it is important for you to know a few facts about the effect of prefixes. In Classical Latin, when a prefix was added to a verb (or noun or adjective, for that matter), it usually raised the stem vowel of the verb:

tángō 'I touch'; contĭ́ngit 'it borders on'
fáciō 'I make'; perfĭ́cō 'I finish'
cláudō 'I close'; inclū́dō 'I include'

If the rules permitted, the stress shifted to the prefix:

cádō 'I fall'; óccĭdō 'I fall down'
tĕ́net 'he holds' rétĭnet '[someone] retains'
prĕ́mō 'I press'; cómprĭmō 'I compress'

Now, here is where the stress change took place. If Vulgar Latin speakers recognized that the verb was a compound, the original stem vowel was restored and the accent shifted back to the stem of the verb. Note how Spanish keeps the Vulgar Latin stress:

CL récĭpit > VL recípit (Sp. recibe)
CL cóntĭnet > VL conténet (Sp. contiene)
CL rétĭnet > VL reténet (Sp. retiene)
CL cónvĕnit > VL convénit (Sp. conviene)

But if the verb was not recognized as a compound, the stress remained where it had been in Classical Latin: CL cóllŏcat (= cum + lŏcat) > VL cóllcat (Sp. cuelga); CL cómpŭtō (= cum + pŭtō) > VL cómputo (Sp. cuento). Needless to say, the Spanish coloco and computo are learned words.

c. The third shift in stress did not affect many words. If a proparoxytonic word had a stop + r in the last syllable, the stress was attracted to the next–to–last syllable. (A STOP is a sound produced first by stopping and then releasing the air from within the mouth; examples include [p, t, k, b, d, g].) This phenomenon is quite easy to grasp through the examples below:

CL íntĕgrum > VL intégru (Sp. entero)
CL cáthĕdra > VL catédra (Sp. cadera)
CL cólŭbra > VL colúbra (Sp. culebra)
CL ténĕbras > VL tenébras (Sp. tinieblas)

The Vulgar Latin Declension System

§18. In order to understand the Vulgar Latin DECLENSIONS (that is, the systems used to show grammatical functions of nouns and adjectives) it is first necessary for you to understand Classical declensions.[12] From Indo–European linguistic stock, Classical Latin

---

[12] Declensions are to nouns what conjugations are to verbs. If you are learning a new Spanish verb and you know that it is "–ir stem changing," for example, you can instantly give any form of any tense. Similarly, if you know that a certain noun belongs to the third declension, you can derive

inherited three genders, a wealth of grammatical endings, and five different declension groups.

The three classical genders were MASCULINE, FEMININE, and NEUTER. Except for male and female beings (hōmo, m 'man' and múlier, f 'woman', for example), the genders were arbitrarily distributed, as the examples below show:

Masculine	Feminine	Neuter
pēs 'foot'	manus 'hand'	caput 'head'
sūcus 'juice'	aqua 'water'	lāc 'milk'
panis 'bread'	mēnsa 'table'	vīnum 'wine'

In Classical Latin, suffixes attached to nouns told their grammatical function. There were six suffixes for the singular and six for the plural. These twelve forms grouped together form a "declension." As an example of the various endings and functions the declension of amīcus, m 'friend' (of the second declension) is given below:

	Singular	Plural
nominative	amícus	amīcī
genitive	amíci	amīcórum
dative	amícō	amícīs
accusative	amícum	amícōs
ablative	amícō	amícīs
vocative	amíce	amīcī

✓ The NOMINATIVE case (that is, a noun with the nominative suffix added) indicates that the noun is the subject of the sentence: **Amīcus est hīc** 'A friend is here'. The GENITIVE case means that the noun possesses (something): **Dōmus amīcī** 'The house of a friend'. The DATIVE case means that the noun is the indirect object: **Dō panem amīcō** 'I give bread to a friend'. The ACCUSATIVE case means that the noun is the direct object: **Videō amīcum** 'I see a friend'.

---

what the genitive plural, or any other form, is. There is a maximum of only twelve declined forms of any noun.

The ABLATIVE case has a number of functions; one of its common uses is as the object of a preposition: **Vadō cum *amīcō*** 'I go *with a friend*'. The VOCATIVE case is used in direct address: **O, *amīce*!** 'Oh, friend!' Only the singular was given here—the plural endings have the same meanings.

§19. Classical Latin nouns fall into five declensions. The first declension is composed almost exclusively of feminine nouns and is characterized by an –*a*– in most of its endings. There is a great number of first declension nouns:

puella,–æ[13] *f* 'girl'

nom.	puélla	puéllæ
gen.	puéllæ	puéllārum
dat.	puéllæ	puéllīs
acc.	puéllam	puéllas
abl.	puéllā	puéllīs

The vocative case in all declensions but the second (such as with *amīcus*, above) is exactly like the nominative form, thus it is not listed here. The function of those forms that are spelled the same becomes apparent in context.

§20. The second declension is comprised of masculine and neuter nouns, and is characterized by the endings given below. There is a great number of second declension nouns as well.

---

[13] In Latin grammars and dictionaries, the genitive singular endings of nouns is listed with the nominative singular: *puella,–æ*. This is particularly useful since the genitive is the best form to use in order to distinguish which declension a noun belongs to. There are five distinct genitive singular endings, one for each declension. Since the nominative form can be misleading, as you will see, the genitive singular ending is essential to tell what the noun's declension is. If you can't distinguish the declension, you don't know what endings to put on the noun.

	servus,–ī *m* 'slave,		dōnum, –ī *n* 'gift'	
	Singular	*Plural*	*Singular*	*Plural*
nom.	servus	servī	dōnum	dōna
gen.	servī	servōrum	dōnī	dōnōrum
dat.	servō	servīs	dōnō	dōnīs
acc.	servum	servōs	dōnum	dōna
abl.	servō	servīs	dōnō	dōnīs
voc.	serve	servī	dōnum	dōna

A few masculine second declension nouns, such as *púer, –ī*, m 'boy' have no *–us* in the nominative singular, but otherwise they follow the pattern regularly.

Notice that the neuter forms, here and in all other declensions have the same form in the accusative that they have in the nominative within each number.

✓ §21. The third declension has masculine, feminine, and neuter nouns, and is more complicated than the first two declensions. Its complexity comes from four causes. First, the gender of the nouns is not automatic as it almost always is in the first two declensions. Second, there are variant sets of case endings. Third, the stressed syllable frequently varies among the singular forms of the declension (the stress stays in the same place throughout the first and second declension singulars). Rules for Classical Latin stress explain why this is so (§16). Fourth, the nominative singular almost always has one syllable less than the remaining four forms of the singular—philologists call this type of declension IMPARISYLLABIC. (If the number of syllables remains constant throughout the singular, the declension is PARISYLLABIC.) The third declension, like the first and second, also includes a large number of nouns.

a. Here are some examples of the imparisyllabic third declension nouns. The first example below (*rĕx*) shows no shift in stress, but the second example (*cívitās*) does. The third example (*córpus*), a neuter, is given to show the neuter endings; its nominative and accusative are characteristically the same in each number, as you'll see on the next page:

rĕx, rḗgis, *m* 'king'   cīvitas, cīvitā́tis, *f* 'state'

nom.	rĕx	rḗges	cī́vitās	cīvitā́tes
gen.	rḗgis	rḗgum	cīvitā́tis	cīvitā́tum
dat.	rḗgī	rḗgibus	cīvitā́tī	cīvitā́tibus
acc.	rḗgem	rḗges	cīvitā́tem	cīvitā́tes
abl.	rḗge	rḗgibus	cīvitā́te	cīvitā́tibus

cŏrpus, cŏrporis, *n* 'body'

nom.	cŏrpus	cŏrpora
gen.	cŏrporis	cŏrpṓrum
dat.	cŏrporī	cŏrpṓribus
acc.	cŏrpus	cŏrpora
abl.	cŏrpore	cŏrpṓribus

b. Finally, here are two parisyllabic examples, among the few in the third declension:

nū́bēs,–is *f* 'cloud'   mā́re,–is *n* 'sea'

nom.	nū́bēs	nū́bēs	mā́re	mā́ria
gen.	nū́bis	nū́b*i*um	mā́ris	mā́r*i*um
dat.	nū́bī	nū́bibus	mā́rī	mā́ribus
acc.	nū́bem	nū́bēs	mā́re	mā́ria
abl.	nū́be	nū́bibus	mā́rī	mā́ribus

Nūbēs and *mare* illustrate yet another feature of the third declension: the genitive plural of both examples ends in *–ium* (instead of *–um*, as in other third declension nouns shown). Examples such as these are known as "*i*–stem" third declension nouns because of the *–i* which ends the stem of the genitive plural.

§22. The fourth declension had only a few nouns, and was characterized by a *–u–* in most endings. Masculine and feminine nouns of this declension shared the same set of endings, but the neuters had a set of their own, as shown on the next page:

	mánŭs, –ūs *f* 'hand,		córnū,–ūs *n* 'horn'	
nom.	mánŭs	mánūs	córnū	córnua
gen.	mánūs	mánuum	córnūs	córnuum
dat.	mánŭī	mánibus	córnū	córnibus
acc.	mánŭm	mánūs	córnū	córnua
abl.	mánū	mánibus	córnū	córnibus

Other common words of this declension include *dōmŭs,–ūs f* 'house'; some kinship terms: *sŏcrŭs,–ūs* f 'mother–in–law', *nŭrŭs, –ūs* f 'daughter–in–law'; the word for 'fruit': *frūctŭs,–ūs* m; and the names of some trees, all of which are feminine: *pīnŭs,–ūs,* 'pine'; *fīcŭs,–ūs,* 'fig tree'.

§23. The fifth declension had very few nouns, and was characterized by the letter *e* throughout the endings. All nouns of this declension were feminine, except *dĭēs,–ḗī* 'day' which could be either masculine or feminine. An odd feature of this declension is that only a small percentage of them, such as *dĭēs,–ḗī* and *rēs,–ḗī* 'thing' had plural forms; the rest were declined only in the singular.

	díēs, –ḗī *m + f* 'day'		mātĕriēs,–ī *f* 'material'
nom.	díēs	díēs	mātĕriēs
gen.	diḗī	diḗrum	mātĕriḗī
dat.	diḗī	diḗbus	mātĕriḗī
acc.	díem	díēs	mātĕriem
abl.	díē	diḗbus	mātĕriē

Some other nouns of this declension are *fĭdēs,–ḗī* f 'faith', and *spēs,–ḗī* f 'hope'.

§24. Vulgar Latin nouns were organized quite differently from Classical Latin nouns. First, of the five main cases of Classical Latin, only two (the nominative and the accusative) were used. Second, only the first three Classical Latin declensions were seen in Vulgar Latin. Third, the neuter gender disappeared.

There seem to be two related reasons why the five Classical Latin cases were reduced to two in the spoken language of the streets. The first is that the endings would have become hopelessly confused through the normal phonetic outcome in Vulgar Latin (§§4, 5, 10); the singular examples below show how the neat grammatical system based on endings would have been destroyed if all cases had been maintained in Vulgar Latin. The genitive, dative and ablative examples below in parentheses *never* existed in Vulgar Latin, and are given only for purposes of the demonstration. Notice also that the transcription has been made as the sounds would have been pronounced (in inscriptions, Vulgar Latin carvers maintained the final *u* even though they pronounced it *o*).

| | First Declension | | Second Declension | |
	Classical Latin	*Vulgar Latin*	*Classical Latin*	*Vulgar Latin*
nom.	puella	puella	servus	servos
gen.	puellæ	(puelle)	servī	(servi)
dat.	puellæ	(puelle)	servō	(servo)
acc.	puellam	puella	servum	servo
abl.	puellā	(puella)	servō	(servo)

In the first declension, the four distinct forms would have been reduced to only two; the nominative, accusative, and ablative—distinct from each other in Classical Latin—would now be confused. In the second declension, the five different forms would have been reduced to three. This time, the dative, accusative, and ablative would have been mixed together.

§25. You might think that because of the latent phonetic confusion of the case endings, Vulgar Latin would not have been able to distinguish grammatical functions, but such was not the case at all. The system that Vulgar Latin used to differentiate grammatical functions is the second reason for the reduction of cases, but in order to explain it, the differences between SYNTHETIC and ANALYTIC language must be given. A synthetic language (such as Classical Latin characteristically was), is one in which grammatical information is attached to the end of words (*serv–ī* = 'of the slave'), and an analytic language (such as Vulgar Latin characteristically was, as well as English and French are), is one where grammatical information precedes the words, or is inferred from syntactic position.

§26. At the outset, Vulgar Latin showed itself to be an analytic language in nouns, adjectives and verbs. In the noun declension system, Vulgar Latin retained the nominative (one of the two most common cases) in the nominative function, i.e., as the subject of a sentence. It also kept the accusative (the other of the two most common cases) in a variety of functions. The Vulgar Latin accusative, aside from its use as a direct object, was also used following certain prepositions to replace analytically the other Classical cases: *de* + *accusative* replaced the Classical genitive case; *ad* + *accusative* replaced the Classical dative case; and any of the other *usual prepositions* + *accusative* replaced the *preposition* + *ablative* use of Classical Latin.

There is a question that arises from the reasoning above: did the phonetic confusion cause Vulgar Latin to become an analytic language? or would Vulgar Latin have been analytic in its structure even if there had been no phonetically confused forms? Evidence seems to favor an affirmative answer to the second part.

§27. The first declension in Vulgar Latin looked like this:

porta 'door'

	Singular	Plural
nom.	porta	porte (portas)
acc.	porta	portas

Due to normal phonetic development, the singular forms shared the same spelling in the first declension (§10). In the plural, *porte* is the normal phonetic development from CL *portæ*, yet there was alternate nominative plural (*portas*) based on the accusative plural form. In Vulgar Latin, since the accusative had taken over the functions of the four OBLIQUE cases (i.e., all of the cases except the nominative), it began to encroach on the territory of the nominative as well. The accusative takeover of the nominative function is shown in this famous, and often misunderstood, gravestone inscription found in the *Corpus Inscriptionum Latinarum*, iii, 3351:

Hic quescunt duas matres, duas filias; numero tres facunt.[14]
"Here lie two mothers and two daughters; that makes three."

Students of Classical Latin would expect to see *duæ fīliæ* since the
two daughters are part of the subject of the sentence, but the
accusative form has taken over the nominative. The third declension nominative plural, *matres*, with its final *–s*, provides a spring-
board for the analogy.

Some people think that "two mothers plus the two daughters"
must equal *four* persons, and not three. But on reflection they will
see that the point of the inscription is that there is a grandmother,
her daughter and her granddaughter all buried together: two mothers
and two daughters, that makes three.

§28a. The second declension masculines were retained in Vulgar
Latin, but the neuters underwent some changes. Below is a typical
masculine noun in Vulgar Latin. Again, the words are transcribed as
they would have been pronounced, rather than the way they would
have been carved:

	amícos 'friend'	
	Singular	*Plural*
nom.	amícos	amíci
acc.	amíco	amícos

The nominative singular and the accusative plural had the same
form, unlike the corresponding Classical Latin forms, which were
different (*amícus, amícōs*); this fact certainly contributed to the
eventual universal takeover of the nominative function by the
accusative.

b. The neuters of the second declension showed two types of
changes. Those that usually were used in the singular changed to
masculine because of the similarity of form:

---

[14] In Classical Latin the text would be "Hic quiēscunt duæ matres, duæ
filiæ, numero trēs faciunt."

CL cŏllum > VL cǫllus (Sp. cuello)
CL násum > VL násus 'nose'
CL vínum > VL vị́nus (Sp. vino)

c. On the other hand, those that were commonly seen in the plural changed to the first declension (feminine) singular since the –a of the neuter plural (§20) was easily confused with the first declension singular:

CL 2nd declension Neuter Plural	VL 1st declension Feminine Singular
pĭrum, pl. pĭra	pị́ra (Sp. pera)
fĕstum, pl. fĕsta	fẹ́sta (Sp. fiesta)
fŏlium, pl. fŏlia	fǫ́lia (Sp. hoja)
lĭgnum, pl. lĭgna	lị́gna (Sp. leña)
sĭgnum, pl. sĭgna	sị́gna (Sp. seña)

The *Appendix Probi* shows a mistaken classical neuter plural (ending in –a) for a first declension (feminine) singular in this example: *vico castrórum non vico castræ. Castra* was a neuter plural with the singular meaning 'camp', so 'of the camp, was "rationally" rendered by the genitive singular of the first declension. (*Vico* meant 'town'.)[15]

§29. The Vulgar Latin third declension inherited some built-in complications from Classical Latin, and showed a number of changes.

a. Since its case endings were the same for both masculine and feminine nouns, some third declension nouns changed gender in Vulgar Latin. Here are examples of Classical masculine nouns that became feminine in the Vulgar Latin of Hispania:

Masculine	Feminine
CL frŏntem	VL frónte (Sp. la frente)
CL fŏntem	VL fónte (Sp. la fuente)

---

[15] This example takes more than a casual glance to understand.

CL paríetem   VL par̦éte (Sp. la pared)
CL serpéntem   VL serpénte (Sp. la serpiente)

b. Third declension neuters became masculine or feminine in the Vulgar Latin of Hispania, but, as the examples from the modern Romance Languages show, genders varied in different areas where Vulgar Latin was spoken. (The Portuguese article *o* shown in the examples is masculine):

Neuter	Masculine or Feminine
CL máre	VL máre (Sp. *el mar*, Ptg. *o mar*, Fr. *la mer*)
CL sále	VL sále (Sp. *la sal*, Ptg. *o sal*, Fr. *le sel*)
CL lac	VL lacte (Sp. *la leche*, Ptg. *o leite*, Fr. *le lait*)
CL mĕl	VL mĕle[16] (Sp. *la miel*, Ptg. *o mel*, Fr. *le miel*)

An inscription in Pompeii shows that the neuter *cadáver* had become masculine since the following adjective was also masculine: *cadaver mortuus* (instead of the neuter *mortuum*).

c. One third declension neuter, *ŏpus*, pl. *ŏpera*, had a first declension doublet already in Classical Latin, where *ŏpera*, the nominative plural of the original form, was used as a new nominative singular. *Opera* was continued as a feminine throughout Romance and gave *obra* in Spanish.

§30. There were two tendencies in the third declension imparisyllabic nouns. Those without a moveable stress (§21a) added a syllable to the nominative (usually making it exactly like the classical genitive in form) to make the declension fit a parisyllabic pattern. This was a device used to "regularize" Vulgar Latin. Examples are on the next page.

---

[16] In Classical Latin, neuter nouns had the same form in the nominative and accusative, such as *lac* and *mĕl*. But when the neuter gender was lost in Vulgar Latin, speakers rebuilt them using typical accusative endings, thus the Vulgar Latin accusative form ends in *–e*. *Lac* was rebuilt on the genitive stem *lact–*.

	Classical Latin	Vulgar Latin
nom.	móns 'mountain'	móntis
acc.	móntem	mónte
nom.	bós 'ox'	bóvis
acc.	bóvem	bóve

The *Appendix Probi* "corrected" some of these rebuilt nominatives: *grus non gruis* 'stork', *pecten non pectinis* 'comb', *glis non gliris* 'dormouse'.

The moveable stress imparisyllabics (§21a) retained the original nominative form, and the original stress:

	Classical Latin	Vulgar Latin
nom.	sérmo 'speech'	sérmo
acc.	sermónem	sermóne
nom.	dólor 'pain'	dólor
acc.	dolórem	dolóre
nom.	rátio 'calculation'	rátio
acc.	ratiónem	ratióne

Typical Vulgar Latin third declension nouns would look like this:

	Non–moveable stress		Moveable stress	
	Singular	Plural	Singular	Plural
nom.	móntis	móntes	dólor	dolóres
acc.	mónte	móntes	dolóre	dolóres

§31. The fourth declension disappeared completely, and its forms were assimilated almost entirely by the second declension, with which it had similarities in form. Most of the words that made this move were either neuter or feminine, but the switch made them almost exclusively masculine.

Classical Latin	Vulgar Latin
Fourth Declension	Second Declension
córnu, *n*	córnus (Sp. *cuerno*)

Classical Latin	Vulgar Latin
Fourth Declension	Second Declension
gĕlu, n	gélus (Sp. hielo)
gĕnu, n	génus. m 'knee'
pínus, f	pínus, m (Sp. pino)
mánus, f	mánus, f (Sp. la mano)

Two fourth declension words, both referring to women, were forced to the first declension, and both are documented in the *Appendix Probi: nurus non nura* (Sp. *nuera*), and *socrus non socra* (Sp. *suegra*).

§32. The few words of the fifth declension were assimilated into the first and third declensions. In Classical Latin some fifth declension nouns had doublets in the first declension: CL 5th decl. *matériēs*, 1st decl. *matéria*; CL 5th decl. *luxuriēs*, 1st decl. *luxuria*. Because of the influence of the doublets, the way was paved for most of the fifth declension to move to the first.

Similarities between the nominatives and accusatives of the fifth declension with those of the third declensions caused the remaining nouns to move to the third declension.

Classical Latin	Vulgar Latin
Fifth Declension	First or Third Declension
matĕriēs	materia, 1st decl. (Sp. madera)
díēs, m	día, 1st decl. (Sp. el día)
rábiēs	rábia, 1st. decl. (Sp. rabia)
sániēs	sánia, 1st decl. (Sp. saña)
fáciēs	fácies, 3rd. decl. (Sp. haz)
fídēs	fídes, 3rd decl. (Sp. fe)

§33. Vulgar Latin, unlike Classical Latin, was partial to nouns with diminutive endings even when the result connoted no diminutive meaning. This predilection is due to a number of causes:

a. Since Vulgar Latin was quite expressive, it made nouns more expressive by adding diminutive suffixes.

CL nĕptis > VL neptícula 'granddaughter'

CL cŭlter > VL cultḗllus 'knife' (cf. Sp. *cuchillo*)
CL ágnus > VL agnḗllus 'lamb' (cf. Fr. *agneau*)

b. Adding a diminutive suffix to a noun was an easy way to change the gender of a neuter, since these suffixes were either masculine or feminine, and never neuter:

CL gĕnu, *n* > VL genṵculu, *m* (Sp. *hinojo*[17])
CL cáput, *n* > VL capḭtia, *f* (Sp. *cabeza*)

c. Vulgar Latin did not favor very short lexical words; the addition of a diminutive suffix added one or two new syllables to make any short word acceptable in length:

CL ácus > VL acṵcula (Sp. *aguja*)
CL ávus > VL aviṵlu (Sp. *abuelo*)
CL ápis > VL apḭcula (Sp. *abeja*)
CL cǽpa > VL cepṵlla (Sp. *cebolla*)
CL ŏvis > VL ovḭcula (Sp. *oveja*)

§34. Classical Latin, unlike Classical Greek, had no definite or indefinite articles, and according to Quintilian, who was from Hispania, did not want any: "Noster sermo articulōs non desiderat" 'Our language does not miss articles', *Institutiones Oratoriæ*, I, 4, 9. But Vulgar Latin, with its need for expressiveness and clarity, began to use weakened Classical demonstratives *ḭllum* and *ḭllam* for the definite articles in Hispania, and the numerals *ṵnum* and *ṵnam* for the indefinite articles.

Adjective Declensions

§35a. Classical Latin adjectives agreed in gender, number, and case with the nouns they modified. There were two types of adjectives. The first type used the endings of the first and second declensions. It used the first declension endings with feminine nouns and

---

[17] *Hinojo* means 'knee' in Spanish most commonly in the expression *de hinojos* 'on bended knee'. The usual word is *rodilla*.

second declension endings with masculine nouns, with neuter variants for neuter nouns. In grammar books, adjectives are identified with the nominative singular ending of all three genders: "*bonus, –a, –um* 'good'."

b. The second type of adjective used third declension "*i*–stem" endings (§21b). It showed the same endings when modifying masculine and feminine nouns (since the corresponding noun declension made no masculine or feminine distinction in form), but in the neuter had a different form shared by the nominative and accusative. In grammar books, adjectives of this type are identified this way: "*fortis, –e* 'strong'." The main entry is the masculine/feminine nominative singular form, and the alternate ending indicates the neuter singular form.

Vulgar Latin (and the Romance Languages) retained both types of adjectives, but, of course, the neuter form disappeared (and therefore in Romance as well), as did all grammatical cases except the nominative and accusative.

c. In a few instances, adjectives based on the third declension moved to the first/second declension type, but with no ultimate success, as these examples from the *Appendix Probi* show:

> tristis non tristus (Sp. *triste*)
> pauper mulier non paupera mulier (Sp. *pobre [mujer]*)
> acer non acrum 'sour'

Typical examples of Vulgar Latin adjectives would look like this:

	béllus, –a 'pretty'		fórtis 'strong'	
nom.	béllus, –a	bélli, –e	fórtis	fórtes
acc.	béllu, –a	béllos, –as	fórte	fórtes

§36. The comparative and superlative degrees of adjectives were synthetic forms in Classical Latin; that is, the comparative or superlative aspect of the adjective was suffixed onto the adjective.

a. In the comparative degree, all Classical Latin adjectives had endings based on the ordinary (not the "*i*–stem") third declension (§21a). This meant that an adjective of the first type (based on the first/second declensions) actually became a *third* declension adjective in the comparative:

First Type	Comparative Degree
bĕllus, –a, –um 'pretty'	bĕllior, –ius 'prettier'
Second Type	
fŏrtis, –e 'strong'	fŏrtior, –ius 'stronger'

The forms *bĕllior* and *fŏrtior* represent the masculine and feminine nominative singular, while *bĕllius* and *fŏrtius* represent the corresponding neuter. Needless to say, the comparatives were declinable in all cases, singular and plural.

b. Classical Latin superlatives, unlike the comparatives, had endings based on the first type of adjective. Thus, adjectives of the third declension became first/second declension superlatives.:

First Type	Superlative Degree
bĕllus, –a, –um 'pretty'	bellĭssimus, –a, –um 'prettiest,
Second Type	
fŏrtis, –e 'strong'	fortĭssimus, –a, –um 'strongest'

c. Finally, a few Classical adjectives—those whose stem ended in a vowel—formed the comparative and superlative differently from the ways mentioned above. Instead of adding endings to the adjective, the word *mágis* 'more' or *máximē* 'most' preceded it:

> idóneus 'suitable'
> mágis idóneus 'more suitable'
> máximē idóneus 'most suitable'

§37. In Vulgar Latin, the comparative and superlative were analytic constructions and not synthetic as in the Classical language. In fact, the system used above (§36c) for adjectives whose stem ended in a vowel was the analytic structure which was adopted by the Romance Languages. Those areas of early Roman conquest, such as Hispania, used *mágis* + adjective, while those areas of later conquest, such as Gaul, used *plūs* + adjective. The

Vulgar Latin comparatives thus set the basis for Romance:

> CL áltior > VL mágis áltus (Sp. *más alto*)
> CL sevérior > VL mágis sevẹ́rus (Sp. *más severo*)

§38. There were a few Classical Latin comparatives that were irregular, four of which were retained by Vulgar Latin:

> CL meliọ́rem > VL meliọ́re (Sp. *mejor*)
> CL maiọ́rem > VL maiọ́re (Sp. *mayor*)
> CL peiọ́rem > VL peiọ́re (Sp. *peor*)
> CL minọ́rem > VL minọ́re (Sp. *menor*)

The Classical Latin superlative in *–ísimus* (§21b) was lost in Vulgar Latin in favor of an analytic construction based on the Vulgar Latin comparative. The reason that Spanish has the suffix *–ísimo* today is that it is learned, taken directly from Classical Latin and restored by scholars during the medieval period.

Latin Pronouns

§39a. Classical Latin had a wealth of demonstrative pronouns. *Hīc, hæc, hōc*[18] pointed out something near the speaker. To refer to something near the person spoken to, the set *ĭste, ĭsta, ĭstud* was used. To allude to something already mentioned, *ĭs, ĕa, ĭd* were used. The pronouns that meant 'the same' were *ídem, ĕadem, ídem*. The intensive pronouns meaning 'oneself' were *ĭpse, ĭpsa, ĭpsum*.

b. Vulgar Latin did not retain all of the Classical demonstratives. *Hīc, hæc, hōc* were largely lost, as were *ĭs, ĕa, ĭd*, most likely due to their lack of phonetic substance. *Iste, ĭsta, ĭstud* replaced the former set (becoming *este, este, esto* in Spanish) and the latter was replaced by *ĭlle, ĭlla, ĭllud* (*él, ella*, and *ello* in modern Spanish). *Ídem, ĕadem, ídem* were lost without leaving a trace while *ĭpse,*

---

[18] The three forms given in this and the following examples represent the masculine, feminine and neuter nominative singular of the pronouns. All pronouns were declinable in all cases, singular and plural, and in all three genders.

ĭpsa, ĭpsum were retained, but without their intensive value (Sp. *ese, esa, eso*).

§40. The Classical relative pronouns (*quī, quæ, quŏd*) and interrogative pronouns (*quĭs, quĭs, quĭd*) which were almost exactly alike in their declensions, except in the nominative forms, became hopelessly confused in Vulgar Latin, resulting in the fusion of the two into VL *qui̧, quȩ, qui̧d*.

The Classical genitive singular of the relative pronouns, *cū̆ius*, which had the same form for all three genders, was continued into Vulgar Latin, but took masculine and feminine endings (as reflected in Sp. *cuyo, cuya*). This is an instance of the retention of a genitive form in Vulgar Latin.

§41a. The development of the personal pronouns for the first and second persons from Classical to Vulgar Latin shows some interesting and even surprising features. First, unlike ordinary nouns, personal pronouns retained the dative case as well as the usual nominative and accusative cases:

	Classical Latin	Vulgar Latin	Classical Latin	Vulgar Latin
nom.	ĕgō 'I'	ȩo	nōs 'we'	no̧s
dat.	mĭ́hī 'to me'	mi̧	nó̄bis 'to us'	no̧s
acc.	mē 'me'	mȩ	nōs 'us'	no̧s
nom.	tū 'you' *sing.*	tu̧	vōs 'you' *pl.*	vo̧s
dat.	tĭ́bī 'to you'	ti̧	vōs 'to you'	vo̧s
acc.	tē 'you'	tȩ	vó̄bis 'to you'	vo̧s

There was a collateral, more emphatic form in Vulgar Latin for the nominative *nōs* and *vōs*: *nōs álteros* and *vōs álteros* (modern Spanish *nosotros* and *vosotros*).

The form *ti̧* is not a direct continuation of *tĭbī* but is analogical with *mi̧*.

The dative *no̧s* and *vo̧s* are attested in the *Appendix Probi*:

nobiscum non noscum 'with us'
vobiscum non voscum 'with you'

(The preposition *cŭm* 'with' usually followed certain Classical pronouns.)

b. The amazing thing about these pronouns in the Vulgar Latin of Hispania was a revolutionary change in function that *mī̧*, *mę* and *tī̧*, *tę* underwent. The continuations of datives *mī̧* and *tī̧* were no longer used exclusively as datives, but became instead *stressed* pronouns for *either* dative or accusative use (as in Spanish *a mí me lo dio* [*mí* = stressed "dative"], *a mí me vio* [*mí* = stressed "accusative"]). The continuations of the accusatives *mę* and *tę* were no longer used exclusively as accusatives, but became instead *unstressed* datives *or* accusatives (Sp. *te lo dieron* [*te* = unstressed "dative"], *te vieron* [*te* = unstressed "accusative"]).

§42. Classical Latin had no personal pronouns *per se* for the third person, but used the *ĭs, ĕa, ĭd* set of demonstratives when personal pronouns were called for. In Vulgar Latin, the *ĭlle, ĭlla, ĭllud* set replaced *ĭs, ĕa, ĭd* (§39a):

		Singular		
---	---	Classical Latin	Vulgar Latin	Spanish
nom.	*m*	ĭlle 'he'	i̧lle	él
	f	ĭlla 'she'	i̧lla	la
dat.	*m + f*	ĭllī 'to him/her'	i̧llí̧	le
acc.	*m*	ĭllum 'him'	i̧llú̧	lo
	f	ĭllam 'her'	i̧llá	la
		Plural		
nom.	*m*	ĭllī 'they' *m*	i̧llos	ellos
	f	ĭllæ 'they' *f*	i̧llas	ellas
dat.	*m + f*	ĭllīs 'to them'	i̧llís	les
acc.	*m*	ĭllōs 'them, *m*	i̧llós	los
	f	ĭllās 'them' *f*	i̧llás	las

Note that the Vulgar Latin *nominative* forms *i̧llos* and *i̧llas* were analogical, based on the accusative forms, and did not come from the Classical nominatives. The shift in stress in certain Vulgar Latin forms should also be noticed, since the Vulgar Latin stress was continued into Spanish.

§43. Finally, the reflexive pronouns. Since this type of pronoun "reflected" the subject, it had no nominative form. The dative and accusative, given below, were the most common cases:

	Classical Latin	Vulgar Latin	Spanish
dat.	mḯhi 'to myself'	mị	mí
acc.	mē 'myself,	mẹ	me
dat.	tĭbi 'to yourself'	tị	ti
acc.	tē 'yourself,	tẹ́	te
dat.	sḯbi 'to him/herself'	sị	sí
acc.	sē 'himself/herself'	sẹ	se
dat.	nṓbis 'to ourselves'	nos	nos
acc.	nṓs 'ourselves'	nos	nos
dat.	vṓbis 'to yourself'	vos	os
acc.	vōs 'yourself'	vos	os
dat.	sḯbi 'to themselves'	sị	sí
acc.	sē 'themselves'	sẹ	se

Since these forms in most cases are identical with the first and second person pronouns (§41), they evolved in much the same way. For example, *sị* is analogical with *mị* and does not continue *sḯbi*.

§44. The Classical Latin possessives were declined like the first type of adjective (*mĕus, –a, –um* 'my', for instance). In Vulgar Latin, only the accusative case of the masculine and feminine remained, all other cases having fallen. Examples below are taken from the singular, although there was a plural form as well.

Classical Latin	Vulgar Latin
mĕum, mĕam 'my'	mẹ́u, mía (§7b)
tŭm, tŭam 'your,	tụ́u, tụ́a
sŭum, sŭam 'his/her'	sụ́u, sụ́a
nṓstrum, –am 'our'	nọ́stru, –a

vĕstrum, –am 'your'   vǫstru, –a

VL *vostru* is analogical with *nostru*.

§45a. Most numbers through 100 were not declinable in Classical Latin; that is, they had the same form for all cases. 'One', 'two', and 'three', however, were. 'One', ū̆nus, –am, –um, was declinable usually only in the singular. 'Two' was *duo, -æ, -o,* declined with some irregular forms (including the masculine and neuter [–o] shown in the model). 'Three' was *trēs, trēs, trĭa,* declined like the plural of the third declension. The result in Vulgar Latin was that only '1' and '2' showed gender distinction, since the neuter was to fall. Examples are shown in the accusative because that was the case that survived:

Classical Latin	*Vulgar Latin*
ū̆num, –am, –um '1'	ū̆nu, ū̆na
dŭo, dŭas, dŭo '2'	dų́os, dų́as
trēs, trēs, trĭa '3'	tręs, tręs

From four to ten the numbers showed little differences:

Classical Latin	*Vulgar Latin*
quáttuor '4'	quáttor
quĭ́nque '5'	cį́nque
sĕx '6'	sęx (§13b)
sĕptem '7'	sę́tte
ŏctō '8'	ǫ́cto
nŏvem '9'	nǫ́ve
dĕcem '10'	dę́ce

VL *quáttor* showed a loss of the second CL *u.*

b. The Vulgar Latin of the Iberian Peninsula made some important changes in the numbers 11 through 19. Although it retained the Classical formation of 11–15, it rejected the Classical Latin formulas for 16 through 19 and provided its own solution:

Classical Latin	Vulgar Latin
úndecim '11'	úndece
duódecim '12'	duódece
trĕdecim '13'	trĕdece
quattuŏrdecim '14'	quattórdece
quíndecim '15'	quíndece
sēdecim '16'	déce et séx
septĕndecim '17'	déce et sétte
duodēvigínti '18'	déce et octo
ūndēvigínti '19'	déce et nóve

c. A major change seen in the development of the tens is the normal loss of –g– (§11b):

Classical Latin	Vulgar Latin
vigínti '20'	viínti
trigínta '30'	triínta
quadragínta '40'	quadraénta
quinquagínta '50'	cinquaénta
sexagínta '60'	sexaénta
septuagínta '70'	settaénta
octogínta '80'	octoénta
nonagínta '90'	novaénta

VL *cinquaénta* is analogical with *cínque* and *novaénta* is analogical with *nóve*.

d. 'One hundred' was *cĕntum*, which was not declinable. Multiples of 100 were declinable like the plural of the first type of adjective: *ducĕntī, –æ, –a*, for example, *Mílle* '1000' was equally not declinable in the "singular," but in multiples it was declined like neuter "*i*–stem" third declension nouns (§21b): *dŭo mília* '2000', for example.

Most Vulgar Latin numbers cited above have never been attested since numbers were overwhelmingly written as *Roman numerals* and not as words.

The Latin Conjugation System

§46. The number of inflected forms of the Classical Latin noun was exceeded only by the number of forms of the Classical Latin verb. Whereas the typical noun had twelve inflected forms, the typical verb had more than 125 forms. The endings of verbs gave even more information than the endings of nouns—they indicated whether the subject was first, second, or third person; singular or plural; identified the TENSE and the MOOD; and distinguished whether the verb was ACTIVE or PASSIVE.

a. There were four conjugation groups in Classical Latin, easily identifiable by the ending of the present active infinitive. The first conjugation ended in –áre (amáre 'to love', laudáre 'to praise'), the second ended in –ére (vidére 'to see', habére 'to have'), the third in –ĕre (pónĕre 'to put', fúgĕre 'to flee'), and the fourth in –íre (veníre 'to come', audíre 'to hear').

The third conjugation had two different groups: those with the first person singular present indicative ending in –ō (pónō 'I put'), and those ending in –iō (fúgiō 'I flee'). This second type retained the –i– in certain tenses.

Of the four Classical conjugations, only three survived in the Vulgar Latin of Hispania, details of which will be given later (§51a).

b. Any Classical Latin verb that was active (vídeō 'I see', laudō 'I praise') could be made passive by substituting a passive ending (vídeor 'I am seen,' láudor 'I am praised'). A complication existed in connection with the active and passive conjugations—there was a type of verb (known as DEPONENT [depp´–uh–nunt]) that was passive in form (i.e., with passive verb endings) but active in meaning: fábulor, with its passive ending, meant 'I speak', and séquor, equally passive in form, meant 'I follow'.

§47. Classical Latin had six indicative active tenses. Examples will be given of audíre 'to hear'. There were the PRESENT (audio 'I hear'), the PERFECT (audívī 'I heard'), the IMPERFECT (audiébam 'I was hearing'), the PLUPERFECT (audívĕram 'I had heard'), the FUTURE (audiam 'I shall hear'), and the FUTURE PERFECT (audívĕrō 'I shall have heard'). Vulgar Latin dropped both Classical future tenses and devised new ways to express them.

There were four SUBJUNCTIVE ACTIVE tenses. The PRESENT (audi-

am 'that I may hear'), the PERFECT (*audīverim*, used after a present or future verb to mean 'that I might hear'), the IMPERFECT (*audīrem*, used after a past tense verb to mean 'that I might hear'), and the PLUPERFECT (*audīvĭssĕm* 'that I might have heard'). Vulgar Latin dropped both the perfect and imperfect subjunctive tenses, replacing them both with the Classical pluperfect subjunctive forms, and it created a new pluperfect subjunctive of its own.

The IMPERATIVE had forms *only* for the second person singular and plural (*audī, audīte* 'hear'). Vulgar Latin retained these, but had to deal with the formation of a negative imperative (§53).

The INDICATIVE PASSIVE shared the same six tenses with the active: the PRESENT (*audior* 'I am heard'), the PERFECT (*audītus sum* 'I was heard'), the IMPERFECT (*audiēbar* 'I was being heard'), the PLUPERFECT (*audītus eram* 'I had been heard'), the FUTURE (*audiar* 'I shall be heard'), and the FUTURE PERFECT (*audītus erō* 'I shall have been heard').

The SUBJUNCTIVE PASSIVE had the four tenses of the indicative as well: the PRESENT (*audiar* 'that I may be heard'), the IMPERFECT (*audīrer* 'that I might be heard'), the PERFECT (*audītus sim* 'that I might be heard'), and the PLUPERFECT (*audītus essem* 'that I might have been heard').

Classical Latin had four PARTICIPLES. The ACTIVE PARTICIPLES were the PRESENT (*audiēns* 'hearing'), and the FUTURE (*audītūrus* 'about to hear'). The PASSIVE PARTICIPLES were the PERFECT (*audītus* '[having been] heard') and the FUTURE (*audiendus* 'about to be heard'). Both active participles fell in Vulgar Latin.

There were *six* different types of infinitives in Classical Latin: the present active (*audīre* 'to hear'), the PERFECT ACTIVE (*audīvisse* 'to have heard'), the FUTURE ACTIVE (*audītūrus esse* 'to be about to hear), the PRESENT PASSIVE (*audīrī* 'to be heard'), the PERFECT PASSIVE (*audītus esse* 'to have been heard'), and the FUTURE PASSIVE (*audītus īrī* 'to be going to be heard'). Of the six Classical infinitives, only the present active remained in Vulgar Latin.

All Classical passives, both indicative and subjunctive, disappeared virtually without leaving a trace (except for the participles), and Vulgar Latin remade its own passives (§61). The Classical deponents either were lost or were rebuilt on an active model (§62).

Each tense had only six persons: three in the singular (corresponding to 'I', 'you' *singular*, and 'he/she') and three in the plural (corresponding to 'we', 'you' *plural*, and 'they'). Classical and Vulgar Latin were like modern English in that there was no distinction made between a familiar and formal 'you'; there was just *tū* for the singular and *vōs* for the plural.

§48. Classical Latin verbs are traditionally identified by four PRINCIPAL PARTS. A number of tenses, participles, or infinitives build on the stem of each principal part. The first principal part is the FIRST PERSON SINGULAR OF THE PRESENT INDICATIVE ACTIVE (*audiō*, for example), the second principal part is the PRESENT ACTIVE INFINITIVE (*audīre*), the third principal part is the FIRST PERSON SINGULAR OF THE PERFECT INDICATIVE ACTIVE (*audīvī*), and the fourth principal part is the ACCUSATIVE FORM OF THE SUPINE (§75a), which is usually listed in the neuter nominative singular form (*audītum*). It is important for students of Classical Latin to learn the principal parts since most verbs are not as consistent in their stems as is *audīre* (*audiō, audīre, audīvī, audītum*); here are examples of verbs with different principal parts: *cádō, cádĕre, cécidī, cásum* 'fall', *dīcō, dīcĕre, dīxī, díctum* 'say', *fáciō, fácĕre, fēcī, fáctum* 'do', and, lastly, the verb with the most unrelated of principal parts, *férō, férre, túlī, látum* 'bear'. Vulgar Latin usually maintained a continuation of the four Classical principal parts.

§49. Finally, Classical Latin had a type of verb known as INCHO-ATIVE [in–coe´–uh–tiv] or INCEPTIVE. Any given verb usually referred to an action in progress, but an inchoative verb referred to the beginning of the action: *hortus flōret* 'the garden is blooming', but *hortus flōrēscit* (the inchoative version) 'the garden begins to bloom,; *tremō* 'I tremble', *tremēscō* 'I begin to tremble'.

All inchoative verbs were of the third conjugation, no matter to which conjugation the basic verbs belonged. Infinitives of the first conjugation became –*áscĕre*, of the second and third became –*éscĕre*, and of the fourth became –*íscĕre* inchoatives: I *amáre* 'to love', > III *amáscĕre* 'to begin to love'; II *flōrére* 'to bloom' > III *flōréscĕre* 'to begin to bloom'; III *trémĕre* 'to tremble' > III *treméscĕre* 'to begin to tremble'; IV *dormíre* 'to sleep' > III *dormíscĕre* 'to begin to sleep'.

The inchoative system was retained in Vulgar Latin but the

notion of the beginning of an action was lost. One grammarian, trying to show his readers how they were misusing verbs, tried to explain: " 'Calesco' is not, 'I am warm' " but rather 'I begin to get warm' (" 'Calesco' non est 'caleo', sed 'calere incipio',", cited in Väänänen, p. 146.) Vulgar Latin even got some new "inchoatives" based on Classical verbs but which were not inchoative in meaning: CL *parēre* became VL *paréscere* (Sp. parecer), CL *obœdīre* became VL *obedéscere* in Hispania (Sp. *obedecer*), CL *merēre* became VL *meréscere* (Sp. *merecer*).

§50. The development of the Classical Latin present active into Vulgar Latin shows tremendous changes, especially in the third conjugation; complete Classical Latin conjugations are given here so that their development can be easily followed:

	I	II	III	III –iŏ	IV
	laudáre	vidēre	pónĕre	fúgĕre	audíre
ego	láudō	vídeō	pónō	fúgiō	audiō
tū	láudās	vídēs	pónis	fúgis	aúdīs
(is)	láudat	vídet	pónit	fúgit	aúdit
nōs	laudámus	vidémus	pónimus	fúgimus	audímus
vōs	laudátis	vidétis	pónitis	fúgitis	audítis
(ei)	láudant	vídent	pónunt	fúgiunt	aúdiunt

Remeber that in the third conjugation, some first person singulars ended in –ō and others in –iō (§46a). This explains why there are two sets of third conjugation verbs above.

§51a. In the Iberian Peninsula, the four conjugation groups of Classical Latin were reduced to three through the loss of the Classical third conjugation (–ĕre). The members of the Classical third conjugation usually moved to the second conjugation in Vulgar Latin, as shown below. Notice the shift in stress in Vulgar Latin:

CL cápĕre > VL capére (Sp. *caber*)
CL comprehéndĕre > VL comprendére (Sp. *comprender*)
CL fácĕre > VL facére (Sp. *hacer*)
CL légĕre > VL legére (Sp. *leer*)

CL pónĕre > VL ponére (So. *poner*)
CL sápĕre > VL sapére (Sp. *saber*)
CL véndĕre > VL vendére (Sp. *vender*)

b. Some Classical Latin third conjugation –*iō* verbs moved to the Vulgar Latin –*ire* conjugation. This type of third conjugation verb was very much like the Classical fourth conjugation (–*īre*) in most tenses, and exactly alike in the present active (except for vowel length), so the change seemed very natural:

CL concĭpĕre (concípiō) > VL concipíre (Sp. *concebir*)
CL fŭgĕre (fŭgiō) > VL fugíre (Sp. *huir*)
CL párĕre (páriō) > VL paríre (Sp. *parir*)
CL recĭpĕre (recípiō) > VL recipíre (*recibir*)
CL succŭtĕre (succŭtiō) > VL succutíre (Sp. *sacudir*)

Not all –*iō* verbs made this shift, however. *Cápĕre* (*cápiō*), *fácĕre* (*fáciō*) (§51a) and *sápĕre* (*sápiō*) went to the Vulgar Latin –*ére* conjugation: *capére, facére, sapére.*

c. A few Classical second conjugation verbs also changed to the Vulgar Latin –*ire* conjugation. Since the CL –*eō* first person singular ending became VL –*iō* through normal phonetic development, these verbs were swept into the –*ire* group along with the third conjugation –*io* verbs:

CL ĭmplére (ĭmpleō = VL –*io*) > VL implíre (Sp. *henchir*)
CL lūcére (lūceō = VL –*io*) > VL lucíre (Sp. *lucir*)
CL rīdére (rídeō = VL –*io*) > VL ridíre (Sp. *reír*)

§52. The Vulgar Latin present indicative shows a number of changes. The minority of Classical Latin verbs which ended in –*iō* in the first person singular (some third conjugation verbs and all fourth conjugation verbs), usually lost the *yod* by analogy with those verbs which had no *yod* (*laudō, vendō*, etc.), such as CL *fáciō* > VL *fáco* > Sp. *hago*. This change also affected the subjunctive (VL *faca* for CL *faciam*).

The first and second person plural forms of the Classical third conjugation were stressed on the stem, unlike the other conjugation groups (véndĭmus, véndĭtis, but laudámus, laudátis). As the Classi-cal Latin third conjugation fell, the stress moved to the endings in vendémus, vendétis to be in line with stress patterns elsewhere. The third person plural endings in –unt tended to give way to –ent. The Peregrinatio shows examples such as absolvent (for the Classical absolvunt 'they loosen'), accipient (for accipiunt 'they receive'), and exient (for exiunt 'they go away'). Spanish forms derive from the endings with –e–; legent develops to Sp. leen, but CL legunt could have only given the form *léon which never existed.

§53. The Classical Latin imperative was easy to form, but only had positive forms. The singular was made by removing the –re from the present infinitive active, and the plural merely by adding –te to the singular command:

láudā 'praise!'	vĭ́dē 'see!'	áudī 'hear!'
laudáte	vĭdéte	audíte

The positive imperative transfered to Vulgar Latin intact.

In Classical Latin, there was no negative imperative per se, and people had to talk around the idea by using the imperative of nólō 'be unwilling' plus the infinitive of the verb in question:

Nólī laudare! 'Be unwilling to praise! = Do not praise!'
Nólīte vidēre! 'Be unwilling to see! = Do not see!'

Nólō was not used in Vulgar Latin. The negative imperative was borrowed from the negative subjunctive (§§65, 66).

§54. The Classical Latin future was a tense destined to be phonetically unstable in Vulgar Latin. It disappeared virtually without leaving a trace[19] as the explanation following these exam-ples show:

---

[19] The second person singular of the future of esse 'to be' was eris; this form is supposed to have given the Spanish eres. If this is true, as it appears to be, eres is the only vestige in any Romance language of the ancient future tense.

I	II	III	IV
laudáre	vidére	pónĕre	audíre
'praise'	'see'	'put'	'hear'
laudábō	vidébō	pónam	áudiam
laudábis	vidébis	pónēs	áudiēs
laudábit	vidébit	pónet	áudiet
laudábimus	vidébimus	pōnémus	audiémus
laudábitis	vidébitis	pōnétis	audiétis
laudábunt	vidébunt	pónent	áudient

a. The first conjugation third person singular (*laudābit*) would be pronounced the same way as the same person of the perfect indicative (*laudāvit*) (§12). The future of the first and second conjugations, with their characteristic –b–, resembled their corresponding imperfect systems (*laudābam, vidēbam*). The first person singular of the future in the third and fourth conjugations was *exactly* like the present subjunctive forms (future *dīcam*, pres. subj. *dīcam*; future *audiam*, pres. subj. *audiam*). Normal phonetic development would cause the forms of the third conjugation future to sound like the corresponding present forms; CL future *dīcēs, dīcet* would come to sound like VL *dices* (= CL *dīcĭs*), VL *dicet* (= CL *dīcĭt*) of the present tense. Finally, there was no unity of conjugation in the Classical future—that is, while the first and second conjugations presented one type of formation (*laudābō, vidēbō*), the third and fourth conjugations presented another (*pōnam, audiam*).

b. With Vulgar Latin's tendency to be analytic rather than synthetic, the language found an analytic construction already in use with which it could replace the ambiguous Classical future. The construction was of the type "*scrībere habeō*" 'I have to write', "*facĕre habet*" '[someone] has to make'. Since anything one *has to* do must be done in the future, the semantic transfer was relatively simple, and the new analytic future became universal in the Western Romance Languages.

The Vulgar Latin conjugation of *habére* 'to have' had shorter forms than its Classical model, possibly because of analogy with other common short verbs (*das, dat*, from *dăre* 'to give', *stās, stăt* from *stāre* 'to stand') as well as from its new use as an unstressed auxiliary:

áio (CL hábeō)   (ab)émus (CL habémus)
as (CL hábes)   abétis (CL habétis)
at (CL hábet)   ant (CL hábent)

Here is an example of this type of future from the Latin Vulgate
Bible (see footnote 4 above), which shows Classical spelling for the
auxiliary:

"Tempestas... tollere habet" 'The storm will take away...'" John
4:1, 2

There is one early example that shows the fusion of the two forms
as in the modern Romance Languages:

Iustinius dicebat: "Daras." [= dare + as]
Justinius said: "You will give." *Fredegarii Chronica*, 85, 27

§55. The fortunate construction with *habére* + *infinitive* was
also able to give rise to a conditional tense (which was unknown in
Classical Latin). In this tense, the imperfect of *habére* was used
following an infinitive:

Sanare te habebat Deus.
God would cure you. Ps.–Aug. *Serm.* 253, 4

§56. The imperfect (or perfect) of *habére*, with the past participle
(= Classical passive perfect participle), was used as an alternate
analytical pluperfect: CL *posuērant* = VL *posita habebant* = Sp.
habían puesto. The Vulgar Latin example just listed comes from the
Peregrinatio.

§57a. In Classical Latin, the imperfect indicative conjugations
were characterized by *–ba–* in the endings:

laudábam	vidébam	audiébam
laudábas	vidébas	audiébas
laudábat	vidēbat	audiébat
laudābámus	vidēbámus	audiēbámus

laudābátis   vidēbátis   audiēbátis
laudábant   vidébant   audiébant

The normal *–ĕre* verbs shared second conjugation imperfect endings (*pōnébam*), but the *–iō* type shared fourth conjugation endings (*fugiébam*). Notice the shift in stress in the first and second person plural forms in the examples above.

b. The Vulgar Latin imperfect indicative showed a few notable differences. The first conjugation, with its *–āba–* endings, remained intact; the other conjugations, however, began to lose the *b*, possibly because of a dissimilation (§149c) of the two *b*'s in the common verbs CL *habēbam* and CL *debēbam* to VL *habea* and *debea*; this dissimilated ending would then spread to all other verbs of the Vulgar Latin *–ere* and *–ire* conjugations. Once this happened, the *–éa* changed to *–ía* according to §7b.

The fourth conjugation *–iēba–* lost its *–i–* in Vulgar Latin by analogy with the more numerous verbs in *–ēbam*; you can see examples of this loss of *–i–* in inscriptions: VL *audeba* (for CL *audiēbam*), *refugebat* (for CL *refugiēbat* '[someone] was escaping'), and *custodebat* (for *custodiēbat* '[someone] was guarding').

Whereas the stress moved forward one syllable in the Classical Latin first and second person plural of the imperfect (*laudábam* but *laudābámus*), in the Vulgar Latin of Hispania the stress leveled out over the same vowel throughout the conjugation (*laudába, laudábas, laudábat, laudábamus, laudábatis, laudábant*).

The irregular Classical imperfects *eram* (of *esse* 'to be') and *ībam* (of *īre* 'to go') were maintained in Vulgar Latin.

§58. In Classical Latin, the perfect tense was used for two different meanings. The first one was that of the perfect proper: 'I have seen, I have said'. The second was the meaning of what Classical grammarians call the AORIST [err´ist] or SIMPLE PAST, (in Spanish, the PRETERITE, 'I saw, I said').

In Vulgar Latin, however, the perfect came to be used only in the meaning of the aorist, the simple past ('I invited', for example). To fill the semantic gap, Vulgar Latin used the present tense of *habére* + *past participle*. Thus, we see in Gregory of Tours (ca. 538-ca. 594):

"Episcopam invitatum habes." 'You have invited the bishop.'

The perfect was the most complicated of the tenses. It had three different types: WEAK, STRONG, and REDUPLICATED.

Weak and strong are not descriptive terms in English, since they have nothing whatsoever to do with strength *per se*. A weak perfect is merely one that is stressed, in all forms, on the ending rather than on then stem (*laud–ávī, aud–ívī*). They are further characterized by a *v* in their endings. A strong perfect, on the other hand, is one that is stressed (in the three singular forms) on the stem rather than the ending (*vīd–ī* 'I saw', *háb–uī* 'I had', *pós–uī* 'I put', *vénī* 'I came,).[20] A reduplicated perfect is one in which the a first syllable of the verb appears twice (usually with a change in vowel): *cádō* 'I fall', *cécĭdī* 'I fell'. Reduplicated perfects are also stong.

a. Most of the weak perfects in Classical Latin were of the first and fourth conjugation.

I	IV
laudávī	audívī
laudāvĭstī	audivĭstī
laudávit	audívit
laudávĭmus	audívĭmus
laudāvĭstis	audīvĭstis
laudāvérunt	audīvérunt

There were no third conjugation weak perfects since the third conjugation was "strong" by nature—witness the infinitives: *pónĕre fúgĕre*. The few second conjugation weak perfects showed the infinitive vowel *–ē–* before the *v* (*delére* 'to destroy', *delévī* 'I destroyed'; *implére* 'to fill', *implévī* 'I filled').

Vulgar Latin weak perfects have a number of important differences. Those of the first and fourth conjugations were continued into Vulgar Latin, but their endings were modified. The first conju-

---

[20] *Weak* and *strong* are translated directly from German. In that language, when the stem of a verb can stand alone without an ending, it is considered "strong" (*Ich kam*), but if it requires an ending to complete its meaning, it is considered "weak" (i.e., unable to stand alone).

gation in Vulgar Latin shows that the –v– and the –i– (or –e–) that follows were lost in the endings of most persons, but only the –v– was lost in the first person singular and only the –i– was lost in the third singular.

laudá(v)i > laudái
laudā(ví)sti > laudásti
laudáv(i)t > laudáut
laudá(vi)mus > laudámus
laudā(ví)stis > laudástis
laudā(vé)runt > laudárunt

The first conjugation third person singular ending, with its –v– having become –u– (áv[i]t > áut) has been attested in Pompeii. Notice also the change in stress in the second and third person plurals above. The fourth conjugation showed the same changes as above in the singular, but had a double development in the plural: either only the –v– was lost, or both the –v– and the –i– (or –e–) following it disappeared:

Singular
audí(v)i > audíi
audī(ví)sti > audísti
audív(i)t > audíut

Plural
audí(v)ĭmus > audiémus
audí(vĭ)mus > audímus
audī(v)ˇstis > audiéstis
audī(vˇ)stis > audístis
audī(v)érunt > audiérunt
audī(vé)runt > audírunt

The fourth conjugation already showed alternate endings for the first person singular in Classical Latin: –ívī and –íī. This latter form provided an analogical basis for CL –āvī to become VL –ai.

b. Strong perfects were divided into three groups. First, there were those with a –u– between the stem of the verb and the usual endings. This type was characteristic of the second conjugation, although there were a few –u– perfects in the third and fourth conjugations as well (*sápĕre* 'to taste', *sápuī* 'I tasted', *aperíre* 'to open', *apérui* 'I opened'.

habére	tenére	tĭmére
'to have'	'to hold'	'to fear'
hábuī	ténuī	tĭmuī
habuístī	tenuístī	tĭmuístī
hábuit	ténuit	tĭmuit
habúimus	tenúimus	tĭmúimus
habuístis	tenuístis	tĭmuístis
habuérunt	tenuérunt	tĭmuérunt

In Vulgar Latin, this type of perfect either was retained (in which case the –u– changed position with the preceding consonant [CL *sápuī* > VL *sáupi* > OSp. *sope*, CL *hábuī* > VL *háubi* > OSp. *ove*]), or the perfect became weak in Vulgar Latin (and thus also in Spanish [CL *tímuī* > VL *timíi* > Sp. *temí*, CL *apéruī* > VL *aperíi* > Sp. *abrí*]).

c. The second group of strong perfects is called sigmatic. The word "sigmatic" derives from the Greek letter Σ 'sigma' (= s). In this type of perfect an *s* (or an *x*) is inserted before the ending. The sigmatic perfect is characteristic of the third conjugation, but a few second conjugation verbs also have sigmatic perfects (*manére* 'to remain', *mánsī* 'I remained').

mĭttĕre	scríbēre	dícĕre
'to send'	'to write'	'to say'
mísī	scrípsī	díxī
mīsístī	scrīpsístī	dīxístī
mīsit	scrípsit	díxit
mísimus	scrípsimus	díximus
mīsístis	scríps̆stis	dīxĭstis
mīsérunt	scrīpsérunt	dīxērunt

The sigmatic perfects remained in Vulgar Latin and a few new ones were even created there, notably CL *quæsīvī* > VL *quési* > Sp. *quise*. The change from weak to strong in the preceding example is often hard for the novice to see; in the Classical example, the stress comes on the ending [after the s] (therefore it is weak); while in the Vulgar Latin example, the stress is on the stem [preceding the *s*] (therefore it is strong).

d. The third group of strong perfects had nothing inserted between the stem and the ending, but the vowel of the stem was usually lengthened and/or raised to a higher point of articulation. This type of perfect was almost evenly divided between the second and third conjugations, although there were a few fourth conjugation perfects of this type, notably *venīre* 'to come', *vénī* 'I came':

fácere	vĭdére	lēgĕre
'to make'	'to see'	'to read'
(ă > ē)	(ĭ > ī)	(ĕ > ē)
fécī	vídī	légī
fēc'stī	vīd'stī	lēgístī
fécit	vídit	légit
fécimus	vídimus	légimus
fēcístis	vīdístis	lēgístis
fēcérunt	vīdérunt	lēgérunt

This group was maintained virtually intact in Vulgar Latin: CL *fécī* > VL *féci*, CL *vídī* > VL *vídi*, CL *légī* > VL *légi*, CL *vénī* > VL *véni*.

e. Finally, there were the REDUPLICATED perfects. This type of perfect was the norm in Ancient Greek, but there were not many in Classical Latin. Most of these were of the third conjugation, but *two* first conjugation verbs, *dáre* 'to give' (conjugated below) and *stáre* 'to stand', *stétī* 'I stood', also had reduplicated perfects. This type of perfect showed great vowel alternation:

cádĕre	cúrrĕre	dáre
'to fall'	'to run'	'to give'
cécidī	cucúrrī	dédī
cēcidístī	cucurrístī	dēdístī
cécidit	cucúrrit	dédit

cĕcídĭmus	cucŭrrimus	dĕdimus
cĕcidístis	cucurrístis	dĕdístis
cĕcidérunt	cucurrérunt	dĕdérunt

All perfects of this type, with the exception of *dĕdi* (from *dăre*) and *stĕtī* (from *stăre*) were rebuilt to fit regular weak patterns: CL *cucŭrri* was rebuilt as VL *currii* and gave Sp. *corrí*. CL *cĕcidi* was rebuilt as VL *cadíi* and gave Sp. *caí*.

§59. The Classical perfect passive participle, like the perfect tense, could be weak or strong, and with the same distribution: the first and fourth conjugations usually had weak perfect passive participles, and the second and third conjugations had strong ones.

a. The perfect participle of the first and fourth conjugations had a stem like that of the infinitive. To the stem was added –*tum* (*laudătum* 'praised', *audítum* 'heard'). Participles were fully declinable, using the system of the first type of adjective (§35a).

The few second conjugation verbs which had a weak passive participle merely added –*tum* to the stem: *delére* 'to destroy', *delé-tum* 'destroyed', *implére* 'to fill', *implétum* 'filled'.

The small number of third conjugation weak particples changed the –ŭ– of the stem to –ū– and added –*tum*: *consŭĕre* 'to sew', *consú-tum* 'sewn', *battŭĕre* 'to fight', *battútum* 'fought'.

b. Strong perfect participles usually had a different stem from either the infinitive or the perfect, and there was usually no vowel (–ā–, –ē–, –ū–, –ī–) between the stem and the ending:

> cápĕre 'to take': cáptum 'taken'
> cláudĕre 'to close': cláusum 'closed'
> dícĕre 'to say': díctum 'said'
> légĕre 'to read': léctum 'read'
> míttĕre 'to send': míssum 'sent'
> pónĕre 'to put': pósitum 'put'
> scríbĕre 'to write': scríptum 'written'
> víncĕre 'to conquer': víctum 'conquered'
> míscére 'to mix': míxtum 'mixed'
> vĭdére 'to see': vísum 'seen'

A few second and third conjugation verbs, however, *did* have regular strong perfect participles ending in *–ĭtum* (but here the *i* was short, not long): *habére* 'to have', *hábĭtum* 'had'; and *bíbĕre* 'to drink', *bíbĭtum* 'drunk'.

One fourth conjugation verb was also strong in the perfect participle: *veníre* 'to come', *vĕntum* > 'come'.

§60. Vulgar Latin favored the weak participles over the strong, thus many strong Classical participles were replaced in Vulgar Latin by weak ones: CL *sénsum* > VL *sentítu* > Sp. *sentido*; CL *sáltum* > VL *salítu* > Sp. *salido*; CL *véntum* > VL *venítu* > Sp. *venido*. A number of strong past participles, however, *were* carried into Vulgar Latin: VL *fáctu* (Sp. *hecho*), VL *díctu* (Sp. *dicho*), VL *pósitu* (Sp. *puesto*), VL *scríptu* (Sp. *escrito*), VL *mórtu* [CL *mórtuum*] (Sp. *muerto*), VL *rúptu* (Sp. *roto*), VL *vístu* [CL *vīsum*] (Sp. *visto*).

Among the weak participles, those in *–átum*, *–útum* and *–ítum* regularly remained, but the participles in *–étum* (representing the Classical second conjugation) disappeared since the second conjugation verbs with weak participles either fell or changed conjugation groups (*delére* fell; *implére* changed conjugations to *–ire*).

§61a. In Classical Latin, there were two ways that the passive was formed, according to the tense involved. A number of tenses (the present indicative and subjunctive, the imperfect indicative and subjunctive, and the future) had a "synthetic passive," that is, the ending of the verb told that it was passive:

> videō 'I see / vide*or* 'I am seen'
> audiē*mus* 'we shall hear' / audiē*mur* 'we shall be heard'

b. The compound, "analytic," passives used a combination of *esse* 'to be' with the perfect passive participle. The workings of this tense often seem particularly confusing to the learner of Classical Latin because the tense of *esse* seems out of step with the meaning of the passive tense itself. For example, the *perfect* passive was built using the *present* of *esse* plus the perfect passive participle, and the *pluperfect* passive was built using the *imperfect* of *esse* and the perfect participle. These examples illustrate this incongruity:

sum 'I am' / auditus sum 'I *was* heard'
eras 'you were' / missus eras 'you *had been* sent'

When you make a literal translation, these passives *do* make logical sense: *audītus* is a perfect passive participle, thus is to be translated 'in the state of having been heard'. So *audītus sum* means 'I am (in the state of) [having been] heard', or, with less verbiage, 'I was heard'; *missus eras* = 'You were (in the state of) [having been] sent, = 'You had been sent'.

Vulgar Latin dropped all of the "synthetic" passives (the *audior* type), and rebuilt the passive based on the Classical analytical (*audītus sum*) formation. In doing so, the past participle came to lose the perfective passive notion it had in Classical Latin; so *audītus sum*, which meant 'I was heard' in Classical Latin, meant 'I am heard' in Vulgar Latin. The Classical construction was just as illogical to Vulgar Latin speakers as it usually is to novice learners of Classical Latin today.

The perfect passive in Vulgar Latin, then, became *laudatus fui* 'I was praised'.

§62. Deponent verbs (§46b), which were conjugated as passives but were active in meaning in Classical Latin, usually became active in form in Vulgar Latin. (The infinitives listed below, with their final long *–i*, are examples of the formation of the Classical present passive infinitive.)

CL fábulor 'I speak'	VL fábulo
fabulắrī 'to speak'	fabuláre (Sp. *hablar*)
lŭctor 'I fight'	lúcto
luctắrī 'to 'fight'	luctáare (Sp. *luchar*)
mŏrior 'I die'	mório
mŏrī 'to die,	moríre (Sp. *morir*)
sĕquor 'I follow'	séquo
sĕquī 'to follow'	sequíre (Sp. *seguir*)

Those Classical deponents which did not go to the regular conjugations were absorbed into the inchoative system (§49): CL *pátior* 'I suffer,' *pátī* 'to suffer' became VL *patescére* (Sp. *padecer*).

§63. There were a few Classical verbs that had more than one stem in the same tense, and a few verbs that had tenses seemingly not built on any of the principal parts (notably the present and imperfect of *ésse* 'to be', the present of *vélle* 'to desire', and the present and imperfect of *īre* 'to go'). Classical Latin grammarians call these the IRREGULAR verbs, and there were only about a half dozen of them.

Four will be given here in, a sampling of tenses, because of their importance to Spanish. Here are their principal parts:

'to be' *sum, ésse, fúī,* ⸺
'to be able' *póssum, pósse, pótuī,* ⸺
'to desire' *vólō, vélle, vóluī,* ⸺
'to go' *éō, īre, íī, ítum*

Note the unique infinitives (lacking *r*) of the first three, as well as their lack of the perfect passive participles.

Present Active Indicative

sum	póssum	vólō	éō
es	pótes	vis	īs
est	pótest	vult	it
súmus	póssumus	vólumus	ímus
éstis	potéstis	vúltis	ítis
sunt	póssunt	vólunt	éunt

Imperfect Active Indicative

éram	póteram	volébam	íbam
éras	póterās	volébās	íbat
érat	póterat	volébat	íbat
erámus	poterámus	volēbámus	ībámus
erátis	poterátis	volēbátis	ībátis
érant	póterant	volébant	íbant

Perfect Active Indicative

fŭī	pótuī	vóluī	íī
fuístī	potuístī	voluístī	ístī
fŭit	pótuit	vóluit	íit
fúimus	potúimus	volúimus	íimus
fŭıstis	potuístis	voluístis	ístis
fuérunt	potuérunt	voluérunt	iérunt

Vulgar Latin did not tolerate as much irregularity as Classical Latin, and it regularized many things: the irregular infinitives were easily rebuilt based on conjugated forms to conform to regular patterns. *Esse* became VL *éssere; velle* became VL *volére* (rebuilt on its perfect form *vóluī*); and *posse* became *potére* (Sp. *poder*) was also rebuilt on its perfect, *pótuī*. The present tense of *potére* was based on its new infinitive, thus: *póteo, pótes, pótet, potémus, potétis, pótent.* Although the conjugation of *íre* already conformed to normal patterns, its conjugated forms were much too short, amounting only to endings. The forms of *íre* were replaced in most tenses in Vulgar Latin by those of *vadére* 'to walk' (CL *vádere*).

Ferre 'to bear', which had the most disparate principal parts (§48), was lost in Vulgar Latin, and it was replaced by *portáre* in some areas and by *leváre* in the Iberian Peninsula (Sp. *llevar*). The compounds of *ferre*, however, did manage to survive by changing to the –*ire* conjugation group: CL *sufférre* became VL *sufferíre*, CL *offérre* became VL *offeríre* (cf. French *offrir*), later to take the inchoative suffix and become *ofrecer* in Spanish.

§64. There were other Classical verbs that were lost since they seemingly did not have enough phonetic substance, and were replaced by longer equivalents in Vulgar Latin. CL *édere* became *comedére* in Hispania (Sp. *comer*), CL *scíre* yielded to VL *sapére* (< CL *sápĕre*), CL *flére* was lost in favor of *ploráre* in Vulgar Latin (Sp. *llorar*), CL *émĕre* fell, replaced by VL *comperáre* (Sp. *comprar*).

§65. The present subjunctive effectively was based on the first person singular of the present indicative, without the –ō (I *laud*–, II *vide*–, III *pōn*–, *fugi*–, IV *audi*–). The third conjugation, not listed below, had the same endings shared by the second and fourth conjugations (–am, –as, –at, etc.):

láudem	vídeam	áudiam
láudēs	vídeās	áudiās
láudet	vídeat	áudiat
laudēmus	videámus	audiámus
laudētis	videátis	audiátis
láudent	vídeant	áudiant

This tense was retained in Vulgar Latin with little change. It was in the *remaining* tenses that the subjunctive showed important changes in Vulgar Latin. The imperfect subjunctive (CL *laudārem, audīrem*) and the perfect subjunctive, with loss of –ve– in the first and fourth conjugations (CL *laudā[ve]rim, audī[ve]rim*) came to have the same pronunciation in Vulgar Latin since the CL –rem and –rĭm would both be VL –re. As a result of this phonetic conflict, both tenses were lost, and the pluperfect subjunctive, with a loss of –vi– (*laudā[vi]ssem, audī[vi]ssem*), moved up to take over the function of the lost perfect and imperfect subjunctives (Väänänen §307).

§66. To make verbs negative, Classical Latin used one of two words, *nōn* or *nē*, depending on the grammatical context. *Nōn* was used for ordinary, "indicative," negation:

Ego Romanus nōn sum. 'I am not a Roman'
Ea amica mea nōn est. 'She is not my friend'

For the type of negation to indicate PROHIBITION, Classical Latin used *nē*:

Monuit eōs nē hoc facerent. 'He warned them not to do it.'
Hortor eum nē veniat. 'I exhort him not to come.'

Sometimes, however, the use of *nōn* encroached on the territory of *nē*. A quotation from Terence (185–159 B.C.), in which prohibition is clearly implied, shows this encroachment: "Non tē credas Davom ludere" 'Don't think you're playing Davos'. Petronius (first century

A.D.), noted for a style which consciously introduced Vulgar Latin grammar and vocabulary (§1), wrote this example in which *nōn* substitutes for *nē*: "et mē nōn facias ringentem" 'and don't make me gnash my teeth'. In the Vulgar Latin of Hispania, however, the complication was resolved when *non* took over both functions.

Other negative words in Classical Latin included *nullus* 'none', *nēmo* 'no one', *nihil* 'nothing', and *númquam* 'never'; all of these fell in Hispania except the last.

Classical Latin had no word that meant "yes." In an affirmative answer, the style was to repeat the verb of the question in the positive form to mean "yes," as in Portuguese. Here is an example from Plautus (ca. 254–184 B.C.): "Tuus servus est? Meus est." 'Is this your slave? Yes.'

A reinforcing word such as *certē* 'certainly', *verum* 'true', or *sīc* 'thus', was sometimes used in the response, and at times these words became the whole answer. This example from Terence shows the genesis of the Spanish *sí*: "Illa maneat? Sīc." 'Is she the one who is staying? Yes.'

Adverbs

§67a. Adverbs were formed in two different ways, depending on which type of adjective they were built. To make an adverb based on the first type of adjective (1st or 2nd declensions), –*ē* was added to the stem of the adjective:

> líberus 'free,—líberē 'freely'
> Romanicus 'Roman'—románicē 'in a Roman way'

To form an adverb based on the second type of adjective (3rd declension), the ending –*iter* was added to the genitive stem:

Nominative	Genitive
fórtis	fórtis 'strong,—fórtiter 'strongly'
félix	félicis 'happy,—fēlíciter 'happily,
céler	céleris 'swift,—celériter 'swiftly'

b. The comparative and superlative of adverbs were formed in this way: –*ius* replaced either –*ē* or –*iter* to make the comparative, and –*íssimē* replaced the same endings to make the superlative:

fórtiter	fórtius	fortíssimē
'strongly'	'more strongly'	'most strongly'

There were a few irregular comparative and superlative adverb formations, notably those of *bene* and *male*:

béne 'well', mélius 'better', óptimē 'best'
mále 'badly', péius 'worse', péssimē 'worst'

§68. Vulgar Latin, as a rule, did not continue the usual Classical formation of adverbs by adding –*ē* or –*iter* to adjectives. There is, however, one curious remnant of the –*ē* adverb which has survived in Spanish as a noun. *Fabulārī románicē* 'to speak in a Roman way [i.e., to speak Latin], became *hablar romance* in Spanish.

In Vulgar Latin, the preferred way to form adverbs was by using *mente* (the ablative of the feminine noun *mens* 'mind') following an adjective (which also, naturally, had to be feminine in form). Originally, the two parts were separated: *bona mente* 'with a good mind = well', *devota mente* 'with a devoted mind = devotedly', *intrepida mente* 'with an intrepid mind = intrepidly'. The comparative and superlative of adverbs in Vulgar Latin were formed like the comparative and superlative of adjectives, preceded by *mágis* or *plūs*.

A number of Classical adverbs (of time, place, etc.) did not derive from adjectives: *étiam* 'even', *íam* 'already', *sīc* 'thus', *támen* 'nevertheless', *sěmper* 'always', *ŭnde* 'from which', *quómodo* 'in what way', *súbitō* 'suddenly', *sémel* 'one time', *póstea* 'afterwards', *hīc* 'here', and others. A few of these (*íam, sīc, sěmper, ŭnde, quómodo*) were continued into Spanish.

Prepositions

§69. Many Classical prepositions were never used in popular speech, and therefore disappeared from the language. *Apud* 'at' gave way to *ad* (Sp. *a*), *ex*, when by itself, yielded to *de* (Sp. *de*), and *ob* to *pro* (Sp. *por*). Vulgar Latin sometimes combined two or three prepositions with similar meaning in its quest for emphasis and phonetic substance; among these were de ex post (Sp. después), *de trans* (Sp. *detrás*), *de in ante* (Sp. *delante*).

Latin Syntax[21]

§70. Because Classical Latin words bore grammatical identification, word order was not as stringent as in an analytic language such as English. For example, no matter where the word *pater* 'father' appeared in the sentence, it had to be the subject since it was in the nominative case. No matter where the word *fīlium* 'son' appeared in the sentence' it had to be the direct object since it was in the accusative case. No matter where the word *videt* 'sees' was in the sentence, the noun in the nominative case would always be its subject. Therefore, all of the following were possible, and all meant 'The father sees the son', each with a slight difference in emphasis.

1. Pater fīlium videt.	4. Fīlium videt pater.
2. Pater videt fīlium.	5. Videt pater fīlium.
3. Fīlium pater videt.	6. Videt fīlium pater.

§71. In practice, however, for a normal sentence, the first example (*Pater fīlium videt*) was the usual pattern: subject, direct object, verb. If there were other elements in a sentence, this was the usual order: 1) subject, 2) indirect object, 3) direct object, 4) adverbial modifiers, 5) verb. For example, "Cīcero amicīs litteras sæpe scrīpsit" 'Cicero often wrote letters to friends'.

Classical Latin syntax placed the most important element at the end of the sentence, as in modern Spanish; in most declarative sentences, the verb was the most important element, and that accounts for its common final position. However, to answer the question "Quem videt pater?" 'Whom does the father see?', the most important element in the answer would be the answer word (*fīlium*), So in this particular case, the second example from above would be the best solution (*Pater videt fīlium*).

Whereas there were a great number of possible syntactic combi-

---

[21] Syntax, i.e., word order, is the most complex and important part of any language. Volumes have been devoted to Latin syntax, so what appears here is really only minimal information.

nations, all of which could be understood, the standard spoken language did not come close to using them all.

Vulgar Latin did not permit the flexible syntax of Classical Latin, but depended, as analytic languages must, on a rather fixed word order. It also showed certain grammatical relationships (again as analytic languages do) largely by prepositions preceding nouns rather than endings following them, as the attested examples in the next sections will show.

§72. The accusative gradually took over the functions of the other oblique cases (§27) by becoming the object of different prepositions. The genitive function was usually seen as *de + accusative*:

> CL gen. mulíeris = VL de muliere 'of a woman,
> CL gen. multórum = VL de multos 'of many'

The dative was assumed by *ad + accusative*:

> CL dat. carnificī = VL ad carnifice 'to the executioner'

The ablative was the case most frequently governed by a preposition in Classical Latin, yet the accusative took over even the ablative use:

> CL abl. ab hortō = VL ab hortu 'from the garden,
> CL abl. cum iūmentō = VL cum iumentu 'with the mule'

§73. Since Classical Latin had a word order that was not absolutely rigid, you can imagine that some device must have been needed to differentiate a declarative sentence from an interrogative one. Such a device did exist.

To make an ordinary declarative sentence into a question, the particle *–ne* was attached to the first word of the sentence:

> Venisne? 'Are you coming?,
> Vidistine meum fratrem? 'Did you see my brother?'

If a positive answer was expected, the word *nonne* began the question:

> Nonne venīs? 'You're coming, aren't you?'
> Nonne vidisti fratrem meum? 'You saw my brother, didn't
> you?'

If a negative answer was expected, the word *num* started the
question:

> Num venis? 'You're not coming, are you?'
> Num vidisti fratrem meum? 'You didn't see my brother, did
> you?'

These question markers fell in Vulgar Latin, and word order
(coupled probably with varied intonation) replaced them.

§74a. One of the distinctive constructions in Classical Latin was
the INFINITIVE WITH SUBJECT ACCUSATIVE. If the action of a subject
and a verb (*ego veniō* 'I come', *tū remanēs* 'you remain') was report-
ed after a verb of saying, thinking, or perceiving, the subject was
recorded in the accusative and the verb turned into an infinitive:

> Ego veniō. Dicunt mē venire.
> 'I come. They say that I come.'
> Tū remanēs. Crēdunt tē remanēre.
> 'You remain. They believe that you remain.'

If the action happened prior to the time of recording, the perfect
infinitive was used:

> Ego vēnī. Dicunt mē vēnisse.
> 'I came. They say that I came.'
> Tū remansistī. Crēdunt tē remansisse
> 'You remained. They believe that you remained.'

b. This construction had another function, which, in the Romance Languages, would be the subjunctive. It is strikingly similar
to its English translation:

Coēgērunt mē ire. 'They forced me to go.'
Coēgimus eōs remanēre. 'We forced them to remain.'

c. In Vulgar Latin this construction was not used. The Vulgar Latin replacement for this lost structure used *quia* or *quod* 'that' plus a conjugated verb. These examples are extremely close to their Romance equivalents:

Nesciebat quia Jesus erat. 'He did not know that Jesus existed.'
Credimus quod mentis. 'We believe that you are lying.'

§75a. Another typical construction of Classical Latin involved the use of the SUPINE. The supine was based on the perfect passive participle and had two forms: the first ended in –*um*, and the second ended in –*ū*. The first form of the supine was used after a verb of motion to express purpose, and is translated by an infinitive:

Veniō lectum. 'I come to read.'
Eunt victum. 'They go to conquer.'

b. The second form of the supine was used after adjectives such as *difficilis* 'difficult', *facilis* 'easy', *ūtilis* 'useful', *turpis* 'shameful', and *bonus* 'good', and is again translated in English by an infinitive:

facilis dictū 'easy to say'
bonus visū 'good to see'
ūtilis factū 'useful to do'

In Vulgar Latin, the supine equally disappeared. The first use of the supine, *veniō lectum* 'I come to read', began to be replaced even in Classical Latin by a construction using the gerund (§47a), *veniō ad legendum*. This construction laid the foundation for the Vulgar Latin solution, *venio ad legere* (Sp. *vengo a leer*). The second use of the supine, *facilis dictū* 'easy to say', was replaced by *facile ad dícere* in Vulgar Latin (Sp. *fácil de decir*).

§76. The Classical Latin subjunctive did not have the same subordinating conjunctions that the modern Romance Languages use. It used *ut* 'in order that, so that' and *nē* 'so that... not' as its main conjunctions.

> Imperat nōbis ut veniāmus. 'He commands us to come.'
> Imperat nōbis nē remaneāmus.
>   'He commands us not to remain.'
> Hoc legimus ut discāmus. 'We read this in order to learn.'
> Hoc dicunt nē eum offendant.
>   'They say this so they won't offend him.'

The conjunctions *nē* and *ut* were lost in Vulgar Latin and were replaced by *quod*. For example, CL *imperat nōbis ut veniāmus* would be *imperat nos quod veniamus* in Vulgar Latin. In addition, infinitives replaced some subjunctives:

> CL Vadunt ut orent = VL Vadent orare 'They come to plead.'
> CL Venit aliquis ut audiat = VL Venit aliquis audire
>   'Someone comes to hear.'

2

Historical Phonetics:
Sound Change Through Time

Stressed Vowels

§77. The stressed Vulgar Latin vowels were very strong and very stable. Each of the seven Vulgar Latin stressed vowels has a corresponding vowel or diphthong in modern Spanish. Vulgar Latin stress overwhelmingly carried through to the modern Spanish word no matter how much phonetic change the word underwent, as the examples below show:

Vulgar Latin	*Spanish*
mátre	mádre
cóllocat	cuélga
artículu	artéjo
rápidu	ráudo
muliére (§7c)	mujér
convénit (§17b)	conviéne
tenébras (§17c)	tiniéblas

§78. The chart on the next page, which follows the outline of the vowel triangle (§3), shows the development of stressed vowels from Classical Latin to Spanish:

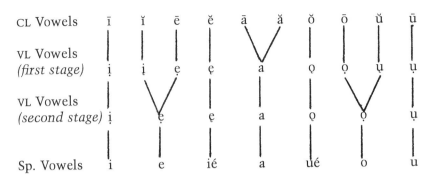

The complete development from Classical Latin to modern Spanish is given for two reasons: first, in the sections that follow, Classical Latin examples will be alluded to frequently, and second, Vulgar Latin examples are usually spelled according to the *first* stage, as explained in footnote 10 of Chapter 1.

Notice that the symmetry of stressed vowel development has continued into Spanish. The two vowels at the extremes of the vowel chart and the one in the middle have remained pure, but the ones flanking the middle have diphthongized in Spanish, and the ones that are second and third from either end have simplified to the close version of the third one in.[1] The development of Spanish vowels in initial, final, and pre- or post-tonic positions is also symmetrical, as you will see.

The sections that follow show in general what happened to the individual stressed vowels. A few special cases and common exceptions are also included, but vowel inflections due to a following *yod* will be treated in later sections (§104-110).

§79. The Vulgar Latin stressed í (from CL ī) remained without change:

fícu > higo   lítigat > lidia
fílu > hilo   lixíva > lejía
fíliu > hijo   scríptu > escrito

---

[1] This is much easier to grasp in the chart than read about.

vínea > viña   víte > vid
vínu > vino

§80a. The Vulgar Latin stressed ę (from CL ĕ, ē, œ) generally remained as e. Vulgar Latin examples from CL ĭ (usually spelled with i in Vulgar Latin transcriptions):

bíbit > bebe   pílu > pelo
cília > ceja   sínu > seno
cíppu > cepo   stríctu > estrecho
círca > cerca   vír(i)de > verde
língua > lengua   vítta > veta

Vulgar Latin examples from CL ē:

cębu > cebo   ręte > red
monęta > moneda   sęta > seda
plęnu > lleno   tęla > tela

Vulgar Latin examples from CL œ:

fędu (CL fœdum) > feo
pęna (CL pœnam) > pena

CL nįvem uncharacteristically became nęve in the Vulgar Latin of Hispania. This latter form developed to the Sp. *nieve.*
b. In hiatus, the VL í (from CL i) rose to į:

vía (CL via) > vía

§81a. The Vulgar Latin stressed ę (from CL ĕ, æ) generally diphthongized to *ié.* The process seems to have been that the Vulgar Latin vowel first lengthened, then diphthongized to [eɛ], and finally the first element became a *yod.*

cęntu > ciento   mętu > miedo
cęrtu > cierto   nębula > niebla
cęrvu > ciervo   pęde > pie

ę́remu > yermo	pę́lle > piel
ę́qua > yegua	pę́rdo > pierdo
fę́sta > fiesta	pę́tra > piedra

Vulgar Latin examples from CL æ:

cę́cu (CL cæcum) > ciego	grę́cu(CL græcum) > griego
cę́lu (CL cælum) > cielo	quę́ro (CL quæro) > quiero

Diphthongization took place whether the stressed syllable was OPEN (that is, ending in a vowel: *pé–de, né–bu–la*) or CLOSED (that is, ending in a consonant, and therefore closed by it: *pér–do, cén–tu*). This feature is unusual since other Romance Languages will diphthongize only in open syllables.

b. In some instances the Vulgar Latin stressed *ę* first became *ié* in the normal fashion, then was reduced to *i* during the period of Old Spanish.

i. When the Vulgar Latin stressed *ę* was in hiatus, it first diphthongized, thus creating an unusual vocalic cluster. This cluster then simplified by eliminating the middle element. Note the shift in stress as well:

meu > m*ie*o > mío
iudeu > iud*ie*o > judío

ii. The Vulgar Latin endings *–ĕllu* and *–ĕlla* developed to *–iello* [yɛłyo] and *–iella* [yɛłya] in Old Spanish. Due to the excessive number of vowel sounds in close proximity, the "middle" element was again lost, leaving *–illo* [íło] and *–illa* [íła]:

VL castę́llu > OSp. castiello > Sp. castillo
VL cultę́llu > OSp. cuchiello > Sp. cuchillo
VL martę́llu > OSp. martiello > Sp. martillo
VL sę́lla > OSp. siella > Sp. silla

Following a consonant cluster known as MUTA CUM LIQUIDA (i.e., a stop or a SPIRANT[2]]+ *l* or *r*), diphthongs usually simplified:

VL intégro > OSp. entriego > Sp. entrego
VL prẹssa > OSp. priessa > Sp. prisa
VL prẹstu > OSp. priesto > Sp. presto

§82. The stressed VL *a* (from CL ă or ā) remained as *a* in Spanish:

ánnu > año	mátre > madre
cápra > cabra	pátre > padre
cáput > cabo	plátea > plaza
flámma > llama	plánu > llano
mánu > mano	sánguine > sangre

§83a. The Vulgar Latin stressed ǫ (from CL ŏ) diphthongized to *ué*:

bǫnu > bueno	mǫrte > muerte
cǫrvu > cuervo	nǫve > nueve
cǫva > cueva	pǫnte > puente
fǫrte > fuerte	pǫrta > puerta
mǫla > muela	sǫrte > suerte

The mechanics of this change are more complicated than the change from stressed *ẹ* to *ié*. Here, the vowel lengthened, then diphthongized to [oó], then the first element became the back semi-vowel [w], yielding *uó* (the stage in which modern Italian has remained: *buono, nuovo*). Certain Old Spanish dialects also document this stage of development: *puode, tuorto*. The *o* element then began to move away from the [w] element, following the outline of the vowel triangle (§3) first to *uá* (OSp. *puarta, uamne* [*hombre*]), then to its final form *ué*.

This diphthongization also took place whether the syllable was

---

[2] A spirant (also called a FRICATIVE) is a sound (unvoiced or voiced) where air is released under pressure through a constricted opening. Unvoiced spirants include [s, ʃ, x, f, θ]. Voiced spirants include [β, đ, ɣ, v, z].

open or closed.

  b. A NASAL consonant (i.e., *m* or *n*) sometimes impeded the diphthongization of the stressed ǫ by closing it to ọ.

cọ́mite > conde
họ́mine > hombre
mọ́nte > monte

In Old Spanish dialects, the first two of the examples above were seen with diphthongized vowels, but none has survived in modern Castilian (OSp. *cuende, uemne* [= *hombre*]).

  However, in many cases the stressed ǫ did diphthongize before a nasal sound:

sǫ́mnu > sueño   pǫ́nte > puente
dǫ́mnu > dueño   frǫ́nte > OSp. fruente
fǫ́nte > fuente

  c. The [w] element of the diphthong was sometimes absorbed by the *muta cum liquida* cluster (§81), leaving only the *e*:

frǫ́nte > fruente > frente
flǫ́ccu > flueco > fleco

§84. Classical Latin *au*, which was commonly ǫ already in Vulgar Latin, developed to *o* in Spanish:

auca > oca   causa > cosa
auru > oro   mauru > moro
caule> col   tauru > toro
paucu > poco   thesauru > tesoro
paup(e)re > pobre

Au first changed to *óu* (the stage which is usually retained in modern Portuguese: *ouro, mouro, pouco, touro*). From here, the diphthong simplified to *o*. The Spanish language, therefore, rejected both the *uó* and the *óu* diphthongs (§83a).

§85. The Vulgar Latin stressed ǫ (from CL ō and ŭ), became o in Spanish.

Vulgar Latin examples from CL ŭ (spelled u in inscriptions):

cepúlla > cebolla	púteu > pozo
cúppa > copa	pútre > podre
lúmbu > lomo	rúptu > roto
músca > mosca	túrre > torre
púllu > pollo	

Vulgar Latin examples from CL ō:

hǫ́ra > hora	tǫ́tu > todo
ratiǫ́ne > razón	vǫ́ta > boda

CL nŭcem should have given noz in Spanish. Sp. nuez goes back to a Vulgar Latin form with ǫ: nǫce.

§86. The Vulgar Latin stressed ų́ (from CL ū) usually remained in Spanish:

acų́tu > agudo	mų́tu > mudo
dų́ru > duro	scų́tu > escudo
fų́mu > humo	sų́cidu > sucio
leg m(i)ne > legumbre	tų́ > tú
mų́ru > muro	ųnu > uno

Initial Vowels

§87. An initial vowel is the unstressed vowel found in the first syllable of a word (ra–tió–ne, sus–péc–ta); it does not necessarily mean that the vowel begins the word, although such is often the case (a–rá–nea, [h]i–ber–nu).

After the stressed vowels, the initial vowels were the strongest group; only rarely was one lost. The chart below shows the development of initial vowels from Classical Latin to Spanish:

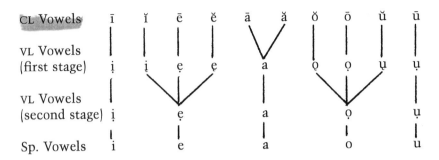

CL Vowels	ī	ĭ	ē	ĕ	ā	ă	ŏ	ō	ŭ	ū
VL Vowels (first stage)	i̯	i̯	ẹ	ẹ̆	a		ǫ	ǫ	u̯	u̯
VL Vowels (second stage)	i̯		ẹ		a		ǫ		u̯	
Sp. Vowels	i		e		a		o		u	

The evolution of initial vowels from Classical Latin to Spanish is again perfectly symmetrical. It should be noticed that all intial *e*'s and *o*'s were ultimately close in Vulgar Latin.

§88. The initial VL *i* (from CL *ī*) remained intact in Spanish:

ci̯vitáte > ciudad   li̯mitáre > lindar
fi̯láre > hilar   ri̯pária > ribera
hi̯bérnu > invierno   ti̯tióne > tizón

Classical Latin *rídĕre* and *dícĕre* developed exceptionally into *reír* and *decir*. In the Vulgar Latin of the Iberian Peninsula, both of these verbs changed conjugation groups to become *ri̯díre* and *di̯círe*. From this stage, the initial vowels dissimilated to *e* (§149d).

§89. The initial *e* (from CL *ĭ*, *ē*, *ĕ*, *æ*) remained *ẹ* in Spanish: Vulgar Latin examples from CL *ĭ* (spelled *i* in transcriptions):

ci̯rcáre > cercar   mi̯nútu > menudo
pi̯scáre > pescar   pli̯care > llegar

Vulgar Latin examples from CL *ē*:

lẹntíc(u)la > lenteja   sẹcúru > seguro

Vulgar Latin examples from CL *æ*:

prẹcóne (CL præcone) > pregón

cẹpúlla (CL cæpullam) > cebolla

§90. The initial VL *a* (from CL ā, and ă) remained intact:

aránea > araña	matur(i)cáre > madrugar
cabállu > caballo	paréte > pared
clamáre > llamar	partíre > partir
laváre > lavar	ratióne > razón

§91. The initial VL *o* (from CL ŭ, ō, ŏ, *au*) gave *o* in Spanish. Vulgar Latin examples from CL ŭ (spelled *u* in transcriptions):

lụcráre > lograr	sụspécta > sospecha
sụpérbia > soberbia	

The change of CL *dŭbitãre* into Sp. *dudar* (instead of the expected *dodar*) has not yet been satisfactorily explained.

Vulgar Latin examples from CL ō:

nọmináre > nombrar	fọrmáceu > hormazo

Vulgar Latin examples from CL ŏ (close *o* in Vulgar Latin):

cọmedére > comer	cọrtícia > corteza
cọróna > corona	sọnáre > sonar

Vulgar Latin examples from CL *au*:

autúmnu > otoño	pausare > posar

§92. The intital VL ụ (from CL ū) remained intact in Spanish:

cụráre > curar	nụb(i)láre > nublar
dụrítia > dureza	pụrítia > pureza
jụd(i)cáre > juzgar	sụdáre > sudar
mụtáre > mudar	

Final Vowels

§93. A final vowel is the unstressed vowel in the last syllable of a word (*fé–ci, amí–cas*). It does not necessarily mean that the vowel must end the word, although such is commonly the case.

Of the groups of vowels discussed so far, the final vowel group is the weakest. The seven Vulgar Latin final vowels (second stage) have been reduced to only three in Spanish, and much of the time a Vulgar Latin final *e* was lost on its way to modern Spanish. The chart below shows the symmetrical development of final vowels from Classical Latin to modern Spanish:

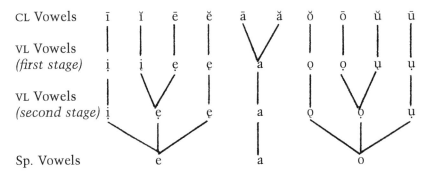

§94. The Vulgar Latin final *i* (from CL *ī*) became e in Spanish:

hábui̯ > hube	pótui̯ > pude
pósui̯ > puse	véni̯ > vine

Spanish words which end in an unstressed *i*, such as *beriberi, bikini, cursi, espagueti, hindi, kaqui, kiwi, mariachi, taxi,* or *yogui,* are either of learned or foreign origin.

§95a. The Vulgar Latin final *e* (from CL *ĭ, ē, ě*) usually disappeared during the period of Old Spanish when following any DENTAL or ALVEOLAR[3] consonant (except *t*): *-d, -l, -n, -r, -z* [dz], and *s*. In Old Spanish dialects, the final *-e* was commonly lost following other consonants as well (*noch, nuef*), but it was restored in all cases in Castilian (*noche, nueve*):

After Romance *d*:

etáte > eda*d*e > edad	réte > re*d*e > red
caritáte > carida*d*e > caridad	salúte > salu*d*e > salud
civ(i)táte > çibda*d*e > ciudad	síte > se*d*e > sed
líte > li*d*e > lid	tenéte > tene*d*e > tened
paréte > pare*d*e > pared	virtute > virtu*d*e > virtud

After *l*:

cáule > col	sále > sal
fidéle > fiel	sóle > sol
mále > mal	víle > vil

If a double *l* became final through the loss of *-e* (which was not the usual case), the *l* could not develop to [ɫ]; *pelle > piel, valle > val*.

After *n*:

bastóne > bastón	precóne > pregón
páne > pan	ratióne > razón
pinnóne > piñón	titióne > tizón

After *r*:

colóre > color	potére > poder
flóre > flor	rumóre > rumor
máre > mar	vendére > vender

---

[3] A DENTAL consonant is one that is formed with the tongue against the teeth (Spanish examples include [d, t]); an ALVEOLAR consonant is one that is produced with the tongue against the ridge behind the teeth (Spanish examples include [n, l, r, s, z]).

pastóre > pastor   veníre > venir

After *s*:

cortése > cortés   revése > revés
mése > mes   trasvése > través
montése > montés   tússe > tos

After a Proto–Spanish *z* (pronnounced [dz]):[4]

crúce > cruze > cruz   nóce > nueze > nuez
déce > dieze > diez   páce > paze > paz
fálce > foz > hoz   perdíce > perdize > perdiz
lúce > luze > luz

b. Due to its role as a verb ending, final *e* did not fall from verbs, even though phonetic circumstances would have allowed it to fall:[5]

Noun	*Verb*
tusse > tos	tussit > tose
colore > color	coloret > colore
luce > luz	lucet > luce
sale > sal	salit > sale

c. If *two* consonants preceded the final *e* in Vulgar Latin, the –*e* had to remain in order to make the final syllable possible:

d(e) un–de > donde   par–te > parte
for–te > fuerte   pa–tre > padre
le–pre > liebre   pon–te > puente

---

[4] Proto–Spanish refers to the pre–literary stage of the language.

[5] During the Middle Ages, for a time, the final *e* DID fall in some verb endings, but it was finally restored to Castilian verbs in all cases. Here are some examples form the present tense: *faz, diz, sal, pon, tien, vien, quier*; and from the preterite: *fiz, pus, quis, vin*. Portuguese has retained the first three of these preterites at this stage of development.

ma–tre > madre   vul–t(u)re > buitre
no–b(i)le > noble

In Old Spanish, the –e was lost after a consonant + d or t (OSp.
dond, fuert) only to be restored later.

  d. If the consonant of the final syllable dropped, causing the
final e to be in hiatus with the preceding vowel, the –e changed to
a *yod*:

bove > buee > buey   lege > lee > ley
grege > gree > grey   rege > ree > rey

However, in the case of verbs where a consonant was lost, and the
final e was the ending of a verb, the –e had to remain intact due to
the requirements of the conjugation system (§173b):

legit > lee   trahit > trae
credit > cree

§96. The Vulgar Latin final a (from CL ā, ă) remained in Spanish:

ámas > amas   fólia > hoja
amíca > amiga   língua > lengua
cília > ceja   spíca > espiga

§97. The Vulgar Latin final ụ (from CL ū) and o (from CL ŭ, ō, ŏ)
became o in Spanish:

Vulgar Latin example from CL ū:

córnụ > cuerno

Vulgar Latin examples from CL ŭ:

lácụ > lago   témpụ > tiempo
mútụ > mudo   vínụ > vino
táurụ > toro

Vulgar Latin examples from CL ō:

ámǫ> amo	plícǫ > llego
mútǫs > mudos	quandǫ > cuando

Vulgar Latin example from CL ŏ:

cǐtǒ > cedo

Words such as *espíritu, ímpetu, miau, ñu, tribu* and *urdu* are of learned, foreign, or onmatopoeic origin.

Pretonic and Posttonic Internal Vowels

§98. Pretonic internal vowels, as the name indicates, are those that are between the initial vowel and the stressed vowel; posttonic internal vowels are between the stressed vowel and the final vowel. Pretonic and posttonic internal vowels had already begun to fall in Vulgar Latin, as seen in the examples from the *Appendix Probi* (§9).

As Vulgar Latin evolved to Spanish, almost every unstressed internal vowel was lost, with the exception of *a*. This loss of vowels is responsible for two major features in the Spanish phonetic system. First, the loss of the posttonic internal vowel made Spanish into a language where the stress on words normally fell on the penult. Italian, on the other hand, retained most posttonic internal vowels, so many of its words are stressed on the antepenult, as this comparative table shows:

Vulgar Latin	Italian	Spanish
dódeci	dódici	dóce
mánica	mánica	mánga
léttera	léttera	létra
nóbile	nóbile	nóble
sémita	sémita	sénda

Second, the loss of the internal unstressed vowels meant that some consonants that had never before been together were now forced to be in contact. Some of these new clusters created phonetic problems which the language had to work out one way or another, as shown below:

artíc(u)lu > artejo   lim(i)te > linde
cómp(u)to > cuento   lum(i)náre > lumbrar
commun(i)cáre > comulgar   másc(u)lu > macho
cúb(i)tu > codo   ráp(i)du > raudo
                                 rét(i)na > rienda

The consonantal evolutions shown above will be discussed as they arise in this chapter.

The chart below illustrates the general outcome of unstressed internal vowels:

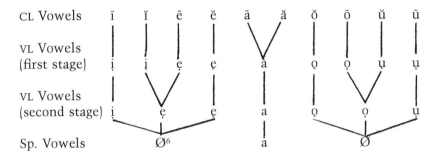

§99a.   In Vulgar Latin, pretonic internal vowels (except *a*) disappeared in most cases:

lim(i)táre > lindar   ver(e)cúndia > vergüenza
lum(i)náre > lumbrar   lab(o)ráre > labrar
sem(i)táriu > sendero   hon(o)ráre > honrar
cat(e)nátu > candado   cos(u(túra > costura
comp(e)rare > comprar   pop(u)lare > poblar
mal(e)díco > maldigo

The few examples with a pretonic internal *a* show that it was retained:

---

calamellu > caramillo   paradisu > paraíso

b. If there were *two* pretonic internal vowels, the one nearest the stress was lost:

caballicáre > cabalgar   humilitáte > humildad
communicáre > comulgar   ingeneráre > engendrar
cuminitiáre > comenzar   recuperáre > recobrar

In *cuminitiáre* there appear to be *three* pretonic internal vowels, but *ti* had become *ts* already in Vulgar Latin.

§100. There are two cases where the pretonic internal vowel was retained, even when the phonetic circumstances would have allowed it to drop. Both reasons are related to analogy.

First, there is the case of infinitives which are based on their conjugated forms. Thus, *rezbir* may be the reasonable phonetic development from VL *recipíre*, but the pretonic internal *i* was forced to remain in the infinitive under analogical pressure from the conjugated forms such as *recibo, recibes*, where the *i* is stressed.

Second, a word may not lose its pretonic interior vowel if another word in the same family is stressed on the vowel in question. For example, VL *maturáre* (Sp. *madurar*) could easily have given *madrar* were it not for the influence of the basic word *maduro*. Similarly, VL *olorósu* (Sp. *oloroso*) would have developed to *oldroso* or *orloso* were it not for the analogical pressure from *olor*.

§101. A *d* or a *g* between vowels often disappeared early (§12). When they fell having been in contact with a pretonic internal *i*, the *i* could not fall and was forced to remain (many times in the form of a *yod*, as in the second and third examples below):

cogitáre > cuidar
litigáre > lidiar
traditóre > traidor

§102. All posttonic interior vowels regularly fell (with the exception of words with a posttonic *a*):

ált(e)ru > otro
artíc(u)lu > artejo
cál(i)du > caldo
cóm(i)te > conde
cómp(u)to > cuento
cúb(i)tu > codo
déc(i)mu > diezmo
díg(i)tu > dedo
dóm(i)na > dueña
ér(e)ma > yerma
fáb(u)lat > habla
fém(i)na > hembra
fráx(i)nu > fresno
gáll(i)cu > galgo
héd(e)ra > hiedra
lép(o)re > liebre

lím(i)te > linde
lítt(e)ra > letra
mán(i)ca > manga
másc(u)lu > macho
néb(u)la > niebla
óc(u)lu > ojo
péd(i)cu > piezgo
póp(u)lat > puebla
pós(i)tu > puesto
ráp(i)du > raudo
rét(i)na > rienda
rób(o)re > roble
sáng(ui)ne > sangre
spéc(u)lu > espejo
vínd(i)cat > venga
vír(i)de > verde

A posttonic internal *a* (which was usually of Greek origin) was maintained in these examples:

aspáragu > espárrago
órphanu > huérfano
pélagu > piélago

ráphanu > rábano
sábana > sábana

§103a. A few words lost their final *e* rather than losing their posttonic internal vowel. When a Latin word is stressed on the antepenult in a syllable closed by an –*r*–, the unstressed internal vowel is retained. Final –*e* is then lost according to §95a. This is easy to see in the examples.[7]

árbore > árbol
cárcere > cárcel

mércuri > miércoles
stércore > estiércol

---

[7] Carmen Pensado (see BIBLIOGRAPHY) discovered this "law." I am grateful to Alex Selimov and Jerry Craddock for pointing it out to me. Some of these words were also affected by dissimilation (*árbol, mármol, estiércol, cárcel, miércoles, tórtola*), explained in §149.

márgine > margen   túrtura > tórtola
mármore > mármol

b. In a few other Latin words with an antepenult *not* closed by –r–, developed in the same way.

júvene > joven   céspite > césped

Vowel Inflection: The Vocalic *Yod*

§104. In Classical Latin, if an *e* or an *i* was in hiatus, each of the vowels was the nucleus of a separate syllable (*ví–ne–am, há–be–at*) (§7a); but in Vulgar Latin the two vowels merged into one syllable, and the *e* or *i* changed to a *yod* (*ví–nia, há–biat*).

The *yod* was unlike any other sound in the development of Spanish in that it could affect neighboring consonants and/or vowels in ways that no other sound could.

The *yod* could influence the adjacent consonants, transforming the their phonetic makeup, or it could affect the preceding vowel, pulling it up a step on the vowel triangle (§3). As the language developed, some later types of *yod* were so strong that they could alter the neighboring consonants *and* raise the preceding vowel.

In the sections that follow, only those *yods* that derive from vowels and affect only the preceding vowel (or sometimes the preceding vowel and consonant) will be discussed.

§105. Students of Spanish have often wondered why –*ir* verbs regularly have unusual changes in certain persons of certain tenses and the –*ar*/–*er* verbs do not. *Dormir*, for example, shows a *u* in *durmieron, durmamos, durmiendo*, whereas *volver* has no vowel change in parallel forms. The reason for this vocalic change lies in the effect exerted by a Vulgar Latin *yod* in certain forms only found the –*ire* conjugation.

In the example given below, the *yod* raised the preceding vowel (*e* or *o*) one step up the vowel triangle (to *i* or *u* respectively). Remember that these initial vowels were close in Vulgar Latin (§87):

servierunt > sirvieron	dormierunt > durmieron
servierant > sirvieran	dormierant > dumieran
serviamus > sirvamos	dormiamus > durmamos
serviendo > sirviendo	dormiendo > durmiendo

Notice that the *yod* was finally lost in the first person plural present subjunctive forms shown above (*serviamus > sirvamos, dormiamus > durmamos*). This was due to analogical pressure from the verbs that had no *yod* in that form (CL *laudēmus, ponāmus*). The *yod* was not lost, however, until it had raised the preceding vowel.

§106. When a Vulgar Latin stressed *ę* diphthongized (§81a), a *yod* was created which almost always raised a preceding initial unstressed *e*:

> cemẹ́ntu > cemiento > cimiento
> decẹ́mbre > deciembre > diciembre
> fervẹ́nte > ferviente > hirviente
> genẹ́sta > yeniesta > hiniesta
> semẹ́nte > semiente > simiente

§107. The *yod* in a Vulgar Latin *ai* cluster first raised the *a* to *e* (giving [ey])—the stage at which Portuguese remained), then the *yod* finally disappeared. Spanish reduced *ei* diphthongs to *e* as much as possible (other examples of this will be seen in §109, 144c):

> amai > amei > amé
> laicu > leigo > lego
> pacai > paguei > pagué
> vaika > veiga > vega

§108. In cases where a *yod* was created by the early loss of a *d*, the *yod* raised the preceding vowel. In the examples given below, the Classical Latin word is given so that the *d*, which would be lost in Vulgar Latin, may be seen.

> CL lĭmpidum > VL lẹmpiu > Sp. limpio

    CL tĕpi*d*um > VL tęp*i*u > Sp. t*i*bio
    CL tŏrbi*d*um > VL tǫrb*i*u > Sp. t*u*rbio

If the *yod* had had no effect, we could have expected *lempio, tebio,* and *torbio* in Spanish.

    §109. The Vulgar Latin clusters *r* + *yod*, *s* + *yod* and *p* + *yod* usually acted in one of two different ways depending on which vowel preceded them. If an *a* or an *ǫ* (CL *ŭ*) preceded the cluster, the *yod* was attracted to and combined with the preceding vowel; it mixed with *a* to give *ai*, then *ei*, and finally *e*, or it mixed with the *o* to give *ói*, then *óe* and finally *ué*. If an *e* preceded the *yod*, on the other hand, the *yod* either remained where it was, but raised the preceding *e* to *i*, much like in §108, or it mixed with the preceding *e* to give *ei* which was later reduced to *e*.

    r + *yod*:

        a*rea* > a*ira* > *eira* > *era*
        augu*riu* > ago*iru* > ago*iro* > agüe*ro*
        calda*riu* > calda*iru* > calde*iro* > calde*ro*
        co*riu* > co*iru* > cue*ro*

    s + *yod*

        ba*siu* > ba*isu* > be*iso* > be*so*
        ca*seu* > ca*siu* > ca*isu* > que*iso* > que*so*
        cera*sea* > cera*sia* > cera*iza* > cere*iza* > cere*za*

    p + *yod*

        ca*pio* > ca*ipo* > que*ipo* > que*po*
        sa*pia* > sa*ipa* > se*ipa* > se*pa*

Here are three examples where the preceding vowel is *e*;

        ce*reu* > ce*riu* > ci*rio*
        pre*sione* > pri*sión*

materia > madeira > madera

In contact with consonants other than *r*, *s*, *p*, the *yod* sometimes affected both the preceding vowel and the preceding consonant. Notice that the *oi* of all examples develops to *ué*, as in *cuero* above:

ciconia > cigoinia > cigüeña
risoneu > risoniu > risoinio > risueño
verecundia > vergoinza > vergüenza (cons. + *d* + *yod* >
    cons. + [z])

§110. Finally, although not a *yod* itself, a final CL *ī* could raise a preceding vowel one step through METAPHONY (a process which causes one vowel to be influenced by another vowel in the same word; in this case, the final CL *ī* [a high vowel] influenced the preceding *ē* to rise). Once it caused the preceding vowel to rise, it changed to *e* in accordance with §94:

CL fēcī > Sp. hice
CL vēnī > Sp. vine

The *Wau*

§111. The *yod*, which was built on the [i] sound, had a companion semi–vowel in Vulgar Latin known as WAU. This semivowel, whose name also derives from that of a Hebrew vowel, was built on the [u] sound. Its phonetic symbol is [w]. The *wau* has been seen in many Latin words already: *aurum, quando, laudat,* for example.

Like the *yod*, the *wau* could raise a preceding vowel, but its workings were neither as extensive nor as vigorous as those of the *yod*. Its effect on consonants was minimal, as will be seen in §§124b, 125b, 126d.

Here are some examples of the workings of *wau*. First, it could raise a preceding vowel: *eguale > igual*. It could also switch places with the preceding consonant, as the *yod* did in §109, and mix with the vowel it came into contact with. These same examples were seen in §58b:

sapui > saupi > OSp. sope
habui > haubi > OSp. ove

As CL víduam developed, the wau raised the preceding vowel and
also changed places with its neighboring consonant to give OSp.
víuda. Modern Spanish phonetic patterns have forced the stress to
move to the u, thus making the original wau into a full vowel:
viúda.

Consonants

§112. As consonants developed from Vulgar Latin to Spanish,
some of them underwent very little change while others were
wholly transformed.

Whereas the most stable vowel from Vulgar Latin to Spanish
was the one that bears the stress, the most stable consonant was the
one that began a word. In the passage from Vulgar Latin to Spanish,
most initial consonants were preserved intact, the notable exception
being the disappearance of most initial fs after the Middle Ages.

The medial consonants were the next strongest group. Vulgar
Latin unvoiced intervocalic stops [p, t, k] tended not only to voice,
but to become spirants [β, đ, γ] in Spanish. The Vulgar Latin un-
voiced double stops pp, tt, cc, tended to simplify to [p, t, k] whereas
Vulgar Latin voiced stops [d, g] tended to disappear on the way to
Spanish. In fact, most CL g's already had become yods in Vulgar
Latin, and these in turn had already begun to fall (§11b). Intervocalic
Latin [b] was strong and did not fall.

When a yod was generated through a consonant cluster, the
consonants usually underwent their most revolutionary changes,
sometimes being altered both in manner and place of articulation.
For example VL [kt], whose [k] element became a yod, evolved to Sp.
[č], and VL [ly] became Sp. [x].

Final position was the weakest. Effectively the only Vulgar Latin
final consonant that remained was the –s. Spanish, of course, has
many more final consonants than –s, largely due to the fall of final
–e.

§113. The initial d, l, m, n, p, r, t passed into Spanish without
any noticeable change:

Initial d

damnare > dañar
debita > deuda
digitu > dedo
dominu > dueño
duru > duro

Initial m

manu > mano
minus > menos
moneta > moneda
monte > monte
mutu > mudo

Initial p

pacat > paga
palu > palo
patre > padre
pectine > peine
porta > puerta

Initial t

tabula > tabla
tauru > toro
terra > tierra
timere > temer
turre > torre

Initial l

laborare > labrar
lacte > leche
lacu > lago
lupu > lobo
lectu > lecho

Initial n

nebula > niebla
nepta > nieta
nominare > nombrar
nova > nueva
nutrire > nodrir

Initial r

rapidu > raudo
ridire > reír
rota > rueda
rotundu > redondo
rugitu > ruido

§114. Since the days of Vulgar Latin, *b* and *v* were both pronounced *b* (§12), and this trait has carried through to modern Spanish:

basso > bajo
bellu > bello
bibit > bebe
bonu > bueno
bucca > boca
vacca > vaca

vacivu > vacío
verrere > barrer
versura > basura
vinu > vino
vita > vida
vult(u)re > buitre

Modern Spanish orthography favors *b–* before *a* or a back vowel, thus *barrer*, *basura* and *buitre* have *b–* instead of the etymological *v–*. This trend also applies internally as well: VL *advocatu* gives Sp. *abogado* and VL *aviolu* gives Sp. *abuelo*.

§115a. The VL *c–* before *a* or a back vowel maintained its [k] sound.

capio > quepo	colore > color
capitiu > cabezo	cǫrvu > cuervo
castellu > castillo	cụna > cuna
carru > carro	cụra > cura

On rare occasions, initial *c* became *g*, as in VL *cattu* > Sp. *gato*.

b. The CL *c–* before *e* or *i* was pronounced [k] in Classical Latin, but became [ts] in Vulgar Latin (§6). This latter sound remained throughout Old Spanish, but later simplified into two different spirants. In Castile, the [ts] sound simplified to a spirant based on [t], giving the modern [θ], and in the south of Spain, the [ts] simplified to the second part of the cluster [s].[8]

cęlu > celo	cereu > cirio
cęntu > ciento	cęrru > cierro
cepụlla > cebolla	cęrtu > cierto
cerásea > cereza	cęppu > cepo

In a few cases, VL *ci–* seems to have developed to *chi–* in modern Spanish. VL *cimice* has given Sp. *chinche*, probably via MOZARABIC pronunciation (i.e., the pronunciation of Christian speakers of early Spanish living in Moorish occupied territory), and apparently VL *ciccu* gave Sp. *chico*.

This brings up the problem of initial [č] in Spanish words. As

---

[8] There is a legend that a certain Spanish king had a lisp and insisted that all of his subjects imitate him in this speech defect. That is, he pronounced [θ] instead of [s]. How can this legend be true since both [θ] and [s] appear in the same word, frequently next to each other, as in *fascinar* and *doscientos*?

the sound system developed from Vulgar Latin to Castilian, the [č] sound evolved in the *middle* of words, but did not usually develop at the beginning of words. Those Spanish words of Latin origin that begin with *ch–* in Castilian have come from other Hispanic dialects or languages (Galician, Portuguese, Catalan, Mallorquin), or from other languages, including Arabic, Persian, French, Russian, English and a number of Indian languages from the Americas. Many Spanish words beginning with initial *ch–* are listed as being of "uncertain origin" in etymological dictionaries.

§116. The initial *f–* remained through the period of old Spanish, but finally disappeared, first pasing through the sound [h], before most vowels. There have been a number of theories suggested as to why this phenomenon took place in Castilian (whereas it did not in Portuguese and Catalan). The theory proposed by Menéndez Pidal is that the loss of *f–* is a direct influence of the Basque language, which has no initial *f*. When Basque speakers attempted to pronounce early Romance words beginning with *f*, they left the first sound off. The Basque country and Castile were close enough together so that a choice possibly had to be made in order to unify pronunciation: should the *f–* remain or not? The language seemingly opted in favor of the Basque solution.[9]

faba > haba	fata > hada
fabulare > hablar	fervere > hervir
facie > haz	fícatu > hígado
factu > hecho	fictu > hito
fastidiu > hastío	ficu > higo
filiu > hijo	fovea > hoya

---

[9] Philologists call this type of phenomenon "substrate influence." A SUBSTRATE language is one spoken in a land before a "conquering language" takes over. As speakers of the substrate language learn the new language, they naturally take some of their old linguistic habits with them. If these habits are widespread enough, they may influence the conquering language. I am not entirely convinced of this theory—how could such a small community influence such a large area? Also, in French, *de foris* has developed to *dehors* without any Basque influence.

fungu > hongo   fumu > humo
furnaceu > hornzo

In very short words, where *f–* was the *only* consonant, it tended to remain, contrary to the above trend: VL *fedu* > Sp. *feo*, VL *fide* > Sp. *fe*. The *f–* also usually remained before a diphthong[10] and always before *r–*:

fęsta > fiesta   fǫra > fuera
fidele > fiel   frenu > freno
fǫcu > fuego   frǫnte > OSp. fruente
fǫnte > fuente

§117a. Initial *g* remained [g] before *a* or a back vowel:

gallu > gallo   gula > gola 'throat'
gaudiu > gozo (§138a) gutta > gota

b. Before *e*, it came to be pronounced [y], becoming *ye–* in Old Spanish, but this [y] has become all but lost in modern Spanish due to two causes. First, since the diphthong *ié* overwhelmingly derives from a stressed VL *ę*, and since an unstressed *ę* cannot diphthongize, Spanish tends not to allow *any* unstressed *ié* diphthongs, no matter what the source. The examples below show that the Old Spanish normal development of VL *ge–* to OSp. *ye–* was forced to be reduced to *e* in the modern language since it was unstressed:

geláre > OSp. yelar > Sp. helar
Gel(o)víra > OSp. Yelvira > Sp. Elvira
genésta > OSp. yeniesta > Sp. hiniesta
germánu > OSp. yermano > Sp. hermano
gingíva > OSp. yencía > Sp. encía

In modern Spanish, the initial *i* of *hiniesta* is due to the raising influence of the *yod* of the following *ie* diphthong.

---

[10] An exception to this is VL *ferru* > Sp. *hierro*, where the *f–* was lost.

c. The second reason that the initial *y* is no longer noticed is that in the examples where the initial syllable is stressed, the vowel of that syllable was VL *ę* which developed to the diphthong *ié* all by itself. The [y] developing from the original *g*– was merely absorbed into the diphthong: *gélu > hielo, gén(e)ru > yerno*.

Words beginning with *ge*– in modern Spanish are learned or foreign: *gente*,[11] *general, genealogía, género, genio, geofísico, geometría, gestiones*.

§118a. Initial *j* before *a* retained its [y] pronunciation in Spanish:

jacere > yacer	Jacobe > Yagüe
jacet > yace	jam > ya

Jamás (from *jam mágis*) came to Spanish via Old Provençal. It was the Old Provençal pronunciation of the *j* which developed into the modern [x] of *jamás*.

b. Before a back vowel, the *j*– developed to its modern [x] sound in a process which must have passed through these stages: [y] > [ž] > [ʒ] > [ʃ] > [x]:

jogu > juego	juntu > junto
judeo > judío	jurat > jura
judice > juez	juvene > joven

Owing to the rustic nature of the implement, the word *yugo* 'yoke' (from VL *júgu*), which is an exception to the above trend, must be a regional development.

The [ʃ] sound was current in Spanish in the 17th century, as shown by the French transliteration of Spanish words. *Quixote* was transliterated *Quichotte* [kiʃɔ́t] and *Chisciotte* [kiʃóte] in French and Italian,[12] and the name of the Cid's wife (*Jimena*) appears as

---

[11] CL *gĕntem* developed regularly to *yente* in Old Spanish.

[12] The Russian version is *Don Kixot* (the *x* is pronounced like the Spanish *jota*) showing that Cervantes' novel was not translated into that language until the Spanish *jota* had completed its evolution.

Chimène [ʃimɛ́n] in *Le Cid* of Corneille.

§119a. Initial *s* usually remained intact:

saltu > soto	sesu > seso
seminare > sembrar	site > sed

CL *serare* which gave Sp. *cerrar* has not yet been convincingly explained.

b. In Mozarabic dialects, initial VL *s* sometimes came to be pronounced [ʃ] (which later developed to [x]); the following developments are attributed to Mozarabic pronunciation:

sapone >jabón	sucu > jugo
sepia > jibia	syringa > jeringa
serba > jerba	

Initial Clusters

§120. Most initial consonant clusters remained intact as Vulgar Latin developed into Spanish:

blandu > blando	frax(i)nu > fresno
blịtu > bledo	fronte > frente
bracciu > brazo	pratu > prado
dracone > dragón	

VL *drappu* was altered slightly to yield Sp. *trapo*. The *gl*– cluster sometimes lost its *g*: VL *glandine* > Sp. *landre* 'glandular tumor', VL *glattire* > Sp. *latir* 'to beat [as a heart]', VL *glirone* > Sp. *lirón* 'dormouse'.

§121. Initial *cl*–, *fl*–, and *pl*– clusters usually went through a palatalization process, and all three came to be pronounced [ɫ]. Apparently the *l* of these clusters had been a palatal sound already in Vulgar Latin and eventually caused a *yod* which gave [kɫ, fɫ, pɫ]; from here the *c*–, *f*–, and *p*– themselves were lost. The spelling *ll*– was taken from the internal *ll*– cluster which had the same pronunciation.[13]

clamat > llama	plenu > lleno
clave > llave	plicare > llegar
flamma > llama	plorare > llorar
plaga > llaga	pluvia > lluvia
planu > llano	

Claro, clave, flor, plaza, plato and *pluma* are usually said to be learned developments (although the iconoclastic Roger Wright [1982:11–12] has some convincing arguments in favor of traditional developments for these words).

§122. The prothetic *e* which began to precede *s* + *consonant* in Vulgar Latin (§6) universally generalized in Spanish:

schola > escuela	sposu > esposo
scribet > escribe	stat > está
scriptu > escrito	stella > estrella
scutu > escudo	strictu > estrecho

Intervocalic Single Consonants

§123. When the voiceless stops [p, t, k] were between vowels, the voiced quality of the vowels surrounding them became contagious and caused the stops to voice to [b, d, g]. This voicing had begun already in Vulgar Latin (§11). Later, the resulting voiced stops went a step farther in Spanish, becoming the voiced spirants [β, đ, γ] in most phonetic environments. The stops [p, t, k] also voiced when between vowel and *r* or *l*.

Several of the examples below illustrate that once the intervocalic stop had voiced, the unstressed vowel next to it fell: *aperire > aberire > abrir, bonitate > bonidade > bondad*. This shows that voicing preceded syncope.

---

[13] A parallel development to illustrate the intermediate stage is seen in Italian, where, for example, VL *clave* became Ital. *chiave* [kyáve]. If the *k*-sound were lost, the form would be quite like modern Spanish.

§124a. The intervocalic *p* voiced to give a spirant *b* in Spanish:

aperire > abrir	rapu > rabo
apic(u)la > abeja	recipire > recibir
capitia > cabeza	riparia > ribera
lep(o)re > liebre	sapere > saber
lupu > lobo	superbia > soberbia
paup(e)re > pobre	

Here are some examples of voicing of *p* between a vowel and *r* or *l*:

aprico > abrigo	capra > cabra
aprile > abril	duplare > doblar

b. If the *p* was between a semi–vowel and a vowel, the voicing was blocked:

capio > ca*i*po > que*i*po > quepo
sapui > sa*u*pi > OSp. sope
sapiam > sa*i*pa > se*i*pa > sepa

c. In some cases, after the *p* voiced to *b* and the following un-stressed vowel dropped, the *b* was thrown in contact with a *d*. When this happened the b VOCALIZED to *u*. (Vocalize means "become a vowel.") If you pronounce the intermediate steps in the developments (the stage with [βd], you will see how close phonetically the spirant *b* is to the [w] sound.

capitále > cabidale > ca*bd*al > caudal
cupidítia > cobidicia > co*bd*icia > coudicia > codicia
lápide > labide > la*bd*e > laude
rápidu > rabidu > ra*bd*o > raudo

The development of *codicia* shows that the *u* which derived from *b* was absorbed by the preceding o since Spanish (unlike Portuguese or Catalan) did not tolerate the óu diphthong. *Laude* and *raudo* show a feature which doesn't seem normal. According to

§§129a and 101, we should expect the intervocalic *d* to disappear in both examples to yield the nonexistent forms *labie* and *rcbio*; it seems to point to a chronological development—unstressed vowels fall before the intervocalic *d* was lost.

§125a. The intervocalic *t* voiced to give the spirant *d* in Spanish. In the examples with final Latin *-te*, once the *t* gave *d*, the final *e* was lost:

catena > cadena	materia > madera
del(i)catu > delgado	metu > miedo
litigare > lidiar	minutu > menudo
moneta > moneda	site > sed
mutare > mudar	totu > todo
pratu > prado	ver(i)tate > verdad
rete > red	vita > vida
rota > rueda	vite > vid
seta > seda	

In the case of VL *portáticu*, after the second *t* voiced to *d* and the *c* voiced to *g*, the unstressed *i* fell, and the result was *portadgo*. From this stage, the pronunciation did not change, but the spelling was modified to *portazgo*. (In modern Spanish, [θ] voices to [đ] before a voiced consonant.)[14]

Here are some examples of voicing of *t* between a vowel and *r*:

latrone > ladrón	putre > podre
matre > madre	utre > odre
patre > padre	petra > piedra

b. When between a semi-vowel and a vowel, the *t* did not voice:

autumnu > otoño	cautu > coto

---

[14] *Portazgo* means 'duty tax'. In Madrid the end of one of the metro lines is PORTAZGO. In olden days it must have been at the edge of town where tolls were collected.

This proves how late the *au* simplified to *o;* it simplified only after the intervocalic *t* changed to *d*, otherwise we might have expected *odoño* and *codo* as developments of the above forms.

§126a. The intervocalic *c* developed in two ways according to which type of vowel followed. If an *a* or a back vowel came after it, the *c* became the spirant *g*, but if a front vowel followed, the *c* became [θ] (or [s]), passing first through the [ts] stage. Here are some examples of a *c* before *a* or a back vowel:

acutu > agudo	fǫcu > fuego
amicu > amigo	formica > hormiga
cęcu > ciego	lactuca > lechuga
ciconia > cigüena	pacat > paga
commun(i)care > comulgar	plịcare > llegar
del(i)catu > delgado	secare > segar
dracone > dragón	securu > seguro
ficu > higo	spica > espiga
focare > hogar	vịnd(i)care > vengar

These examples show the *c* between a vowel and *r*:

lucrare > lograr	sacratu > sagrado
magru > magro	socra > suegra

b. In Vulgar Latin, if the *c* was between a semi–vowel and a mid– or back–vowel, the *c* did not voice (as in §124b): *auca > oca, paucu > poco*. But if the semi–vowel followed the [k], voicing could still take place: *ęqua > yegua, aqua > agua*.

c. When a front vowel followed the *c*, it evolved to the voiced sound [dz], spelled *z*. In the 17th century, the sound unvoiced and changed to its modern [θ] or [s] depending on the region:

dicit > OSp. diz(e) > dice
facere > OSp. fazer > hacer
vicinu > OSp. vezino > vecino

If the front vowel following the [dz] eventually fell, the sound changed its spelling to z in accordance with spelling norms. If a d came into contact with the [dz] because of the fall of a vowel, as in the second example below, the d assimilated into it:

recito > rezdo > rezo
placitu > plazdo > plazo

Similarly, if a final e fell following the [dz], the spelling was changed to z, and it unvoiced to [ts] on its way to [θ] or [s]:

dece > diez	pace > paz
luce > luz	vice > vez
noce > nuez	voce > voz

§127. An f existed between vowels only in Latin compound words (pro–fectu, auri–fece) or in Greek loanwords (raphanu, Stephanu). This f usually voiced to a spirant [β]:

áfricu > ábrego	ráphanu > rábano
auríf(e)ce > OSp. orebze	Stéphanu > Esteban
cóphanu > cuévano	trifol(iu) > trébol
profectu > provecho	

When it was recognized that the word was a compound, the f was treated as initial, and disappeared (§116): defensa > dehesa. A third outcome of the intervocalic f is found in learned words where it naturally remains, as in the modern defensa.

§128. The Vulgar Latin intervocalic b(v) and d became the spirants [β,đ] early.
    a. The b(v) was strong and usually remained:

bibere > beber	cavare > cavar
cibu > cebo	lavare > lavar
habere > haber	neve > nieve
lib(e)rare > librar	nove > nueve
nube > nube	novu > nuevo
nub(i)lare > nublar	vivire > vivir

probare > probar

b. However, the *b(v)* sometimes assimilated into a following back vowel and was lost. This feature began in Vulgar Latin and is seen in examples from the *Appendix Probi.*

esti*vu* > estío	su*b*undare > sondar
ri*vu* > río	vaci*vu* > vacío
sa*b*ucu > sauco	

A few words that ended in *–iva* also lost the *v*, probably due to an analogy with the masculine forms of words such as *vacivu > vacío*, fem. *vacía* (instead of the expected *vaciva*, since *a* is not a back vowel): *gingiva > encía, lixiva > lejía.*

c. When *b(v)* was forced into contact with *d* due to the syncope of a vowel, the *b* vocalized to *u* (as in §124c):

bibitu > bé*b*do > bé*u*do > beodo
civitáte > ci*b*dad > ciu*d*ad
cúbitu > co*b*do > codo
débita > de*b*da > deu*d*a
dúbita > du*b*da > du*d*a
lévitu > le*b*do > leu*d*o

The change in stress (and vowel) in *beodo* has not been convincingly explained (compare with *leudo* where the natural outcome was tolerated). In the developments of *codo* and *duda*, the *wau*s were absorbed into the preceding back vowels. In *ciudad*, the *wau* became a full vowel since when an *i* and a *u* are together, the second one becomes a full vowel and gets the stress, as in *viúda* and *fuíste*: thus *cibdad > cìudad > ciùdad.*[15]

§129a. The Vulgar Latin intervocalic *d* tended to drop in almost every case, as alluded to in §12:

---

[15] The grave accent is used on *ì* and the *ù*, to show secondary stress since the word is stressed on the final *a*.

audire > oír   laudat > loa
audii > oí   limpidu > limpio
cadere > caer   medulla > meollo[16]
crudele > cruel   pede > pie
fastidiu > hastío   rodere > roer
fide > fe   sedere > ser
fidele > fiel   sucidu > sucio
fedu > feo   turbidu > turbio
                        videre > ver

The CL was also sometimes lost between a vowel and *r*; VL *catedra* > *cadera, quadragĭnta* > *cuarenta*.

b. Syncope of vowels apparently was earlier than the loss of –*d*–. The examples below show that once the vowel dropped, the –*d*– was no longer intervocalic and was thus forced to remain:

cal(i)du > caldo   sol(i)dare > soldar
ẹd(e)ra > hiedra   vir(i)de > verde

When the –*d*– preceded the vowel that was lost, and then was placed in contact with another voiced consonant, it merely changed its spelling to *z* as in §125a:

jud(i)care > judgar > juzgar   pẹd(i)cu > piedgo > piezgo

c. Sometimes the Vulgar Latin *d* remained intervocalically, probably so that the word could retain sufficient phonetic substance:

crudu > crudo   nidu > nido
grado > grado   sudare > sudar
modu > modo   vadu > vado

§130a. The Classical Latin intervocalic *g* overwhelmingly became a *yod* in Vulgar Latin, which was usually lost, whether it preceded a front, central, or back vowel (§11b):

---

[16] *Meollo* shows an unusual change of gender.

digitu > dedo   legis > lees
frigidu > frío   magis > más
legale > leal   magistru > maestro
lege > ley   regale > real
legere > leer   sigillu > sello

The –g– could also be lost between a vowel and r: *pigritia > pereza*.

In some words, when an intervocalic –g– was lost before a stressed *i*, the stress shifted to the more open of the two vowels in modern Spanish:

regína > OSp. reína > réina
trigínta > OSp. treínta > tréinta
vigínti > OSp. veínte > véinte

The development of *rígidu* to *recio* is not at all normal. If *rígidu* (with stressed *i*) had paralleled the development of *frígidu* (with stressed *i*), which developed to *frío*, we should have expected *reo* as its outcome. If the word were more semantically associated with *sucidu* (which gave *sucio*), it would be tempting to see an analogy.

b. The –g– did remain in some words:

aguriu > agüero   plaga > llaga
agustu > agosto   rogare > rogar

§131. Other single consonants remained without change except for the single –s–, which was voiced (i.e., [z]) throughout the Middle Ages, after which time it unvoiced to [s].

Intervocalic l   *Intervocalic r*
palu > palo   feru > fiero
pilu > pelo   pira > pera
colore > color   tauru > toro

Intervocalic m   *Intervocalic s*
fumu > humo   usu > uso
ramu > ramo   ausare > osar
timore > temor   formosu > hermoso

Intervocalic n
pinu > pino
cena > cena
lana > lana

Intervocalic Double Consonants

§132. Vulgar Latin double consonants in intervocalic position either simplified or palatalized according to their phonetic nature. This first section deals with those that merely simplified.

a. Intervocalic *cc* simplified to *c* [k]:

bucca > boca   siccu > seco
peccare > pecar   vacca > vaca
saccu > saco

b. Intervocalic *pp* simplified to *p*:

cippu > cepo   puppa > popa
cuppa > copa   stuppa > estopa
drappu > trapo

c. Intervocalic *tt* simplified to *t*:

battire > batir   mittere > meter
cattu > gato   sagitta > saeta
gutta > gota   vitta > veta
littera > letra

d. Intervocalic *ss* simplified to *s* [s]:

grassu > graso   grossu > grueso
passu > paso

Sometimes, however, the *–ss–* palatalized to [ʃ] which later became [x]:

bassu > bajo   recesso > recejo
cessare > cejar   russu > rojo

    pássere > pájaro

The –o of *pájaro* is analogical with other masculine words which
end in –o; the unstressed *a* in the word dates from the formative
period of Romance when there was alternation between *er* and *ar*
(CL *seperāre* > VL *separare*).

    §133a. Intervocalic *ll* palatalized (as initial *cl*, *fl*, and *pl* did in
§121) and developed to the Spanish [ł].

callare > callar	gallu > gallo
castęllu > castillo	mǫlle > muelle
cepųlla > cebolla	pųllu > pollo
cǫllu > cuello	sęlla > silla
fǫlle > fuelle	valle > valle
	vįllu > vello

As the above examples show, the *yod* caused by the palatal *l* did not
affect the preceding vowel in any way, except as noted in §81b*i*
about such words as *castillo* and *silla*.

    b. If a palatal *l* came into syllable or word final position, it lost
its palatal nature (see also §95a in the explanation of *l*):

foll(i)care > holgar	mill(e) > mil
gall(i)cu > galgo	pell(e) > piel

c. Intervocalic *ffl* and *fl* also developed to a palatal *l*:[17]

    afflare > hallar   sufflare > sollar

---

[17] If the *fl* followed a consonant, it could not develop as it would in
intervocalic position, yet it still succeeded in developing into a palatal
sound, the [č], which is even a more complicated development than the
palatal *l*: *inflare > hinchar*. Similarly, a consonant before *pl* caused it to
develop to [č] as well: *implere > henchir, amplu > ancho*. These examples
parallel the Portuguese development of initial *fl* and *pl*: *flamma >* Ptg.
chama; plaga > Ptg. *chaga*, although Portuguese takes the evolution a step
farther, [č] to [ʃ] [ʃáma, ʃága].

§134. Parallel intervocalic *ll*, the Vulgar Latin intervocalic *nn* palatalized in Spanish to *ñ*;

annu > año	pinna > piña
canna > caña	pannu > paño
grunnire > gruñir	

The *m* of the –*mn*– cluster assimilated very early to the *n* so that the cluster could develop as a normal –*nn*– cluster:

autumnu > otoño	dom(i)nu > dueño
damnu > daño	calumnia > caloña

§135a. When a Vulgar Latin intervocalic *sc* preceded a front vowel, the result in Old Spanish was [ts], spelled *ç*. This simplifIed in the sixteenth century to its modern outcome [θ] or [s], depending on the dialect:

crescere > OSp. creçer > crecer
miscere > OSp. meçer > mecer
pascere > OSp. paçer > pacer

b. In cases where a final *e* had fallen following the OSp. *ç*, its spelling changed to *z*:

fasce > OSp. façe > haz   pisce > OSp. peçe > pez

Single Consonant + Vocalic *yod*

§136. In Vulgar Latin (§13), the *t* + *yod* and the *c* + *yod* clusters between vowels (or between *r* and a vowel) were pronounced first [ty] and [ky]; later, both came to be pronounced [ts], the *yod* having expended itself to make the [s] sound. Since the *yod* was lost so early, it couldn't raise the preceding vowel in Spanish, as the examples below demonstrate. In Old Spanish, the Vulgar Latin [ts] voiced to [dz], which later unvoiced to its modern Spanish result [θ] or [s].

duritia > dureza
fortia > fuerza
matea > maza
platea > plaza
puritia > pureza
puteu > pozo

coracea > coraza
facie > haz
furnaceu > hornazo
minacea > (a)menaza
pellicea > pelliza
acutiare > aguzar

§137. The *yod* of the *b(v)*, *d*, *g* + *yod* clusters was never, as a rule, assimilated into any of the three consonants (as it did in the previous section), and thus was able to raise the preceding vowel. This *yod* was not of the strongest type; it usually raised a preceding back vowel, sometimes raised a preceding front vowel, but never raised a preceding *a*.

a. The b(v) + *yod* cluster remained intact most of the time:

aleviare > aliviar
levianu > liviano
noviu > novio

pluvia > lluvia
rabia > rabia

b. Sometimes the *b(v)* disappeared, leaving only the *yod*:

fovea > hoya
habea > haya

rubeu > royo

§138a. The *d* + *yod* cluster tended to lose its initial element in most cases, leaving only the *yod*:

adiutare > ayudar
hodie > hoy

podiu > poyo
sedea > OSp. seya > sea

The *yod* was lost in *seya* to avoid the *ei* cluster.

b. When the *d* + *yod* was no longer intervocalic, or (seemingly) when it followed a CL *u*, the *d* + *yod* developed to [dz] which later simplified to [θ] or [s]:

verecundia > vergüenza
gaudiu > gozo

virdia > berza

Remember that the first *u* in *gaudiu* is a *wau*, therefore *-di-* isn't intervocalic.

§139. The *g* + *yod* cluster always lost its *g*, and the *yod* remained. The *g* was lost because it first became a *yod* itself (§12), and the two *yods* merely merged:

arrugiu > arroyo	fugio > huyo
corregia > correya > correa	Legione > Leyón > León
exagiu > ensayo	

The *yods* were lost in *correya* and *Leyón* again to avoid the *ei* cluster. In *ensayo* there was an erroneous confusion of prefixes (§157a).

§140. The *n* + *yod* cluster and the *gn* cluster both gave [ñ] in Spanish, and both occasionally raised the preceding vowel:
a. Here are some examples with n + *yod*:

aranea > araña	extraneu > extraño
cunea > cuña	seniore > señor
Hispania > España	

b. The *gn* cluster apparently developed as follows: [gn] > [yn] > [ñ]:

ligna > leña	stagnu > estaño
pugnu > puño	tam magnu > tamaño
signa > seña	

The words *reinar* (from *regnare*) and *reino* (from *regnu*), stunted in their development due to the analogical influence of *rey*, attest the second stage in the phonetic evolution of this cluster.

Yod Clusters That Developed to the Modern *Jota*

§141. The *l* + *yod* cluster, which developed to the *jota* in Spanish, had a more complex development than any *yod* cluster discussed so far. It probably evolved in this way: [ł] > [ʒ] > [ʃ] > [ʃ]

> [x]. The *yod* of this cluster only had a minimal effect on the raising of the vowels; only *hoja* and *mujer* below show raised vowels:

alienu > ajeno	fǫlia > hoja
aliu > ajo	mu̧liere > mujer
ci̧liu > cejo	palea > paja
consi̧liu > consejo	ti̧liu > tejo
filiu > hijo	

If the *l + yod* was not intervocalic, it could not develop as above. After a consonant, as the following example shows, it developed to [č]: *cocleare > cuchara.*

§142a. The *c'l* and *g'l* clusters (an apostrophe indicates that a Latin vowel has fallen) developed as the *l + yod* clusters did. Once the unstressed vowel fell, the *c* and the *g* became *yods*, and both clusters developed to [ł] which joined the *l + yod* development. Again, this *yod* only rarely affected the preceding vowel (as in *ojo* below). The initial *ę* of *genuc(u)lu* was not raised because of the *yod*, but rather was probably influenced by the initial *g*.

apic(u)la > abeja	lentic(u)la > lenteja
artic(u)lu > artejo	ǫc(u)lu > ojo
cu̧nic(u)lu > conejo	cuag(u)lu > cuajo
genu̧c(u)lu > hinojo	reg(u)la > reja
oric(u)la > oreja	teg(u)la > teja

If *mirac(u)lu* and *sec(u)lu* had developed in the normal way, they would have become *mirajo and *sejo. Since they were both part of the conservatively-developing ecclesiastic vocabulary, they became *milagro* (OSp. *miraglo* [§151a]) and *siglo*.

b. If an an *n* or an *s* preceded these clusters, they usually developed to [č]:[18]

cing(u)lu > cincho	masc(u)lu > macho
conc(u)la > concha	trunc(u)lu > troncho
manc(u)la > mancha	

c. The –t'l– cluster, because it was so uncommon, sometimes was transformed into c'l in Vulgar Latin, and this c'l developed normally. The *Appendix Probi* corrects: *vetulus non veclus*.

CL rotulare > VL roclare > Sp. (ar)rojar
CL větulum > VL veclu > Sp. viejo

Viejo presents an unsolved problem: why did the ẹ diphthongize when the *yod* was supposed to prevent diphthongization? We should have expected *vejo*. Histories of the language usually say that *viejo* is a borrowing from Aragonese (where such diphthongs occur), yet it seems unlikely that such an essential, common word could be a borrowing.

For another outcome of the t'l cluster, see §151b, §143.

§143. The Vulgar Latin [ks], which also developed to *jota* in Spanish, gave rise to a *yod* able to raise a preceding a to e. Up to this point, no *yod* had been able to raise a preceding a. The development of this cluster appears to have been: [ks] >[ys] > [sy] > [ʃ] > [x].

axe > eje	laxus > lejos
cọxo > cojo	lixiva > lejía
dịxi > dije	mataxa > madeja
exemplu > ejemplo	maxịlla > mejilla
laxare > dejar	taxone > tejón

---

[18] The *N'gl* cluster shows a few curious developments: *spong(u)la > esponja* shows intervocalic development of *g'l*; *sing(u)los > sendos* shows a change of *l* to *d*; *singulariu > señero*, *ung(u)la > uña* show a development to *ñ*. *S'cl* also has a few aberrant developments: *musc(u)lu > muslo* shows loss of *c*. *Mesc(u)lare > mezclar* is semi–learned.

The initial *d* of *dejar* is an unresolved question in the Iberian Peninsula. French and Italian retain the original *l* (*laisser, lasciare*), while Spanish shows initial *d*, and Portuguese shows **deixar** in the modern language and **leixar** in older Portuguese.

When the *i* of *fraxinu* fell, the *x* was no longer intervocalic. The *yod* that developed in this word when *x* became [ys] merged with the *a* to make *ai* which in turn became *ei* and then *e*, leaving the *s* intact: *fraxinu* > *fresno*.

The *CT* Cluster

§144a. The –*ct*– cluster, which developed to [č] in Spanish, also gave rise to a very powerful *yod* that could raise *a* to *e*. The development of the [kt] seems to have been [kt] > [yt] > [ty] > [č]:

despẹctu > despecho	nọcte > noche
dịctu > dicho	pẹctu > pecho
dụctu > ducho	profẹctu > provecho
factu > hecho	strịctu > estrecho
iactare > echar	tẹctu > techo
lacte > leche	trụcta > trucha
lactuca > lechuga	vervactu > barbecho

As powerful as this *yod* was, it sometimes did (as in *dicho*) and sometimes did not (as in *estrecho*) raise a Vulgar Latin *į* to Sp. *i*. *Iactare* did not develop to *yechar* for the reasons stated in §117b.

b. When the –*ct*– followed vowels at the extreme ends of the vowel triangle (the *į* and the *ụ*), the *yod* was absorbed or lost, leaving the *t* intact:

exsuctu > enjuto	frịctu > frito
fịctu > hito	fructu > fruto

c. In contact with a consonant, the –*ct*– cluster could not develop as it would between vowels. The *c* fell in Vulgar Latin (§15c), and was sometimes able to raise the preceding vowel:

jụn(c)tu > junto	pụn(c)tu > punto

Pectine offers an interesting case. When the unstressed vowel dropped, leaving *pect'ne*, the *–ct–* cluster, although less constricted than when the *n* preceded it, could still not develop fully. The *c* became *yod* and the *t* fell: *pect'ne* > *peine* (the *i* of *peine* is retained here extraordinarily in order to avoid an unfortunate homonym).[19]

The word *collacteu* 'foster brother or sister' presents another interesting development, showing how two conflicting clusters developed. The *–ct–* cluster (*collacteu*) would normally yield [č], but the t + *yod* cluster (*collacteu*) developed to [ts] before this change was possible; the *c* could do nothing else but assimilate to the *t* and fall: *collacteu* > *collactso* > *collatso* > *collazo*.[20]

Clusters with *L*

§145. When a VL *l* preceded a consonant, much of the time it vocalized to *u*, which is a close acoustic relative to *l*. When *a* preceded the *l*, the cluster developed in this way: [al] > [au] > [o]. When *u* preceded the *l*, the cluster passed through these stages: [ul] > [úu] > [u]:

altariu > otero	falce > hoz
alt(e)ru > otro	falcino > hocino
calce > coz	saltu > soto
culm(i)ne > cumbre	talpa > topo

If *–al–* came into contact with a consonant because of the loss of a vowel, the cluster developed to *au*: *cal(i)ce* > *calce* > *cauce*; *sal(i)ce* > *salce* > *sauce*. *Topo* has undergone an unusual change in gender.

---

[19] My friend Francisco Rico of the Real Academia de la Lengua says that the "unfortunate homonym" is too recent to cause the retention of *–ei–* in *peine*. You look it up. You be the judge.

[20] This interesting conflictive development was pointed out by my teacher and friend Carlos Otero in his *Evolución y revolución en romance* (Barcelona: Ariel, 1971). By sheerest of coincidences both his first and last names are discussed in coming sections 145 and 148b. *Collazo* nowadays means 'farmhand'.

§146. The –*lt*– cluster preceded by *u* acted in a different way from the way it did above. The *l*, instead of changing into a *wau* (in which case it would be absorbed by the preceding *u*), changed to a *yod* by dissimilation (§149d). The *yod* then acted on the *t* to form [č], and raised the ṵ to ṳ. Here is the apparent development of the cluster: [ult] > [uyt] > [uty] > [uč].

ascṵltare > escuchar   mṵltu > mucho
cṵltẹllu > cuchillo

When the –*ult*– cluster was followed by a consonant, as in *vult're*, it could not develop as above. Its evolution was arrested at the second step shown above: *vúlture* > *vúlt're* > *búitre*. There was then a normal shift in stress to the *i* giving Sp. *buitre*. *Muy* (from *mṵlt[u]*) also shows arrested development at the second step.

Final Consonants

§147a. Most Vulgar Latin final consonants were lost along the way to Spanish:

Final *d*

ad > a   aliquod > algo
illud > ello   istud > esto

Final *t*

aut > o   dicit > dice
laudat > loa   stat > está

Final *c*

dịc > di   nẹc > ni
sịc > sí

Final *b*

sub > OSp. so

Nẹc (with its open *e*) would have developed to *ne*. The form *ni* is doubtless analogical with other short words ending in *–í* such as *sí*.

b. The final *m* was already generally lost in Vulgar Latin (§10). But the final *m* in monosyllabic words was retained and changed to *n*, most likely because Spanish has no final BILABIAL consonant ("bilabial" means 'articulated with the two lips.'):

<blockquote>

cụm > con   tam > tan

quẹm > quien
</blockquote>

This rejection of final *m* accounts for the Spanish *–n* in borrowings such as *Jerusalén, harén, Matuselén, Adán,* and *Belén.*

§148a. Vulgar Latin final *l, r,* and *x* did not fall:

Final *l*	Final *r*	Final *x*
fẹl > hiel	inter > entre	sẹx > seis
mẹlle > miel	quattuor > cuatro	
	sẹmper > siempre	

The final *r* in the above examples switched places with the preceding vowel. The [ks] of *sẹx* changed its [k] element into a *yod* which prevented the diphthongization of the preceding vowel: [seks] > [seys]. The *x*, when *intervocalic*, developed to [x], of course, but in *sẹx*, we have a case of the survival of final *x*. Its development was thus stunted at the first stage of development as seen in §143 above.

b. Vulgar Latin final *s* universally remained in verb forms as well as in noun and adjective plurals:

<blockquote>

fab(u)las > hablas   patres > padres

formosos > hermosos
</blockquote>

Old Spanish carried over some third declension neuter singular forms ending in *s* (§21a), but since the language rejected singular forms with final *s*, the etymological *s* was lost:

<blockquote>

Singular

corpus > OSp. cuerpos > cuerpo
</blockquote>

opus > OSp. huebos (§153b)
pectus > OSp. pechos > pecho
tempus > OSp. tiempos > tiempo[21]

In names such as *Carolus* > *Carlos* the final *s* was retained
(§156). The *h–* of *huebos* is of course not etymological. It was placed
before a vocalic *u* in Old Spanish as an orthographic signal to
distinguish the vowel *u* from the consonant *v*, both of which were
spelled *u*; without the *h*, *huebos* might have otherwise been read as
vebos. Other examples which show an added orthographic *h–* are:
orphanu > *huérfano, ossu* > *hueso, ovu* > *huevo*.

Dissimilation, Assimilation and Metathesis

§149. DISSIMILATION is the process whereby, in a word with two
like sounds, one of the two sounds is altered or eliminated.

a. As the Spanish language developed, it did not usually allow
two *r*'s, two *l*'s or two nasals (*m*s or *n*s) in the same word, and
usually changed the manner of articulation of the second of the two
sounds, although sometimes the first was altered.

r – r > r – l	*n – n > l – n, n – l, n – r*
ar*b*ore > ár*b*o*l*	de in ante > de*l*ante
car*c*ere > cár*c*e*l*	ing(ui)ne > ing*l*e
mar*m*ore > már*m*o*l*	hispa*n*ione > españo*l*
ro*b*ore > ro*b*le	sang(ui)ne > sa*n*gre
ste̜rcore > estiérco*l*	
l – l > r – l, l – r	*n – m > l – m, r – m*
ca*l*ame̜*ll*o > caramillo	án(i)ma > a*l*ma
*l*oca*l*e > *l*ugar	mi*n*(i)mare > mermar

b. When a vowel was lost due to syncope between *m* and an *n*,
the *n* dissimilated to *r* most of the time, then a *b* was generated
between the *m* and the *r* in order to the new cluster pronounceable

---

[21] French, on the other hand, retains the final *s* in *corps* and *temps*, and
you can hear the *s* in expressions such as *de temps en temps*.

and also to conserve the *r* as a single tap. (Without the *b*, the *r* would have to be pronounced as a multiple trill, as in *honra*.)

costum(i)ne > costumbre	lum(i)ne > lumbre
culm(i)ne > cumbre	nom(i)ne > nombre
fem(i)na > hembra	sem(i)nare > sembrar
hom(i)ne > hombre	

In *communicare*, an ecclesiastical word, since there was no syncope between *m* and *n* (§99b), the *n* dissimilated to *l*: *commun(i)care* > *comulgar*.

c. Another type of dissimilation was very strong, causing one of the consonants to disappear completely instead of merely changing its point of articulation.

> bobe > boe > buey
> propriu > propio
> trasvese > través
> trem(u)lare > trem'lare > tremblare > temblar[22]

In the last example, it was not until the *b* developed that the dissimilation took place. It is a case of dissimilation of two *muta cum liquida* clusters (defined in §81b*ii*) (*tr – bl* > *tr – b*).

d. Occasionally vowels also dissimilated, but not with the pattern of predictability that consonants show:

dicire > decir	ridire > reír.
formosu > hermoso	verrere > barrer
rotundu > redondo	vicinu > vecino

§150a. ASSIMILATION (the opposite of dissimilation) is the process where two unlike sounds in a given word become the more similar. FULL ASSIMILATION is where one sounds grows to be identi-

---

[22] Spanish *orquesta* also shows a dissimilation of this type. Portuguese has *orquestra*, but has dissimilated *registada* 'registered' (compare Sp. *registrada*).

cal with another sound in the same word; one example of this is
il(i)cina > *encina* (*l – n* > *n – n*).

b. PARTIAL ASSIMILATION is where one sound, put in contact with
another due to the syncope of a vowel or the loss of a consonant,
has to adjust its point of articulation to match that of the following
consonant:

com(i)te > con*de*   lim(i)tare > lin*d*ar
com(pu)tare > con*t*ar   sem(i)ta > sen*d*a
ven(di)care > ven*g*ar (n = [ŋ])

Ralph Penny (1983) points out that *contar, hostal* and *mascar* show
evidence of an ancient partial assimilation whose cause has long
since been lost. You would correctly expect the *–t–* of *computare*
and *hospitale* to voice to *d*, and the *–k–* of *masticare* to voice to *–g–*.
Since voicing precedes syncope (compare the developments of *conde,
vengar, lindar,* and *senda* above), you could logically expect the
forms **compdar, *ospdale,* and **mastgar* in an early stage of
development. It was at this stage that a partial assimilation took
place—an unvoiced consonant (*p* and *t* in the examples here) caused
the following voiced consonant to unvoice:

com*p*(u)tare > com*p*(u)*d*are > com*pd*ar > com*pt*ar > con*t*ar
    (*pd > pt > t*)
hos*p*(i)tale > hos*p*(i)*d*ale > os*pd*ale > os*pt*al > hos*t*al
    (*pd > pt > t*)
mas*t*(i)gare > mas*t*(i)gare > mas*tg*ar > mas*tc*ar > mas*c*ar
    (*tg > tc > c*)

Once the fourth stage was reached above, the three consonants
(*–mpt–, –stc–*) were reduced to two through the loss of the middle
element (recall the loss of the middle element in §81b*ii*).

c. Sometimes a consonant cannot properly adjust to the point of
articulation of the following consonant and instead, a *third* consonant is generated between the two (similar to §149b above):

hum(e)ru > hom*b*ro   trem(u)lare > tem*b*lar
pon(e)ré > pon*d*ré   val(e)ré > val*d*ré

sal(i)ré > saldré   ven(i)ré > vendré
ten(e)ré > tendré

If the first consonant is alveolar (l, n) a d is generated; if it is bilabial (m), a b is generated.

§151a. METATHESIS is the process where one or two sounds change position. When only one consonant changes place in a word (crepare > quebrar), it is called SIMPLE METATHESIS. When two consonants switch places with each other (animalia > alimaña), it is called RECIPROCAL METATHESIS.

animalia > alimaña   oblitare > olvidar[23]
crepare > quebrar   maturicare > madrugar
integrare > entregar   parabola > palabra
mirac(u)lu > milagro   peric(u)lu > peligro

b. After a vowel has been lost, awkward consonant clusters are sometimes created. Metathesis is often the easiest way to resolve these clusters:

ac(e)re > arce   col(o)rare > corlar
capit(u)lu > cabildo   gen(e)ru > yerno[24]
cat(e)natu > candado   ret(i)na > rienda
spat(u)lu > espalda   tit(u)lare > tildar
ten(e)ru > tierno   ven(e)ris > viernes

Capit(u)lu, spat(u)lu and tit(u)lare show a different solution to the t'l cluster from the one in §142c. These (due to the voicing of t) obviously show a later syncope.

c. There was a special metathesis in the few verbs ending –ificare. The f voices to b, then vocalizes to u—at that point the

---

[23] Since the sounds are together, this could also be a case of simple metathesis.

[24] French retains the Latin order of consonants in its development of generu to the modern gendre, but notice that a d had to be put in once the e was lost to allow the transition between the two consonants per §150c.

metathesis takes place.

> pacif(i)care > pacibgar > paciugare > (a)paciguar
> santif(i)care > santibgar > santiugar > santiguar

d. VL *fábr(i)ca* deserves special mention. When the unstressed *i* fell, the word was placed in a phonetic conflict which was not resolved until metathesis affected it *twice* and the *b* vocalized to *u*:

> fabr(i)ca > fabrga >
> [simple metathesis 1:] frabga >
> [vocalizaion:] frauga >
> [simple metathesis 2:] fragua

3

Historical Morphology: Form Change Through Time

The Development of Nouns

§152a. In Vulgar Latin, nouns had two distinct cases, the nominative and the accusative (§§27–30). When the Vulgar Latin of Hispania evolved into Old Spanish, the nominative case was lost in almost every instance, and the accusative case—which was much more common than the nominative, given its diversified role in Vulgar Latin—was overwhelmingly the only one to survive.

b. Here are some examples which developed from the Vulgar Latin first declension. They include a number of forms that it inherited from different Classical Latin sources; for example, second declension neuter plurals (*pira, vota,* §28c), third declension nouns made into the first declension by addition of a diminutive suffix (*apic[u]la, oric[u]la,* §33c), ordinary fourth declension nouns (*sŏcrus*) and those with diminutive suffixes (*acuc[u]la, capitia,* §77b), and fifth declension nouns (*dia, materia,* §32):

acṵc(u)la > aguja	orịc(u)la > oreja
apịc(u)la > abeja	pẹrna > pierna
capịtia > cabeza	pịra > pera
cepụlla > cebolla	pọrta > puerta
dịa > día	sŏcrus > suegra
matẹria > madera	vọta > boda

c. The following examples are from the Vulgar Latin second declension. They include some masculine forms inherited from the

Classical Latin second declension neuter (*balneu, collu, vinu,* §28b) and some forms from the fourth declension (*cornu, frax[i]nu, manu* §31):

amicu > amigo	dom(i)nu > dueño
balneu > baño	filiu > hijo
castellu > castillo	frax(i)nu > fresno
collu > cuello	manu > mano
cornu > cuerno	vinu > vino

d. The examples below are from the Vulgar Latin third declension. The sampling includes forms that derived from the Classical Latin fifth declension (*facie, fide,* §32):

calle > calle	hom(i)ne > hombre
carcere > cárcel	lacte > leche
civ(i)tate > ciudad	latrone > ladrón
dolore > dolor	mare > mar
facie > haz	parete > pared
fide > fe	ratione > razón
fonte > fuente	rege > rey

§153a. The third declension, as usual, shows more complications than the other ones. Many third declension nouns which served both masculine and feminine genders eventually added an analogical *–a* to the feminine in Old Spanish to differentiate the genders; this differentiation has remained in the modern language:

hispanione > OSp. español *f* > española
infante > OSp. infante *f* > infanta
latrone > OSp. ladrón *f* > ladrona
parente > OSp. pariente *f* > parienta
pastore > OSp. pastor *f* > pastora
seniore > OSp. señor *f* > señora

b. Some nouns that had been third declension neuters created a problem because their accusative form ended in *–s* in the singular (§21a). This final *–s* carried through Vulgar Latin and into Old

Spanish where these forms are seen:

> corpus (*sing.*) > OSp. cuerpos (*sing.*)
> pectus (*sing.*) > OSp. pechos (*sing.*)
> opus (*sing.*) > OSp. huebos (*sing.*)
> tempus (*sing.*) > OSp. tiempos (*sing.*)

These were eventually "logically" regarded as plurals in Old Spanish, and analogical singulars, without –s, were created: *cuerpo, pecho, tiempo* (§148b). *Huebos* was not continued into modern Spanish. (*Huebos es* was a fixed expression meaning 'it is necessary'.)

    c. Those Vulgar Latin third declension neuter accusative forms that ended in a consonant (other than –s) were rebuilt with final –e, by analogy with the commoner third declension masculine and feminine nouns with final –e in Vulgar Latin (such as VL acc. *hom(i)ne, civ(i)tate, dolore, ratione, monte*). The first five Vulgar Latin forms below appear to be built on the model of *hom(i)ne*.

> CL culmen > VL culm(i)ne > Sp. cumbre
> CL examen > VL exam(i)ne > Sp. enjambre (§157b)
> CL inguen > VL ing(ui)ne > Sp. ingle
> CL nomen > VL nom(i)ne > Sp. nombre
> CL piper > VL pip(e)re > Sp. pebre
> CL sulphur > VL sulph(u)re > Sp. (a)zufre

§149b describes how –*m(i)ne* in some of the above examples became –*mbre*. The *n – n* of *inguine* dissimilated to *n – l* (§149a).

§154. The fourth and fifth declensions have left no direct trace through normal development since they both changed declensions in Vulgar Latin, but the Spanish language has taken some learned fourth and fifth declension forms from Classical Latin:

Fourth Declension	*Fifth Declension*	
espíritu	especie	superficie
tribu	serie	caries
ímpetu	altiplanicie	

§155a. The plural form of nouns usually offered no complications since it was almost always the direct development of the Vulgar Latin accusative plural:

amicos > amigos	capitias > cabezas
calles > calles	civ(i)tates > ciudades
dǫm(i)nos > dueños	pǫrtas > puertas
filios > hijos	rationes > razones
pęrnas > piernas	ver(i)tates > verdades

b. Those neuter singulars which had Classical Latin plurals which ended in –a, took analogical plurals in in Vulgar Latin ending in –os or –es and these were contineud into Spanish.

CL balneum, pl. balnea > Sp. baño, baños
CL cǒllum, pl. cǒlla > Sp. cuello, cuellos
CL cǒrnu, pl. cǒrnua > Sp. cuerno, cuernos
CL mare, pl. maria > Sp. mar, mares
CL vīnum, pl. vīna > Sp. vino, vinos

c. Second declension neuter plurals that became Vulgar Latin first declension singulars (§28c), built analogical plurals by adding an –s:

VL cịlia > Sp. ceja, pl. cejas
VL fęsta > Sp. fiesta, pl. fiestas
VL fǫlia > Sp. hoja, pl. hojas
VL pịra > Sp. pera, pl. peras
VL sịgna > Sp. seña, pl. señas
VL vascella > Sp. vajilla, pl. vajilllas
VL vota > Sp. boda, pl. bodas

Vestiges of Latin Cases Other Than the Accusative

§156. Whereas most Spanish nouns have evolved from the accusative case of Vulgar Latin, a few fossils from other cases have managed to survive in Spanish.

a. The nominative has been preserved in pronouns associated with the nominative, as well as in a few names:

egō > yo   tū > tú
ĭl(le) > él   Car(o)lus > Carlos
ĭpse > ese   Deus > Dios
ĭste > este   Marcus > Marcos

There is a number of learned nominatives, of course, which were taken directly from Classical Latin, such as *abdomen, cadáver, carácter, cráter, crisis, tórax, espécimen, régimen.* Notice that the last two words already have proparoxytonic stress in Latin; when made plural in Spanish, they would be come to be stressed *four* syllables back, which the language does not tolerate in nouns—that accounts for the change in stress in the modern Spanish plural forms: *especímenes, regímenes.*[1]

b. The genitive is seen in fossilized forms in a few words, most notably in the days of the week:

(dies) martis [= Mars' day] > martes
(dies) jovis [= Jupiter's day] > jueves
(dies) veneris [= Venus' day] > viernes

By analogy with the above third declension forms ending in *–is*, the first declension *(dies) lunæ* [= Moon's day] became *lunis* which gave Sp. *lunes.* The second declension *(dies) mercuri* [= Mercury's day] became *mercuriis* which gave *miércoles* in Spanish (with dissimilation *r – r* to *r – l*). (*Sábado* comes from VL *sábbatu* and *domingo* comes from *(dies) domín(i)cum.*

Other vestiges of the genitive (shown in italics) are seen in:

comite *stabuli* > 'count of the stable' > condestable
filiu *ecclesiæ* 'son of the church, > feligrés 'parishioner'
pedis ungula 'nail of the foot' > pezuña 'foot of cloven
   hoof animal'

---

[1] The third irregular Spanish plural is *carácter – caracteres*, which is not proparoxytonic in the singular.

forum *judicum* 'court of the judges' > *Fuero Juzgo*[2]
Campus *Gothorum* 'Field of the Goths' > Toro 'Spanish city name'

c. The only remains of the Latin dative in Spanish are found in the development of the dative pronouns: *(il)lī > le, (il)līs > les.*

d. There are a few vestiges of the ablative case fossilized in a small number of Spanish words:

> CL hāc horā > OSp. agora[3]
> CL hōc annō > Sp. hogaño
> CL locō > Sp. luego
> CL quōmodō > Sp. como

Prefixes and Suffixes

§157a. There was sometimes a confusion or accumulation of prefixes as Vulgar Latin developed into Spanish. The first two examples show that the prefix *ex–* was substituted for *a(b)s–*:

> a(b)scondere > esconder   ascultare > escuchar

The following examples reveal that *in–* influenced the words:

> exagiu > in(e)xagiu > ensayo
> exam(i)ne > in(e)xam(i)ne > enjambre
> exemplu > in(e)xemplu > OSp. enxiemplo

In this example, the prefix *in–* mixed with the initial *i–*:

> hībĕrnu > inbẹrnu > invierno

b. A few suffixes were occasionally confused, the more common ones overpowering the less common ones:

---

[2] The *Fuero Juzgo* is a famous ancient Spanish lawbook based on Roman jurisprudence.
[3] Modern Spanish *ahora* derived from *ad horam.*

capellanu (+ –ane) > capellán
foll(i)catianu (+ –ane) > holgazán
tosoria (+ –aria) > tijera
certitud(i)ne (+ –um[i]ne) > certidumbre
cos(ue)tudine (+ –um[i]ne) > costumbre
mans(u)etudine(+ –um[i]ne) > mansedumbre
multitud(i)ne (+ –um[i]ne) > muchedumbre

The Latin suffix –*aticu* developed normally to –*azgo* (§125a), as in *afflaticu* > *hallazgo*, *portaticu* > *portazgo*. But the French result (–*age*), was also borrowed by Spanish as –*aje*, shown in these loanwords: *garaje*, *portaje*, *salvaje*, *viaje*. The *i* of *tijera* may be due to the influence of the *i* of VL *cisoriu* 'scissors', although it seems quite tenuous.

Articles

§158a. The Spanish definite articles derive from the Latin demonstratives *ille, illa, illud*,[4] which had already begun to be used in the function of definite articles in Vulgar Latin (§34). The singular articles have their origin in the nominative forms of these demonstratives, while the plural articles were taken from the accusative forms. (The same alternation—nominative used in the singular and accusative in the plural—will be seen in the Spanish demonstratives, §162). In the Vulgar Latin of Hispania, the demonstratives used as articles lost one syllable in every form, usually the *il–*, except in the masculine singular:

CL ĭlle > VL i̯l > Sp. el
CL ĭllōs > VL los > Sp. los
CL ĭlla > VL la > Sp. la
CL ĭllas > VL las > Sp. las
CL ĭllud > VL lu > Sp. lo

b. A few words should be said about the feminine article *el* (as

---

[4] Notice that the neuter form (*illud*) was retained, contrary to the tendency to drop neuters.

in **el** *águila,* **el** *agua,* **el** *alma*); it did not derive from the second syllable of *ílla,* but from the first, as the examples below show:

ílla aqua (= [ilákwa]) > el agua
ílla aquila (= [ilákwila]) > el águila
ílla anima (= [ilánima]) > el alma

Because of the fusion of the two *a*'s, the initial *i* of *ílla* was forced to remain. In Old Spanish, *el* was used before *any* initial *a,* stressed or not, but gradually it came to be used only before a stressed *a*– (that is, nowadays we say *la* **avenida,** *la* **agricultura** since the intial *a* is not stressed).

§159. The indefinite articles which began to come into existence in Vulgar Latin (§34), remained in Spanish

unu > un	una > una
unos > unos	unas > unas

Unu lost its last syllable due to its PROCLITIC nature (that is, its use as an unstressed short word which forms a unit with the following word). When it is no longer proclitic, the lost syllable returns: *Yo tengo un coche bueno pero ella tiene* **uno** *mejor.*

Adjectives

§160. The accusative forms of Vulgar Latin adjectives evolved into Spanish adjectives without complication.

a. The first group of adjectives, based on the first and second declensions, maintains the differences between masculine and feminine genders in its forms (§35a):

bibitu,–a > beodo,–a	grossu,–a > grueso,–a
bonu,–a > bueno,–a	integru,–a > entero,–a
delicatu,–a > delgado,–a	limpidu,–a > limpio,–a
duru,–a > duro,–a	mutu,–a > mudo,–a
extraneu,–a > extraño,–a	securu,–a > seguro,–a
fedu,–a (CL fœdum) > feo,–a	strictu,–a > estrecho,–a
formosu,–a > hermoso,–a	tepidu,–a > tibio,–a

b. The second group of adjectives, based on the third declension, does not usually show a difference in gender:

crudele > cruel	paup(e)re > pobre
equale > igual	regale > real
fidele > fiel	stab(i)le > estable
felice > feliz	turpe > torpe
forte > fuerte	vir(i)de > verde
grande > grande	

Before a noun, *grande* becomes *gran*, a relic of the Old Spanish shortened *grant*. The third declension adjectives ending in *–or* in Old Spanish began to take an analogical feminine *–a* around 1300, much as in §153a. Examples include *entendedora*, *habladora*.

c. The adjective *mismo* is an interesting problem. In Classical Latin, to say 'I myself' all that was needed was to attach the particle *–met* to the pronoun: *egomet*. To be more emphatic, the adjective *ipse* 'self' was added: *egomet ipse*. With the passage of time, the original emphasis wore off this construction, so *ipse* was made into a superlative: *egomet ipsissimus*. This construction became so well used that *metipsíssimus* could be used by itself. (In Classical Latin, *–met* could not be separated from the pronoun to which it was attached.) In Vulgar Latin, the form developed to something like this: *medissíssimu*. It was at this point that HAPLOLOGY took place. Haplology, a strong type of dissimilation, is the process whereby two like syllables (*ississ* in this case) are reduced to one, and the result was *medis(i)mu*.[5] It developed to *medesmo* (*–iss[i]mu* contained a short *i* in Latin), then to *mesmo*, which was the most common form of the word through the era of Cervantes and is also the current form in Portuguese and in the French *même*. So far, everything has been rather easy to explain. It is the unusual change from *mesmo* to *mismo* which has not yet been satisfactorily resolved (perhaps there was an assimilation in constructions such as

---

[5] There are many examples of haplology in Italian, but very few in Spanish. A modern example is *tenista* 'tennis player' (which should be *tenisista*).

a mí mesmo > a mí mismo).

§161a. The comparative and superlative systems did not basically change since Vulgar Latin times (§37):

> magis fidele > más fiel
> magis felice > más feliz
> magis securu > más seguro
> il magis fidele > el más fiel
> la magis felice > la más feliz
> las magis securas > las más seguras

Magis evolved to *mais* in Old Spanish. Certainly its common proclitic use helped to simplify it to *más*.

b. The irregular comparatives (§38) developed normally:

maiore > mayor	minore > menor
meliore > mejor	peiore > peor

It should be noticed that these third declension words ending in *–or* did not add an analogical *–a* in the feminine form (contrary to §§153a, 160b).

Demonstratives

§162. The demonstratives that remained in Vulgar Latin (§39ab) were continued into Spanish. It was the nominative form that gave rise to the Spanish singular forms, but it was the accusative form that became the Spanish plural.

Singular (= nom.)	*Plural* (= acc.)
iste > este	istos > estos
ista > esta	istas > estas
ipse > ese	ipsos > esos
ipsa > esa	ipsas > esas
istud > esto	
ipsud > eso	

The etymology of *aquel, –la, –los, –las* has been suggested as *eccu ille.* (*Ecce* [meaning *he aquí* in Spanish] was used in Classical Latin preceding demonstratives for emphasis, and its linguistic descendants are current in a number of modern French and Italian forms.) Arriving at the stage *equel*, the initial *e* could have dissimilated to *a. Atque ille* has also been postulated, and makes *aquel* easier to derive phonetically, but semantically (*atque* = 'and even') it is weak.

Relatives and Interrogatives

§163. From the Vulgar Latin relative and interrogative pronoun declension, the only members to survive were the nominative singular *qui*, the accusative singular *quem*, and the neuter singular *quid*. The first two developed to *qui* and *quién* in Spanish, and were used interchangeably in Old Spanish both as singulars or plurals, nominatives or accusatives. In the 14th century, however, *qui* fell into disuse. During the 16th century, an analogical plural was created for *quién: quiénes*.

The neuter *quid* developed into the interrogative *¿qué?* and the unstressed *quem* also became *que* (*la chica que veo*); the two *que*'s working together were able to oust other related Latin words: *melius quam > mejor que, credo quia > creo que* (574c).

Other interrogatives developed without complication:

de unde? > ¿dónde?	quando? > ¿cuándo?
quale? > ¿cuál?	quomodo? > ¿cómo?

Positive and Negative Words

§164. Several Classical Latin positive and negative words were dropped and new ones formed in Vulgar Latin. The past participle *natus* 'born' used in a negative sense gave rise to two of the new formations in Hispania: *(res) nata* '([no]thing) born' replaced CL *nihil* 'nothing'. CL *nemo* 'no one' was replaced by a form of *(hominem) natum* '([no] man) born' = 'no one' explained below. CL *etiam* was replaced by *tam bene*.

aliqu'unu > alguno	(res) nata > nada
aliquod > algo	semper > siempre

iam > ya[6]	tam bene > también
numquam > nunca	tota via > todavia

To complete this list, there are three words which require some explanation: *alguien, ninguno and nadie.*

CL *áliquem* would have developed to *algue* in Spanish, but it changed its stress based on the model of the stressed monosyllable *quem* (Sp. *quién*), giving *alguién.* To make its stress uniform with *algo* (and other positive and negative words), the stress then moved back to its original place: *álguien.*

Nec + unu gave rise to *ningun(o).* *Necunu* would develop normally to *neguno,* but two things happened to it. First, an *n* appeared that made it *nenguno* in Old Spanish. This *–n–* could be analogical with the *–n* of *bien, sin, con, en,* but it also seems plausible that the initial *n–* might have nasalized the entire syllable, causing another *–n–* to be created before the *g,* much like the Portuguese *muito* [mwĩntu], which is pronounced with an *–n–* preceding the *t.* The second feature, the appearance of *i* in the first syllable, is analogical with *ni.*

The process by which *natu* changed into *nadie* is not usually explained convincingly. Traditionally, *nado* + the *i* of *qui* is said to have been given OSp. *nadi;* and *nado* + the final *e* of *este, ese* was supposed to have given OSp. (rare) *nade.* A merging of the two was *supposed to* have developed to *nadie.* I believe that *nadie* was influenced by the positive *alguien,* and resulted in *nadien,* which lost its final *n* early by dissimilation with the initial *n* (§149c). (The modern substandard *nadien* may be a continuation of this form.)

Possessives

§165. The possessives developed into two distinct sets in modern Spanish: a stressed set where the possessive is a stressed word and follows the noun (*este amigo* **mío**), and an unstressed set where the possessive precedes the noun as a proclitic (**mi** *amigo*). Whereas the two sets are differentiated in modern Spanish in all forms except *nuestro* and *vuestro,* they were quite close in form in

---

[6] See §205b for more about *iam.*

Old Spanish as the developments below show. It could even be postulated that the forms of the "unstressed" set were actually stressed in Old Spanish since the "unstressed" VL *meu, nostru* and *vostru* show stressed vowel development in Old Spanish.

Whereas Classical Latin possessives had the same vowel quality in both the masculine and feminine forms of the singular (*mĕum, mĕam; tŭum, tŭam; sŭum, sŭam*), in Vulgar Latin, the feminine form showed a close vowel (*mẹu, mịa; tụu, tụa; sụu, sụa*),[7] this feature affected both sets of possessives.

a. The stressed possessives developed in this way from Vulgar Latin to Old Spanish:

mẹu > mieo > OSp. mío	mẹos > mieos > OSp. míos
mẹa > OSp. mía	mẹas > OSp. mías
tụu > OSp. to	tụos > OSp. tos
tụa > OSp. tua	tụas > OSp. tuas
sụu > OSp. so	sụos > OSp. sos
sụa > OSp. sua	sụas > OSp. suas
nọstru > OSp. nuestra	nọstros > OSp. nuestros
nọstra > OSp. nuestra	nọstras > OSp. nuestras
vọstru > OSp. vuestro	vọstros > OSp. vuestros
vọstra > OSp. vuestra	vọstras > OSp. vuestras

In Old Spanish, *mío* existed along with *mió*, the latter being actually a normal development, parallel to that of *Deus*, which gave *Diéos, Díos*, and finally *Diós* (§81b*i*).

The feminine form of the possessives was dominant; based on the forms *tua(s)* and *sua(s)*, the Old Spanish *to(s)* and *so(s)* became *tuo(s)* and *suo(s)*. These latter forms are rarely seen in the old language because of another analogy which affected all of the forms. *Tuyo(s)* and *suyo(s)* were created by analogy based either on *cuyo* or the *i* of *mio*. Already in the *Poema del Cid*, *tuyo* and *suyo* are commonly seen.

b. In Vulgar Latin, some of the unstressed possessives began to

---

[7] §78 gives an attested example where the *e* of *mea* actually rose to *i*, yielding VL *mia*.

appear in shortened form due to proclitic use; they developed into
Old Spanish in this way:

męu > OSp. mío	męos > OSp. míos
męa > OSp. míe, mi	męas > OSp. míes, mis
tų > OSp. to	tųs > OSp. tos
tųa > OSp. túe, tu	tųas > OSp. túes, tus
sų > OSp. so	sųs > OSp. sos
sųa > OSp. súe, su	sųas > OSp. súes, sus
nǫstru > OSp. nuestro	nǫstros > OSp. nuestros
nǫstra > OSp. nuestra	nǫstras > OSp. nuestras
vǫstru > OSp. vuestro	vǫstros > OSp. vuestros
vǫstra > OSp. vuestra	vǫstras > OSp. vuestras

The final *e* of *míe(s)* is said to be due to an assimilation of the *–a*,
approaching the point of articulation of the *i*. The final *e* of *túe(s)*
and *súe(s)* would then be analogical with *míe(s)*. Here again, the
masculine forms conformed to feminine development and became
mi(s), *tu(s)* and *su(s)* in modern Spanish.

Nuestro and *vuestro*, which had no hiatus problem to complicate their development, evolved the same way in both sets of
possessives.

Numbers

§166. The cardinal numbers offer few problems in their development from Vulgar Latin to Spanish. The numbers *unu*, *duos* and
tres were declinable in Vulgar Latin (§45a), but in Spanish only *uno*
differentiates between masculine and feminine.

a. The development of 1 – 10 from Vulgar Latin to Spanish is as
follows:

unu, –a > uno, –a	sex > seis
duos > dos	sette > siete
tres > tres	octo > ocho
quatt(u)or > cuatro	nove > nueve
cinque > cinco	dece > diez

The phonology of *cuatro* and *seis* is explained in §148a. The final *o* of *cinco* is analogical with the *–o* of *cuatro*.

  b. The development of 11–19 is as follows:

und(e)ce > once	dece et sex > dieciséis
dod(e)ce > doce	dece et sette > diecisiete
tred(e)ce > trece	dece et octo > dieciocho
catord(e)ce > catorce	dece et nove > diecinueve
quind(e)ce > quince	

Normal phonetic development would have caused *dod(e)ce* and *tredece* to become *doz* and *trez* (§95a, and compare French *douze* and *treize*), but analogy with *once* (where the *e* could not fall since the *c* began the last syllable, and there would be no syllable possible without the *e*), and also the need to keep the forms fully divorced phonetically from *dos* and *tres*, caused the *e* not to fall.

  c. The tens showed this development from Vulgar Latin:

viínte > veínte > véinte	sexaénta > sesenta
triínta > treínta > tréinta	settaénta > setenta
quadraénta > cuarenta	octoénta > ochenta
cinquaénta > cincuenta	novaénta > noventa

Veinte and *treinta* need some explanation. The final long *i* of CL *vīgíntī*, in accordance with §110, raised the stressed short *i* (which normally would have developed to *e*) to *i*. The final *i* eventually became *e* itself, and the result was *viínte*. There was then a dissimilation of the two *i*'s (as in CL *vīcīnum* > Sp. *vecino*, §149d). From there, the stress shifted to the more open vowel to give *véinte*. Since CL *trīgínta* does not end in a long *i*, it should have given Sp. *trienta*; but it modeled itself after *veinte*, and the result was *treinta*.

  d. The plural hundreds derive from the accusative plural (with final *os* and *as*) and therefore distinguish between masculine and feminine genders. *Ciento* '100 even' has inherited its invariable nature from Classical Latin.

> centu > ciento, cien
> ducentos > OSp. dozientos > Sp. doscientos
> trecentos > OSp. trezientos > Sp. trescientos

quadragintos (not continued)
quingentos > quinientos
sexcentos > seiscientos
septengentos (not continued)
octingentos (not continued)
nongentos (not continued)

Cien is a carryover from Old Spanish apocopated *çient* (as modern *gran* is a continuation of OSp. *grant*). APOCOPE [uh–póck–uh–pee] is just the loss of a final vowel.

Analogy with *dos* and *tres* caused *dozientos* and *trezientos* to change to *doscientos* and *trescientos*. *Quinientos* and *seiscientos* reflect normal development (although *quiñentos* would be a more etymological spelling for the former; compare Portuguese *quinhentos*, with similar pronunciation.)

The remaining forms (*cuatrocientos, setecientos, ochocientos, novecientos*) are analogical with the basic number to which was added *–cientos*. Note how *sete–* and *nove–* properly show pretonic vowel development.

e. In the thousands, *mille* gave *mil* in accordance with §133b. The Latin system of using the neuter plural for multiples of thousands (*due milia, tria milia,* §45d) was naturally lost. Instead, Old Spanish expressed them this way: *dos vezes mil, tres vezes mil.* Modern Spanish has eliminated the word *veces; dos mil, tres mil.* *Míllón* was an Italian "invention" (It. *milione*) which Spanish borrowed during the Middle Ages.

§167. The ordinal number system in Spanish shows learned forms exclusively starting with *sexto.* CL *primus* and *tertius* were replaced by VL *primariu* and *tertiariu.*

primariu > primero	sextu (learned *sexto*)
secundu > segundo	septimu (learned *séptimo*)
tertiariu > tercero	octavu (learned *octavo*)
quarto > cuarto	nonu (learned *noveno*)
quintu > quinto	decimu (learned *décimo*)

The old language continued *septimu* as *sietmo, octavu* as

ochavo, and *decimu* as *diezmo*. (*Ochavo* is retained in the language as the name of an old coin, and *diezmo* is continued in the meaning 'tithe'). *Noveno* is taken from the Latin distributive number system. (*Docena* and *decena* are other examples reflecting the Latin distributive system.)

Personal Pronouns

§168a. The personal pronouns evolved from Vulgar Latin with some interesting developments. Here is how the nominative first and second person pronouns developed from Vulgar Latin to Spanish:

> ego > eo > yo
> tu > tú
> nos > OSp. nos (+ otros) > nosotros
> vos > OSp. vos (+ otros) > vosotros

Eo became *yo* in accordance with §41a; *nos* and *vos* had emphatic collateral forms in Vulgar Latin, *nos alteros* and *vos alteros* (§41a), and it was these forms that finally replaced *nos* and *vos* at the end of the Middle Ages in Hispania.

Usted comes from an eroded development of **vuestra merced** through shortened forms such as *vuasted* and *vusted*. *Ustedes* is an analogical plural built on *usted*. (*Vuestra merced* shows why *usted* is frequently abbreviated **Vd.**)

b. In Vulgar Latin, the first and second person object pronouns developing from the Classical Latin dative case (Sp. *mí, ti, nos, os*) became the *stressed* direct or indirect object pronouns, and the pronouns that came from the Classical Latin accusative case (Sp. *me, te, nos, os*) became the *unstressed* direct or indirect object pronouns (§41b). Spanish has maintained this distinction everywhere except in the plural of the stressed set where subject pronouns have been substituted:

Stressed (= dat.)	*Unstressed* (= acc.)
mi > mí	me > me
ti > ti	te > te
nos > (nosotros)	nos > nos
vos > (vosotros)	vos > os

Os is said to have developed due to the phonetic conflict caused in reflexive commands. The *–dv–* of *venidvos* (and all other such commands) proved to be too cumbersome phonetically, so the *v* fell: OSp. *venidos*.

c. The third person pronouns developed from the same Latin demonstratives which gave rise to the definite articles (§158a), but with certain variations. The Vulgar Latin distinctions between the dative and accusative pronouns remains in the Spanish unstressed pronouns, unlike those of the preceding section:

Nominative (Subject Pronouns)—Stressed

il(le) > él	illos > ellos
illa > ella	illas > ellas
illud > ello	

Dative (Indirect Object Pronouns)—Unstressed

(il)li > le	(il)lis > les

Accusative (Direct Object Pronouns)—Unstressed

(il)lu > lo	(il)los > los
(il)la > la	(il)las > las

The dative and accusative pronouns lost a syllable due to their proclitic nature, but the nominative pronouns (excepting *él*) did not lose a syllable since they were the stressed set. *Il(le)* apparently lost the final *e* due to the tendency of final *e* to fall (§§95, 133b).

Since CL *ĭllī, ĭllīs*, with long final *i*, gave VL *(il)li, (il)lịs*, the forms **li* and **lis* might be expected in Spanish, but because these pronouns were used proclitically, the i was treated as unstressed, and the modern forms became *le* and *les*.

Because all of the forms of the dative and accusative were used for unstressed third person object pronouns (unlike the singular pronouns of section *b* above), the stressed object pronouns were taken from the only remaining source, the subject pronouns. A fortunate outcome from using the subject pronouns here is that they allow distinctions that would otherwise be impossible: *lo veo a él; lo veo a usted.*

d. The problem of *se lo* (= *le lo*) puzzles every generation of learners of Spanish. The historical development will explain this strange structure.

When two Classical Latin object pronouns were grouped together, the dative preceded the accusative: CL *illī illum, illī illās*. As these two pronouns developed, the first one lost its initial vowel as it did when it stood alone. But since the two pronouns were fused together, the "initial" *i* of the second pronoun was not lost because it was really no longer in initial position. The development of the examples at this point in Vulgar Latin could be imagined as *lielo, lielas*. As these evolved into Old Spanish, the initial *l* + *yod* developed to [ʒ] (as the same cluster did in *muliere* > OSp. *muger* [muʒɛr]. In Old Spanish these sets looked like this: *gelo, gelas* [ʒélo, ʒélas]. In accordance with §141, [ʒ] evolved to [ʃ], which is close to the [s] sound. The change from [ʃélo, ʃélas] to [sélo, sélas] was easily made, especially since there was a good analogy with the reflexive *se*, which appeared in similar syntactic patterns: *gelo dio (a ellal)*, *se lo dio (a sí misma)*. The plural form, which was seen in a few Old Spanish examples in variants of *leslo* (a normal development since there was no Vulgar Latin *yod* as in the singular), was overpowered by the singular form, and in modern Spanish *se lo* represents both *le* + *lo* and *les* + *lo*.

e. *Mecum, tecum* and *secum* (§41a, note) developed to *micum, ticum*, and *sicum* in the Vulgar Latin of Hispania, corresponding to the stressed object pronouns of *b* above. These developed phonetically in the normal way to give *migo, tigo* and *sigo*. Since *cum* had been so transformed (into *go*) and looked nothing like *con* (which was the usual phonetic outcome of *cum* when standing alone, §147b), the preposition *con* was prefixed to *migo, tigo* and *sigo* to yield the modern forms *conmigo, contigo* and *consigo*; thus CL *cum* is represented twice in the modern Spanish forms.

The Development of Verbs

Infinitives

§169. The Spanish language inherited almost all Vulgar Latin infinitives with only a few complications.

a. The Vulgar Latin *–are* infinitives passed into Spanish smoothly. Among the examples below, *fabulare* was deponent in Classical Latin (§62):

circare > cercar   lucrare > lograr
clamare > llamar   mesurare > mesurar
coll(o)care > colgar   mutare > mudar
fab(u)lare > hablar   nom(i)nare > nombrar
lavare > lavar   plicare > llegar

The –*ar* verbs are the most common and the most regular in the language, and virtually every new verb that has come into the language, be it based on an adjective, a noun, or a newly created word, is an –*ar* verb: *faxear, fechar, fotografiar, fusilar, igualar, mejorar, ocasionar, telefonear.*

Andar is a very mysterious infinitive; its origin has never been identified with certainty, although there are a number of theories about it. The least likely conjecture is the one that derives it (through metathesis) from *adnare* 'to swim to'. More reasonable is the theory that says that the noun *ambitus* 'detour' gave rise to an infinitive *ambitare* which would then give *andar* through normal phonetic evolution (*ambitare* > *ambidare* > *ambdar* > *andar*). Semantically, the best choice is *ambulare* 'to walk', but this form would have developed to *amblar*. If there had been a change of suffix in Vulgar Latin which had made *ambulare* into *ambutare*, then *andar* would be the normal development.

b. The Vulgar Latin –*ere* infinitives usually passed into Spanish without difficulty. The sampling below includes examples from the Classical Latin second conjugation (–*ēre*), as well as from the Classical third conjugation infinitives (CL *bíbĕre, comédĕre, fácĕre, légĕre, pónĕre, sápĕre, véndĕre,* §51a), a few Vulgar Latin inchoatives that derived from non–inchoative Classical infinitives (CL *carēre, obœdīre, parēre,* §49b), and the Vulgar Latin infinitive *potére,* which replaced the irregular CL *posse* (§63):

> bibére (CL bíbĕre) > beber
> carescére (CL carēre) > carecer
> comedére (CL comédĕre) > comer
> debére > deber
> facére (CL fácĕre) > hacer
> jacére > yacer
> habére > haber

legére (CL légĕre) > leer
obedescére (CL obœdīre) > obedecer
parescére (CL parēre) > parecer
ponére (CL pónĕre) > poner
potére (CL pósse) > poder
sapére (CL sápĕre) > saber
tenére (CL ténĕre) > tener
timére (CL tímĕre) > temer
vendére (CL véndĕre) > vender
vịdére > ver

The Vulgar Latin infinitive *éssere* (which replaced CL *esse*) was not continued into Spanish; Sp. *ser* derived from CL *sedēre* 'to sit'.

There are two remnants of the CL *–ĕre* infinitives surprisingly left in Spanish. CL *fácĕre* and *dīcĕre* had a double development; the first was their conjugation group change to OSp. *fazer* and *dizer*, but there was another development which maintained the Classical Latin stress.

fácere > fácre > fáre > OSp. far > Sp. har
dícere > dícre > díre > dir

These alternate infinitives are seen exclusively in the formation of the future and conditional tenses in Spanish: *haré, diría*.

c. Vulgar Latin *–ire* infinitives also transfered to Spanish intact. The sampling below includes those infinitives that Vulgar Latin inherited from the CL *–io* third conjugation (*fúgiō, –ĕre; páriō, –ĕre; recipiō, –ĕre,* §51b), those that derive from the Classical second conjugation (CL *implēre, lucēre, ridēre,* §51c), and VL *sequire*, which was deponent in Classical Latin (*sequī,* §62):

audíre > oír
dormíre > dormir
fugire (CL fúgére) > huir
glattíre > latir
implíre (CL implēre) > henchir
lucíre (CL lucēre) > lucir
parire (CL parĕre) > parir

partíre > partir
recipíre (CL recipĕre) > recibir
ridíre (CL ridēre) > reír
sentíre > sentir
sequíre (CL séqui) > seguir
servíre > servir
veníre > venir

There were other Classical Latin third conjugation infinitives which joined the above. The –gĕre infinitives switched to –ir in Spanish for reasons that are not clear: CL cíngĕre > Sp. ceñir, CL rĭngĕre > Sp. reñir, CL spárgĕre > Sp. esparcir. Those –ĕre infinitives with ī in the stem also became –ir verbs in Spanish, sometimes with vocalic dissimilation (§149d), as in the first two of the following examples: CL dīcĕre > VL dicíre > Sp. decir, CL frīgĕre > VL frigíre > Sp. freír, CL scríbĕre > Sp. escribir, CL vīvĕre > Sp. vivir. Classical Latin pétĕre had a double set of perfects, one based on the –ire verbs (petīvī) and the other based on the –ĕre verbs (pétuī). It was probably due to its –ire perfect that the rest of the conjugation switched to the –ire pattern: Sp. pedir.

The Present Indicative

§170. The present indicative, although it forms a fairly consistent system in modern Spanish, has quite a complicated history. In fact, it is precisely *because* the language strove to regularize the conjugations and maintain a constant stem throughout the present indicative that most of the historical complications have come about. The pressure to regularize the conjugations was so great that normal phonetic evolution was actually stunted in many cases. Indeed, whereas phonetic "laws" are quite strong in themselves, morphological "laws" are even stronger and of more consequence, as the sections below will explain.

For the time being, model conjugations will be given which show no complications after the Vulgar Latin stage. Where the Vulgar Latin form differs significantly from the Classical form, the latter will be given in parentheses. In §50 there are examples of complete Classical Latin present indicative conjugations.

§171a. This is the normal development of the present indicative from Vulgar Latin to Spanish of the verbs deriving from the Classical Latin first conjugation, *-āre*:

> clámo > llamo
> clámas > llamas
> clámat > llama
> clamámus > llamamos
> clamátis > OSp. llamades > Sp. llamáis
> clámant > llaman

The only unusual feature found above concerns the *-atis* > *-áis* development. In the fifteenth century, the *-d-* of *-ades* disappeared, and the *-e-* changed to *yod*. Ordinarily, the *-d-* deriving from *-t-* was not lost in Spanish (§125a). The loss of *-d-* also affected the endings of the remaining conjugations (*-etis* > *éis*, and *-itis* > *-ís*).

b. Because there are many *-are* verbs which changed their tonic *ŏ* to *ué* or their *ĕ* to *ié*, a few verbs which had an *ō* or an *ē,ĭ* in Classical Latin have diphthongized by analogy, especially those verbs in which *-ns* follows the vowel in question:

CL cōlat > Sp. cuela	CL rĭcat > Sp. riega
CL cōnstat > Sp. cuesta	CL sēminat > Sp. siembra
CL mōnstrat > Sp. muestra	CL pēnsat > Sp. piensa

On the other hand, some verbs which should have diphthongized show a simple vowel in modern Spanish:

CL confŏrtat > Sp. conforta	CL vĕtat > Sp. veda

A few verbs which did have diphthongs in Old Spanish have lost them in modern Spanish since the diphthongs follow *muta cum liquida* (§81c): CL intĕgrat > OSp. *entriega* > Sp. *entrega*, CL præstō > OSp. *priesto* > Sp. *presto*.

c. The Classical Latin verb *lĕvāre* presents an interesting development. In Old Spanish it developed to *levar* and was conjugated *lievo, lievas, lieva, levamos, levades, lievan*. It is easy to see that the four forms with *li-* became confused with *ll-*. Finally the whole conjugation, including the infinitive and the *nosotros* and *vosotros* forms, changed to the *ll–* pronunciation and spelling.[8]

d. The Classical Latin verb *jŏcārī* presents a real phonetic problem in the modern Spanish *jugar*. It has been suggested that the verb could have derived from VL *jugare*, but in that case, the Old Spanish result would have had no diphthongized forms (which it did have in fact: OSp. *juego, juegas, juega, juegan*). It has also been suggested that *jugar* represents a Leonese development where the diphthong *ué* has generalized into the infinitive, then simplified to *u*; VL *jocare* would have given Leon. *juegar* and then simplified to *jugar*, as in VL Leon. > *cuentar* > Leon. *cuntar*. It does not seem likely, however, that such a common verb would come from a dialect. The answer seems to be that the would–be *o* of the infinitive changed to *u* in self defense. The only other common infinitive that begins with *jo–* is *joder* 'to fornicate', and anyone who began to utter the infinitive meaning 'to play' with initial *jo–* risked laughter from his audience.[9]

§172. Here is the normal development of the present indicative from Vulgar Latin to Spanish of the verbs deriving from the Classical Latin second conjugation, *–ēre*:

> débo (CL debeō) > debo
> débes > debes
> débet > debe
> debémus > debemos
> debétis > OSp. debedes > Sp. debéis
> débent > deben

---

[8] *L* + *yod* in intervocalic position developed to *jota* (§141), but there were no cases of it in initial position. In any case, this cluster came about much too late to develop to *jota*.

[9] See my article *"Jugar: Étymologie scabreuse"* (1992). I am indebted to the attentive Kurt Baldinger for his endorsement of this analysis, which I explained to him, point by point, during our lengthy wait in a Polish police station—we were there to report some thefts. We had a good time during this discussion, but the police were consternated by our mirth.

It was pointed out in §51c that in some verbs, the –e– of the Classical Latin first person singular was slow to drop and became a *yod*, the result being that these verbs moved to the Vulgar Latin –ire conjugation. The –e– in the usual case, as in the model conjugation above, fell without leaving a trace. Other examples of this include: CL *tímeō* > Sp. *temo*, CL *móveō* > Sp. *muevo*.

CL *vídeō*, which kept –eo, developed to *veyo* in Old Spanish (§129a). The vowel cluster was then reduced by the removal of the middle element, and the modern *veo* came into existence. CL *vides, videt, vidēre* gave *vees, vee, veer* through Cervantes' time (he died in 1616). When the infinitive simplified to *ver*, the other forms made an analogical change to conform to the new infinitive: *ves, ve*. This development contrasts with *lee* and *cree* in §173b, where the infinitive continues the vowels of the conjugated forms.

§173a. This is the normal development from Vulgar Latin to Spanish of the verbs deriving from the Classical Latin third conjugation, –*ĕre*:

> bíbo > bebo
> bíbes (CL bíbis) > bebes
> bíbet (CL bíbit) > bebe
> bibémus (CL bíbimus) > bebemos
> bibétis (CL bíbitis) > OSp. bebedes > Sp. bebéis
> bíbent (CL bíbunt) > beben

In Vulgar Latin, the Classical Latin third conjugation merged with the Classical second conjugation (§51a)—this included second conjugation verb endings as well as second conjugation stress (§52).

b. With the fall of intervocalic *d* and *g* (§§129a, 130a), one might expect CL *crédit* to develop to Sp. **crey* and *légit* to give **ley*, in accordance with §95d. However, due to the morphological pressure to maintain consistent verb endings, these two verbs did not give in to normal phonetic development, and became *cree* and *lee*.

§174. This is the normal development of the present indicative from Vulgar Latin to Spanish of the verbs from the Classical fourth conjugation, –*īre*:

dórmo (CL dŏrmiō) > duermo
dórmis > duermes
dórmit > duerme
dormimus > dormimos
dormítis > OSp. dormides > Sp. dormís
dórment (CL dormiunt) > duermen

The *yod* in the Classical Latin first person singular ending was usually lost in Vulgar Latin (§50), but in many instances, the *yod* was slower to disappear than it was in the model above, in which case it caused some phonetic and morphological difficulties, as will be explained in §176; Other examples which show early loss of the *yod* include: CL *apériō* > Sp. *abro* (§175), CL *fĕriō* > Sp. *hiero*, CL *partiō* > Sp. *parto*.

OSp. *–ides* would have given *–íes*, *–iés* with loss of *–d–*. But in this case, since *–ades* gave *–áis*, *–ides* followed suit yielding *–íis* which simplified to *–ís*. The Vulgar Latin third person plural ending is analogical with the *–ent* of the *–ēre* conjugation (§172).

§175. A few more comments should be made about the leveling of Classical Latin stress in Vulgar Latin. In Classical Latin, a verb would be stressed in some persons on the first syllable of the stem (*áperis*, *súccutis*), and in other persons on the second syllable of the stem (*apério*, *succútio*). This variance of stress evened out in Vulgar Latin, but not in a uniform way. Some verbs unified their stress based on the first person singular: VL *ápero*, *áperis*, *áperit*, and others unified their stress based on the pattern of the remaining forms: VL *sucúto*, *sucútis*, *sucútit*. This Vulgar Latin stress was maintained in Spanish: *ábro*, *ábres*, *ábre; sacúdo*, *sacúdes*, *sacúde.*

Since Spanish always stresses the present tense verbs on the penult (except for the *vosotros* form), "learned" verbs which have been added into the language do not maintain "learned" stress, but are modified it to fit the normal Spanish pattern:

CL cólloco > Sp. colóco
CL commúnico > Sp. comuníco
CL consídero > Sp. considéro
CL víndico > Sp. vindíco

The first, second and fourth of these in their traditional developments, have maintained the original Latin stress:

CL cŏ́ll(o)cō > Sp. cuélgo
CL commū́n(i)cō > Sp. comúlgo
CL vĕ́nd(i)cō > Sp. véngo

§176a. The present tense of *–ir* verbs shows quite a bit of inflection and analogy not seen in *–ar* and *–er* verbs. It was stated in §52 and again in §174 that the *yod* of the first person singular endings in some third and most fourth conjugation present indicatives were not retained in Vulgar Latin (CL *faciō* > VL *faco* > Sp. *hago*, CL *partiō* > VL *parto* > Sp. *parto*). However, when the stem vowel of a Vulgar Latin *–ire* verb was a close *e* (deriving from CL *ē* or *ĭ*), the VL *yod* raised it to *i* before it disappeared. This effect is seen universally in the earliest Castilian texts. Thus VL *metio* became *mido* already in Old Spanish. On the other hand, you would expect that VL *metis*, *metit* and *metent* would become *medes*, *mede* and *meden* in Spanish since no *yod* followed their close *e*. These forms do not exist in Spanish, and for a very good reason. In the *–ar* and *–er* conjugations, where there is a vowel change, it affects *all four* strong forms, as these examples show:

–ar		–er	
siento	sentamos	vuelvo	volvemos
sientas	sentáis	vuelves	volvéis
sienta	sientan	vuelve	vuelven

By analogy, the *–ir* verbs with an inflected first person singular followed the model of the *–ar* and *–er* verbs and placed an *–i–* in the remaining strong forms. Thus:

Vulgar Latin	Spanish
métio	mido
métis	mides
métit	mide
metímus	medimos
metítis	medís
métent	miden

This analogical feature affecting the second and third persons singular and third person plural is again seen in the earliest Castilian texts.

This phenomenon also affected verbs with a *yod* which came to the VL *-ire* from other sources, as this sampling shows:

CL implēre,	VL implēre > Sp. henchir
ímpleō	VL implio > Sp. hincho
	VL implis > Sp. hinches (anal.)
	VL implimus > Sp. henchimos
CL concipĕre,	VL concipire > Sp. concebir
concípiō	VL concipio > Sp. concibo
	VL concipis > Sp. concibes (anal.)
	VL concipimus > Sp.concebimos

The Spanish result of CL *recípĕre*, practically a twin of *concípĕre*, has generalized the *i* everywhere whereas *concípĕre* has not:

CL recipĕre,	VL recipire > Sp. recibir (anal.)
recípiō	VL recipio > Sp. recibo
	VL recipis > Sp. recibes (anal.)
	VL recipimus > Sp.recibimos (anal.)

b. The above deals with *-ir* verbs with a Classical Latin close *e* as their stem vowel. But what about those *-ir* verbs which had an open *e*?

You would expect that the Vulgar Latin *yod* would raise the open *e* to a close *e* in the first person singular only, but that the remaining three strong forms, lacking a *yod* in their endings, would be develop a diphthonigized vowel, thus, these conjugations (which do not exist exactly as given below) could have been expected:

Vulgar Latin	Spanish	Vulgar Latin	Spanish
sérvio	*servo	séntio	*sento
sérvis	*sierves	séntis	sientes
sérvit	*sierve	séntit	siente
servímus	*servimos	sentímus	sentimos
servítis	servís	sentítis	sentís
sérvent	*sierven	séntent	sienten

Since neither *servir* nor *sentir* is conjugated as phonetically predicted, how can the existing Spanish conjugations of these two verbs be explained? Again, it is analogy at work, and both examples show a different type of analogy. *Servir* has merely modeled itself after the *medir* type, using this ratio formula: *medimos : servimos :: mido : x (= sirvo)*. Once *sirvo* was formed, *sirves, sirve, sirven* followed suit, as explained in *a* above. Other verbs that work like servir are *vestir*, from CL *věstīre* (Sp. *visto*, not *vesto*), and *embestir* from CL *ĭnvěstīre* (Sp. *embisto*, not *embesto*).

The more common case is what happened with *sentir*. Here, the first person singular simply yielded to the morphological pressure exerted by the other strong forms and took an analogical *–ie–*. Other verbs that work like sentir include *herir*, from CL *fěrīre* (Sp. *hiero*, not *hero*) and *mentir*, from CL *měntīre* (Sp. *miento*, not *mento*).

c. A number of Classical Latin verbs which had no *yod* in the first person singular joined the Vulgar Latin *–ire* conjugation, and many of these, by analogy, followed the "inflected" conjugation described above in *a*. The Classical Latin infinitives and first person singulars are given for better comparison:

Classical Latin	Modern Spanish
cĭngěre, cĭngō	ceñir, ciño
dīcěre, dicō	decir, digo
pétěre, pětō	pedir, pido
régěre, régō	regir, rijo
sěquī, sěquor	seguir, sigo

d. The other type of –*ire* conjugation inflection was where close *o* was raised to *u* in the Old Spanish first person singular. In these verbs, the first person was so powerful that all forms of the verb, every person of every tense, not just the strong forms of the present (as in *a* above), eventually took the *u* as their theme vowel. In the examples below, from CL *sŭbīre* and *coŏpĕrīre*, the modern Spanish forms reveal analogical generalization of the *u*:

Vulgar Latin	Old Spanish	Spanish
sųbire	sobir	subir (anal.)
sųbio	subo	subo
sųbis	sobes	subes (anal.)
sųbit	sobe	sube (anal.)
sųbimus	sobimos	subimos (anal.)
sųbitis	sobides	subís (anal.)
sųbent	soben	suben (anal.)
cọp(e)rire	cobrir	cubrir (anal.)
cọp(e)rio	cubro	cubro
cọp(e)ris	cobres	cubres (anal.)
cọp(e)rit	cobre	cubre (anal.)
cọp(e)rimus	cobrimos	cubrimos (anal.)
cọp(e)ritis	cobrides	cubrís (anal.)
cọp(e)rent	cobren	cubren (anal.)

This phenomenon affected verbs with a *yod* that joined the Vulgar Latin –*ire* conjugation from other Classical Latin sources, as this sampling shows:

CL cōmplēre,   VL cọmplíre > OSp. complir > Sp. cumplir (anal.)
  cōmpleō   VL cọmplio > OSp. cumplo > Sp. cumplo
               VL cọmplis > OSp. comples > Sp. cumples (anal.)
               VL cọmplímus > OSp. complimos > Sp. cumplimos (anal.)

CL fŭgĕre,   VL fųgire > OSp. foir > Sp. huir (anal.)
  fŭgiō   VL fųgio > OSp. fuyo > Sp. huyo
               VL fųgis > OSp. foes > Sp. huyes (anal.)
               VL fųgímus > OSp. foimos > Sp.huimos (anal.)

CL sŭfferre,   VL sufferíre > OSp. sofrir > Sp. sufrir (anal.)
   sŭfferō   VL sufferio > OSp. sufro > Sp. sufro
                 VL sufferis > OSp. sofres > Sp. sufres (anal.)
                 VL sufferímus > OSp. sofrimos > Sp. sufrimos (anal.)

CL *sŭfferre* was a compound of the irregular *ferō (ferre)*; it changed to the *–ire* conjugation in Vulgar Latin (§63).

e. In the case of VL *dormio* and *morio* (CL *morior*, a deponent verb), we could have expected the *yod* to raise the open *o* to a close *o* in Spanish giving these hypothetical forms: *dormo and *moro. The Spanish *duermo* and *muero* are obviously analogical forms with the remaining strong forms with *–ué–*. This process is similar to the one described in section *b* above (with *siento*).

§177. In a number of first person singular forms in Spanish, a *g* has appeared where there seemingly is no reason for its being there. These forms fall into two different groups: 1) *caigo, oigo, traigo*, and 2) *vengo, pongo, tengo, salgo, valgo.*

a. The outcome of VL *cadeo* (CL *cadō*) and *audio* was *cayo* and *oyo* in Old Spanish; *traho* resulted in OSp. *trayo* through the addition of *y* to avoid hiatus.[10] The common and important Old Spanish verbs *digo* and *fago*, whose *g* is etymological, deriving from VL *dico* and *faco* (CL *faciō*), imposed a non–etymological *g* into *cayo*, *oyo* and *trayo*, causing them to become *caigo, oigo* and *traigo*.

b. The second set requires a different explanation as to why the *g* appeared when there was no apparent etymological reason. Certainly the Latin forms below could not directly result in the Spanish forms with *g*:

> VL venio – Sp. vengo
> VL tenio (CL tĕneō) – Sp. tengo
> VL valio (CL valeō) – Sp. valgo
> VL ponio (CL pōnō) – Sp. pongo
> VL salio – Sp. salgo

---

[10] Philologists call this spontaneously generated type of vowel an EPENTHETIC [epp-un-thétt-ick] vowel.

In the Vulgar Latin forms above, the *yod* could not have its effect in either of the two ways usually open to it. First, its action was thwarted because morphological pressure prevented it from mixing with the previous consonant, which would thus have impaired the consonantal unity of the stem of the verb (176), and would have caused the first person singular forms to develop into these non-existent examples: *teño, *poño, *sajo, *veño (although in Portuguese, *tenho, ponho* and *venho* [remember that Portuguese *nh* sounds like Spanish *ñ*] are the normal developments). The *yod* was again thwarted since in four of the five verbs it could not release its energy by inflecting the preceding vowel—only *-ire* verbs with an *e* or *o* as their stem vowel would allow inflection and of the five verbs, only *venio* met these requirements. (In *venio* the open *e* WAS raised by the *yod* to a close *e*, thus there is no diphthong in that form.) Three of the other verbs are from the *-ere* conjugation, and the remaining verb, although from the *-ire* group, has *a* as its theme vowel, thus none of the remaining four was susceptible to inflection. Since the *yod*'s energy HAD TO BE released, it was forced to find a third way—a new way—to expend itself. Since a *g* can become a *yod* (§§139, 172b, 142a), it is plausible that a *yod* that is seeking a new outlet for its energy, can become a *g*, especially since there was a nice analogy in Old Spanish of verbs which presented an etymological *g* in similar phonetic surroundings: *frango* (VL *frango*), *plango* (VL *plango*), *tango* (VL *tango*). Thus, the *g* in the five Spanish verbs above appears to derive from a *yod*.[11]

---

[11] In this paragraph, I have restored my explanation of this phenomenon from the first edition. It made sense to me, and seemed to be a daring solution to this sticky problem. Since a few reviewers didn't like it, I changed it to a very non–committal, traditional explanation in the second edition. Joel Rini, whose opinions I value, convinced me to put back the original explanation in this edition, for which I am grateful. If you disagree with it, here is the second edition's explanation. The reference below to Italian is relevant to the above explanation as well:

    The usual explanation given for the appearance of the *-g-* is that the forms *vengo, tengo,* and *pongo* are analogical with Old Spanish forms which did show an etymological *-ngo,* such as *frango, plango,* and *tango. Valgo* and *salgo* (with their final *-lgo*) would then be

§178. Another interesting set of first person singular forms were OSp. *oyo* (modern *oigo*) and *fuyo* (modern *huyo*), whose *y* developed regularly from VL *audio* and *fugio*. This *y* was powerful in two ways. First, it propagated itself to the remaining strong forms of the present: *oyes, oye, oyen; fuyes, fuye, fuyen*. (The Vulgar Latin forms could not give rise to a *y* by themselves: *audis, audit, audent; fugis, fugit, fugent*.) Second, the *y* infiltrated into the strong forms of learned verbs such as *construir*, none of whose forms, not even the first person singular, had an etymological right to a *y*:

CL cónstruo—Sp. construyo   CL cónstruis—Sp. construyes
CL cónstruit—Sp. construye   CL cónstruunt—Sp. construyen

Among other verbs that follow this pattern are *argüir, concluir, construir, contribuir, destruir, diluir, disminuir, excluir, incluir, influir, obstruir, sustituir*.

§179. The modern verb forms *doy, soy, voy, estoy*, which have a final *y*, developed to their normal phonetic result in Old Spanish without *y*:

VL do > OSp. do
VL sum > OSp. so[12]
VL vao (CL vadō) > OSp. vo
VL sto > OSp. estó

---

tenuously analogical with these forms. Because Italian shows the same features (It. *vengo, tengo*, and *valgo*), the reason for the –g– must be larger than just a Spanish phenomenon (but compare Portuguese *venho, tenho, valho* which show a direct development without complications). Since all of these forms have a *yod* in the Vulgar Latin ending, we can suspect that the –g– is related to the *yod* in some way, but a convincing solution has yet to be discovered.

[12] *Son* would be the expected result from *sum*, as *tam* > *tan, quem* > *quien* (§147b), but *–n* was dropped in order to differentiate *so* from the third person plural *son* (< *sunt*). Italian has the same form for both persons with no problems: *io sono, egli sono*.

The earliest documentation of any of these four forms with final *y* is *doy* and dates from the early thirteenth century—the final *y* refers to the indirect object, as some of the examples below show. This Spanish *y* (<CL *ibī* 'there') is similar to the French adverbial *y* of *j'y vais*:

> do y la otra heredat a este monasterio (Staaff, p. 39)
> do.hy. cuanto eredamiento a Sancta Maria de Piasca (Staaff, p. 39)
> do.y. ueinte uaccas (Staaff, p. 77)
> do i por mi alma... vi tabladas (*Doc. ling.*, p. 124)
> do hi conmigo quanto he (*Doc. ling.*, p. 134)[13]

It was not until the sixteenth century that the –*y* became permanently attached to *do* and spread to *so* and *vo*, both of which were related to *do* since all three were common monosyllabic first person singulars. (The *y* of *estoy* is analogical with *soy*.)

During this same period, *ha* 'there is, there are' also took a final *y*, which made it similar to the French construction *il y a* (Fr. *y* + *a* [as pronounced, not as spelled] = Sp. *ha* + *y*).

§180a. The present tense of the verb *ser* developed from the Classical Latin *esse* conjugation with some modification:

> CL sum > OSp. so > Sp. soy (§179)
> CL es (not continued); eris > Sp. eres
> CL est > Sp. es
> CL sŭmus > Sp. somos
> CL estis (not continued); VL sŭtis > OSp. sodes > Sp. sois
> CL sŭnt > Sp. son

Both CL *es* and *est* would have developed to *es* in Spanish; to avoid

---

[13] Staaff, Erik, *Étude sur l'ancien dialecte léonais (d'après des chartes du XIIIᵉ siècle)*, Uppsala: Almqvist & Wiksell, 1907; Ramón Menéndez Pidal, *Documentos lingüísticos de España* (Vol. 1, Reino de Castilla), Madrid: Centro de Estudios Históricos, 1919.

this confusion, the language retained the Classical Latin future (of *esse*) *eris* 'you will be' which developed to *eres*. This lone form is the only vestige of the Classical Latin future tense in Spanish, indeed, the only vestige of the Classical future in any of the major Romance Languages (n. 19, p. 58). CL *estis* was lost in Spanish, probably because its root was based on the singular *es, est,* and not on the plural forms; *sutis,* based on *sumus* and *sunt,* was created, which gave *sois* in Spanish through normal phonetic evolution.

b. The Classical Latin infinitive *īre* was continued (Sp. *ir*), but none of its present tense conjugation has survived to modern Spanish—most of its forms would have been too short or too confusing: CL *ego eō* would have developed to Sp. **yo yo,* for example. *Imos* (from CL *īmus*) and *ides* (from CL *ītis*) were the only forms of *īre* that were retained in Old Spanish.

It was the present indicative of CL *vádĕre* 'to walk' which replaced the present indicative of *īre* in Spanish:

CL vadō > VL vao > OSp. vo > Sp. voy (§179)
CL vadis > VL vas > Sp. vas
CL vadit > VL vat > Sp. va
CL vádimus > VL vamus > Sp. vamos
CL váditis > VL vatis > Sp. vais
CL vadunt > VL vant > Sp. van

§181. The conjugation of CL *habēre* lost a syllable in the Vulgar Latin strong forms (§54b):

CL habeo > VL aio > Sp. he
CL habes > VL as > Sp. has
CL habet > VL at > Sp. ha
CL habemus > VL abemus > OSp. (av)emos > Sp. hemos
CL habētis > VL abetis > Sp. habéis
CL habent > VL ant > Sp. han

Restoration of the *h*– in Spanish is purely learned.

The development of the first person singular has been traditionally very obscure. The final *o* of the Vulgar Latin form had to be lost early for *ai* to become *ei* (as in Portuguese *hei*) then to simplify to *(h)e.* Compare *probai* > *probei* (cf. Portuguese *provei*) > *probé* (§107). If the *o* had remained, *aio* would have given simply *hayo*, or possibly *haigo* by analogy with other verbs. The obscure point is the loss of –*o*. Joel Rini (1995) has said that the –*o* fell because of haplology (§160c) caused when the pronoun was in postverbal position: *aio yo*. This created "an awkward series of reduplicated syllables, certainly destined for some sort of abbreviation or repair." A logical next step would be to eliminate the only –*o* that *could be* eliminated (the one in *aio*) and the result would be *ai*. From there *he* would develop phonetically in the usual way (§107).

In Old Spanish, *avemos* was regularly used for the main verb and for the auxiliary, whereas *emos* was used for the formation of the future. It is this latter form which has survived in modern Spanish, both as an auxiliary (*lo hemos hecho*) and as the future ending (*lo haremos*).

§182. VL *sapére* has also given rise to a problem in the first person singular. *Sapio*, according to normal phonetic development pattern (§109), should have given **sepo*, as *sapiam* has given *sepa*. The usual explanation for *sé* is that it is analogical with *he*. This seems to be the most likely possibility since other Romance Languages have the same parallel in forms: It. *so, ho*; Port. *sei, hei*, Fr. *sais, ai* [sɛ, ɛ].

The Present Subjunctive

§183. The endings of the Classical Latin present subjunctive had the characteristics that the Spanish subjunctive was to retain: the –*are* conjugation had endings based on *e*, and the remaining conjugations had endings based on *a* (§65). Here are typical developments from Vulgar Latin to Spanish:

–*are*	–*ere* (from CL –*ēre*)
clámem > llame	tímam (CL timeam) > tema
clámes > llames	tímas (CL timeās) > temas
clámet > llame	tímat (CL timeat) > tema
clamémus > llamemos	timámus (CL timeāmus) > temamos
clamétis > llaméis	timátis (CL timeātis) > temáis
cláment > llame	tímant (CL timeant) > teman

–ere (from CL *–ĕre*)	*–ire*
bíbam > beba	pártam (CL partiam) > parta
bíbas > bebas	pártas (CL partiās) > partas
bíbat > beba	pártat (CL partiat) > partamos
bibámus > bebamos	partiámus (CL partiāmus) > partamos
bibátis > bebáis	partiátis (CL partiātis) > partáis
bíbant > beban	pártant (CL partiant) > partan

The stem of the subjunctive was influenced by the stem of the indicative, and specifically by the first person singular. If *pacare* and *plicare*, for example, had developed according to phonetic convention, *pacem* would have given **pace* in Spanish, and *plicem* would have given **llece* (instead of *pague* and *llegue*), as noted in §126c, but the morphological pressure from the indicative prevented this normal phonetic change from taking place.

The *yod* which was lost in the first person singular of the present indicative of the Classical Latin *–ēre* conjugation (CL *tímeo* > VL *tímo*) was equally lost in the subjunctive in Vulgar Latin.

Those Spanish verbs which have a *–g–* in the first person singular of the indicative, whether it is etymological or not, have a *–g–* in all of the present subjunctive forms. In these same verbs, if there was no diphthongization in the first person singular of the present indicative (as in *tengo, vengo* below), there was no diphthongization in any form of the present subjunctive either. This again illustrates the immense influence of the first person singular of the present indicative.

CL dīcō > Sp. digo
CL dicam > Sp. diga
CL tĕneō > Sp. tengo
CL tĕneat > Sp. tenga
CL vĕniō > Sp. vengo
CL vĕnias > Sp. vengas

§184a. In the *–ire* subjunctive conjugation, if the stem vowel was an *i*, *a* or *u*, the *yod* of the first and second person plural fell without leaving a trace, as in VL *partiamus* > Sp. *partamos* above.

b. If, however, the stem vowel of the *–ire* conjugation was an *e* or *o*, the *yod* of the first and second person plural raised it to *i* or *u*, then disappeared:

Vulgar Latin	*Spanish*
met*i*amus	m*i*damos
met*i*atis	m*i*dáis
sent*i*amus	s*i*ntamos
sent*i*atis	s*i*ntáis
dorm*i*amus	d*u*rmamos
dorm*i*atis	d*u*rmáis

Since Vulgar Latin initial vowels were close (§87), the *yod* only had to raise the *e* and *o* one step on the vowel triangle.

§185. The irregular present subjunctives in Spanish have a different stem from the first person singular present indicative.

a. The subjunctive of *esse* (CL *sim, sīs, sit, sīmus, sītis, sint*) would have developed into forms that were too short or too confusing in Spanish; the present subjunctive of CL *sedēre* replaced this conjugation:

> VL sedeam > OSp. seya > Sp. sea
> VL sedeas > OSp. seyas > Sp. seas
> VL sedeat > OSp. seya > Sp. sea
> VL sedeamus > OSp. seyamos > Sp. seamos
> VL sedeatis > OSp. seyades > Sp. seáis
> VL sedeant > OSp. seyan > Sp. sean

The Old Spanish stage, containing a vowel cluster beginning with *ey*, dropped the *yod* as usual. Another example of this *yod* loss is seen in the development of ver: VL *videas* > OSp. *veyas* > Sp. *veas*.

b. The present subjunctive of *ire* (CL *eam, eās, eat, eāmus, eātis, eant*) was equally lost, and for the same reasons as above. The subjunctive of *vadere* replaced it. In Old Spanish this subjunctive took an epenthetic *y* to remedy the unusual hiatus created by the loss of *d*, although you do occasionally see the etymological forms of the first and second persons plural in Old Spanish without *y*: *vaamos, vaades*.

vadam > vaya	vadamus > vayamos
vadas > vayas	vadatis > vayáis
vadat > vaya	vadant > vayan

The etymological result of *vadamus*, however, has survived as the positive *nosotros* imperative: ¡*vamos!*

c. The present subjunctive of *habēre* shows an unusual loss of *b* before *yod* (§137b). The loss of *b* apparently occurred in Vulgar Latin, similar to what happened in the indicative (§181):

CL habeam > Sp. haya	CL habeāmus > Sp. hayamos
CL habeās > Sp. hayas	CL habeātis > Sp. hayáis
CL habeat > Sp. haya	CL habeant > Sp. hayan

d. The present subjunctive of *dăre* and *stāre* present a minor phonological problem. In all other *–are* subjunctives, the endings are unstressed (except for the first and second person plural), so it makes no difference that the first and third person singular and the third person plural have a CL *ĕ*, whereas the second person singular shows a CL *ē*; both *e*s will result in *e* in Spanish (§93). However, in the case of *dăre* and *stāre*, the endings contained the stressed vowels in these persons, so their first and third person singular and third person plural could have developed to **die, *die, *dien* and **estié, *estié, *estién,* but morphological pressure was too great to allow this "irregularity":

CL dĕm > Sp. dé	CL dēmus > Sp. demos
CL dēs > Sp. des	CL dētis > Sp. deis
CL dĕt > Sp. dé	CL dĕnt > Sp. den
CL stĕm > Sp. esté	CL stēmus > Sp. estemos
CL stēs > Sp. estés	CL stētis > Sp. estéis
CL stĕt > Sp. esté	CL stĕnt > Sp. estén

Imperatives

§186a. In Classical Latin, the imperatives existed only in the positive form, the negative form being expressed with the verb *nolī(te)* 'be unwilling', + *infinitive* (§53). But Classical Latin also used the JUSSIVE subjunctive (*Frater meus id faciat!* 'Let my brother do it!') as a type of imperative, both for the positive and for the negative. This subjunctive use laid the foundation for the Vulgar Latin *non* + *subjunctive* to replace the CL *nolī(te)* + *infinitive* construction as the negative form of the imperative (§53).

The Spanish language continues the Classical Latin positive imperatives in the *tú* and *vosotros* forms: CL *clamā* > Sp. *llama*, CL *clamāte* > Sp. *llamad*, as well as the Vulgar Latin use of *non* + *subjunctive* for the negative (*no llames, no llaméis*).

b. The positive imperatives require a few special notes concerning their phonological features.

First, among those –*ir* verbs which have a vowel alternation (*servir–sirvo, mentir–miento, dormir–duermo*), analogy was as much at work in the *tú* imperatives as it was in the present indicative (§176a–d). The *tú* imperatives of these verbs, instead of developing to their normal phonetic result, were based on the strong forms of the present indicative. Thus, the *tú* commands *sirve, miente* and *duerme* are analogical with *sirvo, miento* and *duermo*. If normal phonetic evolution had taken place, CL *sĕrvī, mĕntī* and *dŏrmī* would have developed to a hypothetical Sp. **serve, *sente* and **dorme* since final long *i* normally raises a preceding open vowel one step up the vowel triangle (§110).

c. In Classical Latin, there were a few *tū* imperatives which had no ending at all, for example *fac* (from *facĕre*), *dīc* (from *dīcĕre*), *dūc* 'lead' (from *dūcĕre*), and *es* (from *esse*). Of these, only *dīc* has survived into Spanish: *di*. It is possible that *di* influenced other common commands, causing them to lose their final *e* by analogy, contrary to §95b.

> VL dị̄c > Sp. di
> VL face > Sp. haz
> VL pone > Sp. pon
> VL salị̄ > Sp. sal
> VL tẹnị̄ (CL tĕnē) > Sp. ten
> VL vẹnị̄ > Sp. ven

VL *Teni* was apparently analogical with *venī*; the CL *tĕnē*, with no final *ī* to prevent diphthongization, would have developed to **tien(e)*. CL *fac* would have developed to Sp. **fa* (§147a).

d. Finally, there is the case of *ve (ir)* and *sé (ser)*. VL *vade* replaced the extremely short Classical imperative *ī*, and lost its *d* to give this development: *vade > vai > vei > ve*. The plural command of *īre (īte)* was continued into Spanish: *id*. The imperative forms of VL *esse (es* and *este)* were lost and replaced in Vulgar Latin by the imperatives of *sedēre* (VL *sede* and *sedéte)*, which, through normal phonetic evolution, gave Sp. *sé* and *sed*.

The Inchoative Flexion

§187a. The inchoative flexion (§49) which gained new members in Vulgar Latin while losing its inceptive notion, continued to gain new members on the way to Spanish. In the inchoative conjugation, the first person singular ending, *–sco*, should have remained *–sco* in Spanish as well, but due to an analogy, it developed to *–zco*.

> VL paresco > OSp. paresco > Sp. parezco
> VL paresces > Sp. pareces
> VL parescet > Sp. parece
>
> VL parescemus > Sp. parecemos
> VL parescetis > Sp. parecéis
> VL parescent > Sp. parecen

This is one instance where the first 1st. pers. sing. yielded to analogical pressure applied by the rest of the conjugation. Since the consonant before the ending in inchoative verbs developed to [θ] everywhere but in the first person singular, where it was [s], this form gave in, and traded its etymological *–sco* for an analogical *–zco*.

b. There was a number of verbs represented both by *–ir* and inchoative infinitives in Old Spanish, and in almost every case the inchoative is the only form to survive:

(CL dormīre)	OSp. adormir–adormesçer
(CL fallĕre)	OSp. fallir–fallesçer
(CL florēre)	OSp. florir–floresçer
(CL offĕrre)	OSp. ofrir–ofresçer
(CL patī)	OSp. padir–padesçer
(CL perīre)	OSp. perir–peresçer
(CL stabilīre)	OSp. establir–establesçer

Of the double infinitives, only *aburrir* and *aborrecer* (from CL *abhorrēre*) survive in both forms in Spanish since the two became differentiated semantically.

   c. The inchoative flexion became quite aggressive in Old Spanish, imposing itself onto verbs which were never inchoative, but merely happened to have an infinitive ending in *–cer* or *–cir*. VL *jacer, jaco* (CL *jaceō*) developed fairly regularly in Old Spanish to *yaçer, yago*, but soon the inchoative flexion infiltrated into this verb, and the modern outcome is *yacer, yazgo*. Other examples include:

Vulgar Latin	Spanish
cognoscére, cognosco	conocer, conozco
complacére, complaco	complacer, complazco
conducíre, conduco	conducir, conduzco
reducíre, reduco	reducir, reduzco
traducíre, traduco	traducir, traduzco

Cognoscere, although it looks as if it might have originally been an inchoative verb, was not (the *o* of *–oscere* is the clue—no inchoative had an *–oscere* infinitive).

   d. Many new verbs which were built on nouns or adjectives went to the inchoative flexion, much of the time with the addition of the prefix *en–* (*em–*).

(bello)	embellecer
(blanco)	emblanquecer
(claro)	clarecer
(favor)	favorecer
(mane = mañana)	amanecer
(negro)	negrecer
(oscuro)	oscurecer
(pobre)	empobrecer
(rico)	enriquecer
(tarde)	tardecer
(verde)	verdecer
(viejo)	envecejer

Outcome of the Future Passive and Present Active Participles

§188. The accusative case of Classical Latin future passive participles (one of its uses is shown in §75b), also called the GERUN-DIVE, survived in Spanish as the present participle or gerund:

> CL clamandum > Sp. llamando
> CL bibĕndum > Sp. bebiendo
> CL movĕndum > Sp. moviendo
> CL audiĕndum > Sp. oyendo

Of the four conjugations, only the –*ire* group had a Vulgar Latin *yod*; this *yod* remained and was able to raise a pretonic *e* to *i* or *o* to *u*:

> VL dǫrmiendu > Sp. durmiendo
> VL mętiendu > Sp. midiendo
> VL mǫriendu > Sp. muriendo
> VL sęrviendu > Sp. sirviendo
> VL vęniendu > Sp. viniendo
> VL vęstiendu > Sp. vistiendo

The gerunds from the Classical Latin second and third conjugations were later to develop a *yod* due to the diphthongization of the open *e: moviendo, bebiendo,* but this *yod* developed too late to raise the preceding vowel; the –*ire yod* had a head start of several centuries to raise the vowel.

The Classical Latin verb *posse* (VL *potére*) had no future passive participle, so the gerund of Sp. *poder* had to be specially constructed. It was built on the preterite stem: *pudiendo.* In Old Spanish, gerunds were sometimes built on the preterite stem: *toviendo, dixiendo, oviendo, supiendo.* All of these except *pudiendo* reverted to their normal developments in modern Spanish (*teniendo, diciendo, habiendo, sabiendo*); *pudiendo* did not change, however, since it had no etymological form to fall back on.

CL *esse* 'to be' had no future passive participle either. Sp. *siendo* derives from *sedęndu* of *sedēre.*

The future passive participle of CL īre was *eundum,* which was "regularized" to *iendu* in Vulgar Latin to give *yendo* in Spanish.

Syntactically, the Classical Latin notion of the gerund was carried into Spanish, as seen in this example: *Yendo a Madrid, me detuve en Segovia.* But also, the gerund gave rise to the progressive tenses in Spanish: *Estoy leyendo, siguen durmiendo, iban trabajando.*

§189. The Classical Latin present active participle has survived as a noun or adjective, having lost its verb quality:

> CL cantāntem > Sp. cantante
> CL ponēntem > Sp. poniente
> CL tenēntem > Sp. teniente
> CL dormiēntem > Sp. durmiente

The diphthong *ie* of Sp. *teniente* and *poniente* has no etymological basis (owing to the long *e* in Classical Latin) but is rather analogical with the *–ire* conjugation and/or with the gerunds.

The Latin *yod* of the *–īre* group was again able to raise the preceding *e* or *o* in all cases: *sirviente* (< *sĕrviēntem*), *durmiente.*

The Imperfect Indicative

§190a. The Classical Latin *–āba–* endings came into Spanish intact, but the CL *–(i)ēba–* endings simplified to *–ea–* in Vulgar Latin (§57b); the phonetic result in Spanish is *–ía–*.

In the examples below, it should be noticed that the stress, which varied in Latin, regularized over the same vowel in Spanish in every conjugation:

> VL clamába > Sp. llamaba
> VL clamábas > Sp. llamabas
> VL clamábat > Sp. llamaba
> VL clamabámus > Sp. llamábamos
> VL clamabátis > Sp. llamabais
> VL clamábant > Sp. llamaban
>
> VL debéa (CL debēbam) > Sp. debía
> VL debéas > Sp. debías
> VL debéat > Sp. debía

VL debeámus > Sp. debíamos
VL debeátis > Sp. debíais
VL debéant > Sp. debían

VL bibéa (CL bibēbam) > Sp. bebía
VL bibéas > Sp. bebias
VL bibéat > Sp. bebía
VL bibeámus > Sp. bebíamos
VL bibeátis > Sp. bebíais
VL bibéant > Sp. bebían

VL dorméa (CL dormiēbam) > Sp. dormía
VL dorméas > Sp. dormías
VL dorméat > Sp. dormía
VL dormeámus > Sp. dormíamos
VL dormeátis > Sp. dormíais
VL dorméant > Sp. dormían

The *vosotros* form *–abais* did not simplify from OSp. *–ábades* until the seventeenth century. (In the present indicative, OSp. *–ades* simplified to *–áis* in the fifteenth century, §171a.)

b. In the thirteenth century, sometimes the imperfect of the *–er* and *–ir* verbs changed their endings and stress: *–ía* first became *–íe* as the *a* assimilated to the *i*, then the stress moved to the *e* (as in CL CL *mulíerem* > VL *muliére*). The first person singular withstood this change, however:

tenía	teniémos
teniés	teniédes
tenié	tenién

This stress pattern is borne out by two facts. First, some forms show an inflected pretonic vowel due to the newly formed *yod*: OSp. *sirvié* for *servía*. Second, the imperfect ending *–ie* rhymed with *–é*, which proves it had to be pronounced *–ié* and not *–íe*.

c. The irregular imperfects in Spanish inherit their irregular features from Classical Latin.

The development of the imperfect of CL *esse* into Spanish shows

no diphthongization of the CL *ĕ* because of the unstressed nature of
the verb *ser*:

CL ĕram > Sp. era	CL ĕrámus > Sp. éramos
CL ĕras > Sp. eras	CL ĕrátis > Sp. erais
CL ĕrat > Sp. era	CL ĕrant > Sp. eran

The "irregular" imperfect of CL *īre* was continued in Spanish,
and developed normally (except for the shift in stress in the first and
second person plural forms):

CL íbam > Sp. iba	CL ibámus > Sp. íbamos
CL íbas > Sp. ibas	CL ibátis > Sp. ibais
CL íbat > Sp. iba	CL íbant > Sp. iban

The Spanish irregular imperfect *veía* reflects the regular outcome of the imperfect of *veer* in Old Spanish. There was no phonetic reason for *veía* to lose any vowel (as there was in such forms as
veer, vee, veemos, where two like vowels merged) so it was carried
over into modern Spanish intact

The Outcome of the Perfect

§191a. The weak perfects of Vulgar Latin from the –*are* conjugation (§58a) developed normally into Spanish:

VL clamái > Sp. llamé
VL clamásti > Sp. llamaste
VL clamáut > Sp. llamó
VL clamámus > Sp. llamamos
VL clamástis > OSp. llamastes > Sp. llamasteis
VL clamárunt > Sp. llamaron

The Old Spanish second person plural ending –*stes* is etymological; the change to –*steis* in modern Spanish is analogical with all
other tenses where there is an *i* in the *vosotros* ending.

b. Old Spanish retained the double development in the plural
from the Vulgar Latin –*ire* conjugation (§58a), but modern Spanish
has kept only one form for each person. The first and second person

plural forms derive from those Vulgar Latin forms which had left out the Classical –vi–, while the third person plural form is based on the Vulgar Latin form which eliminated only the –v–:

Classical Latin	Vulgar Latin	Old Spanish	Modern Spanish
partí(v)i	partíi	partí	partí
parti(ví)sti	partísti	partiste	partiste
partví(i)t	partíut	partió	partió
partí(v)imus	partiémus	partiemos	——
partí(vi)mus	partímus	partimos	partimos
parti(v)ístis	partiéstis	partiestes	——
partí(vi)stis	partístis	partistes	partisteis
parti(v)érunt	partiérunt	partieron	partieron
partí(vé)runt	partírunt	partiron	——

In Old Spanish, those plural forms in the –ir conjugation which had a *yod* regularly raised the preceding *e* to *i*, or the preceding *o* to *u*. However, the plural forms which had no *yod* could not inflect the preceding *e* or *o*; thus:

Vulgar Latin	Old Spanish	Vulgar Latin	Old Spanish
petiemus	pidiemos	petimus	pedimos
petiestis	pidiestes	petistes	pedistes
petierunt	pidieron	petirunt	pediron
dormiemus	durmiemos	dormimus	dormimos
dormiestis	durmiestes	dormistes	dormistes
dormierunt	durmieron	dormirunt	dormiron

Modern Spanish, which has retained the *yod* only in the third person, shows an inflected vowel only in that plural form. In the singular, where VL –*íut* yielded –*ió*, inflection was universal: *petíut > pidió, dormíut > durmió.*

§192. Of the remaining two Classical Latin conjugations (–*ēre* and –*ĕre*), only the –*ēre* group had weak perfects, and there were only very few of them (§58b). The few that there were either disappeared from the language (*delēre, delēvī* 'destroy', for example, was not continued) or changed conjugation groups (*implēre, implēvī* 'fill', became *henchir, henchí; complēre, complēvī* 'complete', became *cumplir, cumplí*). Spanish has not inherited one *-ere* weak perfect from Classical Latin, yet there is a great number of weak perfects belonging to the Spanish *-er* conjugation. It is evident, then, that a large percentage of Classical Latin strong perfects were rebuilt based on the weak system, as you will now see.

The Development of Classical Latin Strong Perfects

§193. When a Classical Latin strong perfect (mostly of the *-ēre* and *-ĕre* conjugations) was rebuilt on a weak pattern, it took the endings of the *-ire* weak perfects owing to the phonetic and formal similarities among the conjugations involved.

In Classical Latin, the strong perfects really only had three "strong" forms; the first and third person singular and the first person plural. (In §58cd there are good examples of this.) In Spanish, the strong preterites have only two strong forms: the first and third person singular. The plural forms, now all weak, took analogical *-ir* weak endings.

The remarks that have been made in this section apply to all sections that follow dealing with the perfect.

§194a. Those strong *-u-* perfects (§58b) which changed to fit the weak pattern, show the development that follows. Examples are from CL *timēre*:

Classical Latin	Vulgar Latin	Spanish
tímui	timíi	temí
timuísti	timísti	temiste
tímuit	timíut	temió
timúimus	timímus	temimos
timístis	timístis	temisteis
timuérunt	timiérunt	temieron

The Spanish examples show the *-ire* endings described in the preceding section. If the strong conjugation had been maintained, the forms would have been quite confusing: the third person singular and the first person plural would have duplicated the present indicative forms: *teme, tememos.*

Other strong –*u*– perfects that became weak include: *aperīre* (*apéruī* > *abrí*), *cooperīre* (*coopéruī* > *cubrí*), *debēre* (*débuī* > *debí*) *dolēre* (*dóluī* > *dolí*), *jacēre* (*jácuī* > *yací*), *valēre* (*váluī* > *valí*). *Merēre* (*méruī*) and *parēre* (*páruī*) became inchoatives (and therefore weak) in Spanish: *merecer* (*merecí*) and *parecer* (*parecí*).

b. The strong –*u*– perfects which remained strong were due to undergo quite a bit of change in order to do so, and their resulting history is somewhat complex.

The logical place to start is with the development of the perfect of *habēre* from Classical Latin to Old Spanish:

Classical Latin	Old Spanish
hábui	ove
habuísti	oviste
hábuit	ovo
habúimus	oviemos
habuístis	oviestes
habuérunt	ovieron

In this verb, as with VL *cápui* (CL *cépī*) and CL *sápuī* below, the *wau* (–*u*–) has been attracted to the preceding vowel and has mixed with it to yield *o*: CL *hábuī* > VL *aubi* > OSp. *ove* (*v* is merely a variant graph for the *b* sound). This process is similar to the one where a *yod* is attracted to and mixes with a preceding vowel, as in *capio* > *caipo* > *queipo* > *quepo, sapiat* > *saipat* > *seipa* > *sepa* (§109). The other –*u*– perfects with an *a* in the stem were VL *cápui* > OSp. *cope* and CL *sapuī* > OSp. *sope.*

Notice that the third person *habuit* should have developed to *ove*, but if it had, it would have been exactly like the first person singular form. The weak conjugations provided an analogical *o* to avoid this confusion. The final unstressed *o* is a universal feature in all "strong" Spanish preterites (except *fue*).

The perfect of *habēre* was to have an analogical influence on a few Spanish verbs. CL *ténuī* (from *tenēre* 'to hold') never gave *tene* in Old Spanish; instead, it modeled itself after *ove* and became *tove.*

Similarly, the reduplicated perfect *stētī* (from *stāre*), while developing to its expected *estide* in Old Spanish, it also had an analogical preterite based on *ove*: *estove*. The mysterious *andar* equally developed an analogical preterite: *andove*. Old Spanish occasionally showed other analogical *–ove* preterites: *crove* from *creer* and *crecer*, *sove* from *ser*.

OSp. *ove*, *tove*, *cope*, *estove* and *andove* still require a further development to become the modern *hube*, *tuve*, *cupe*, *estuve* and *anduve*.

c. When the *wau* of the Classical Latin perfects *pótuī* (from CL *posse*) and *pósuī* (from CL *pónĕre* 'to place') mixed with the preceding *o*, the result was *u*:

Classical Latin	Old Spanish	Classical Latin	Old Spanish
potui	pude	posui	puse
potuistī	pudiste	posuistī	pusiste
pótuit	pudo	pósuit	puso
potúimus	pudimos	posúimus	pusimos
potuístis	pudistes	posuístis	pusistes
potuērunt	pudieron	posuērunt	puisieron

Pude and *pudo* are seen in the earliest Spanish texts.

The *u* of these two verbs was very powerful, and caused all of the verbs in the preceding section to exchange their etymological *o* for an analogical *u*:

Old Spanish		Modern Spanish
ove		hube
tove		tuve
cope	+ puse	cupe
sope	pude	supe
estove		estuve
andove		anduve

§195a. Among the sigmatic perfects (§58c), several were lost early and rebuilt on the weak pattern, using the infinitive's stem, and taking the weak *–ir* endings:

CL ardēre, ársī > Sp. arder, ardí
CL erigĕre, eréxī > Sp. erguir, erguí
CL torquĕre, tórsī > Sp. torcer, torcí

b. Other sigmatic perfects were common in Old Spanish, but were finally ousted and new weak perfects were rebuilt, based on the infinitive:

Classical Latin	Old Spanish	Spanish
cinĕgre, cínxī	ceñir, cinxe	ceñir, ceñí
coquĕre, cóxī	cocer, cóxe	cocer, cocí
mittĕre, misī	meter, míse	meter, metí
ridĕre, rísī	reír, ríse	reír, reí
scribĕre, scrīpsī	escribir, escrísse	escribir, escribí
tingĕre, tínxī	teñir, tínxe	teñir, teñí

c. The few sigmatic perfects that have survived into modern Spanish were CL *díxī* (*dīcĕre*), compounds of CL *dūxī* (*dūcĕre*), VL *quési* [for CL *quæsívī*] (*quærĕre*), and *tráxī* (*trahĕre*).

Classical Latin	Spanish	Classical Latin	Spanish
díxī	dije	tradúxī	traduje
dīxísti	dijiste	tradūxístī	tradujiste
díxit	dijo	tradúxit	tradujo
díximus	dijimos	tradúximus	tradujimos
dīxístis	dijisteis	tradūxístis	tradujisteis
dīxĕrunt	dijeron	tradūxĕrunt	tradujeron

The third person plural of these verbs in Old Spanish (*dixieron, traduxieron* [diʃyéron, traɗuʃyéron]) show a *yod* which was eventually swallowed up by the palatal [ʃ]. The *yod* was equally swallowed up by the palatals which end the stems in the modern Spanish preterites of the *ciñeron* and *bulleron* type.

Other compounds of *dūcĕre* include: *aducir, conducir, deducir, introducir, producir.*

VL *quési* appears to have had a close *e* which was raised by the final close *i* to develop to modern Spanish *quise.* The phonetic outcome of *tráxī* should have been *treje* (§143), but the *a* is analogical with that of *traer.*

§196a. Among the third type of strong perfects, which usually showed only a vowel inflection (§58d), all but three were rebuilt based on the infinitive and using the endings of the *–ir* weak conjugation. These examples show some of the rebuilt forms:

Classical Latin	Spanish
legĕre, légī	leer, leí
recipĕre, recépī	recibir, recibí
rumpĕre, rúpī	romper, rompí
vincĕre, vícī	vencer, vencí

Sédī, the strong perfect of *sedēre*, fell out of use and was replaced by the perfect of *esse (fuī)*, explained below in §198.

b. The three strong perfects of this type which remained, *vidēre*, *facĕre* and *venīre*:

Classical Latin	Spanish
vīdī	vi
vīdístī	viste
vīdit	vio
vīdīmus	vimos
vīdīstis	visteis
vīdērunt	vieron

Classical Latin	Old Spanish	Spanish
fēcī	fize	hice
fēcísti	feziste	hiciste
fēcit	fezo	hizo
fécimus	fezimos	hicimos
fēcístis	fezistes	hicisteis
fēcérunt	fizieron	hicieron
vēnī	vine	vine
vēnísti	veniste	viniste
vēnit	veno	vino

vénimus	venimos	vinimos
venístis	venistes	vinisteis
venérunt	vinieron	vinieron

In the preterites of *fácĕre* and *venīre*, Old Spanish shows the expected phonetic outcome, with only the first person singular (§110) and the third person plural (§§193, 105) having the right to an inflected vowel. However, as usual, in modern Spanish, the powerful first person singular form caused the whole conjugation to take the inflected vowel by analogy.

§197a. All but two of the reduplicated perfects (§58e) were rebuilt on the weak pattern, based on the infinitive. Here are examples of rebuilt reduplicated perfects:

Classical Latin	*Spanish*
cadĕre, cécidī	caer, caí
credĕre, crédidī	creer, creí
currĕre, curúrrī	correr, corrí
mordĕre, momórdī	morder, mordí
tendĕre, teténdī	tender, tendí
vendĕre, véndidī	vender, vendí

b. The two reduplicated perfects that stayed in the language are said to be *dĕdī* (from *dăre*) and *stetī* (From *stāre*). The development of the perfect of *dăre* is given below. But this verb seems to have just kept the initial *d–* and taken analogical *–ir* endings.

CL dĕdi > Sp. di
CL dĕdísti > Sp. diste
CL dĕdit > Sp. dio
CL dĕdimus > Sp. dimos
CL dĕdístis > Sp. disteis
CL dĕderunt > Sp. dieron

Normal development would have resulted in the diphthongization of the short *e* in the strong forms.

Stetī is only marginally continued, since its normal outcome,

OSp. *estide*, was first modified to OSp. *estove*, on the analogy of *ove*, then to Sp. *estuve* on the analogy of *pude* (§194bc).

§198. *Fui*, the preterite of both *ser* and *ir* in Spanish, requires some explanation. The perfect of CL *īre* (*iī, īstī, iit, imus, īstis, iērunt*) was short–lived, owing to its reduced phonological makeup, but why it was replaced by the perfect of *esse* is the question which has to be answered.

According to Corominas' *Diccionario crítico*, the solution goes back to Classical Latin, where, in popular usage, the perfect of *esse* could be used with *in + accusative* to mean 'went':

> Pretores in provinciam... fuerunt. 'The officers went into the province'
> in Mediam fui sæpius... 'I went more often to Media...'

In popular Latin, the accusative case used with a place showed "movement toward," so "the officers were [moving] toward the province" means "the officers went into the province." Modern French offers an equivalent of this in its (frowned upon but common) *J'ai été au théâtre* for the more standard *Je suis allé(e) au théâtre* 'I went to the theater'.

Here is the standard development of the conjugation:

> CL fúi > Sp. fui
> CL fuístī > Sp. fuiste
> CL fúit > Sp. fue
> CL fuímus > Sp. fuimos
> CL fuístis > Sp. fuisteis
> CL fuéunt > Sp. fueron

The forms *fui, fuimos* and *fuisteis* have taken analogical *–ir* endings; the modern result through normal development would have been *fue, fuemos, fueron* (these forms are actually listed as standard in Nebrija's Spanish grammar of 1492).

The Development of the Imperfect Subjunctive

§199a. Already in Vulgar Latin, the perfect and imperfect subjunctive, due to a threatened homonymy, were beginning to fall and were replaced by the Latin pluperfect subjunctive (§65).

The loss of *–v(i)–* in the perfect (§58a) was universal in Vulgar Latin in the *–are* and *–ire* conjugations. Since the pluperfect subjunctive derives from the perfect stem, it, too, lost its *–v(i)–* in the *–are* and *–ire* conjugations:

Vulgar Latin	*Spanish*
clamá(vi)sse	llamase
clamá(vi)ssēs	llamases
clamá(vi)sset	llamase
cmama(vi)ssémus	llamásemos
clama(vi)ssétis	llamaseis
clamá(vi)ssent	llamasen
deb(u)ísse	debiese
deb(u)ísses	debieses
deb(u)ísset	debiese
deb(u)issémus	debiésemos
deb(u)issétis	debieseis
deb(u)íssent	debiesen
bibísse	bebiese
bibisses	bebieses
bibísset	bebiese
bibissémus	bebiésemos
bibissétis	bebieseis
bibíssent	bebiesen
dormi(v)isse	durmiese
dormi(v)isses	durmieses
dormi(v)isset	durmiese
dormi(v)issémus	durmiésemos
dormi(v)issétis	durmieseis
dormi(v)issent	durmiesen

In all cases, the first and second person plural moved their stress back one syllable in Spanish so that the stress would be on the same vowel throughout the conjugation.

In the fourth conjugation, the *yod* created in the ending inflected the preceding *e* or *o* in the normal way: VL *metiesse* > Sp. *midiese,* VL *moriesse* > Sp. *muriese.*

Again, the *–ire* endings imposed themselves on the *–ere* conjugations. (If the *–ere* forms had developed normally, their conjugations would be based on **debese* and **bebese.*) The Spanish forms in *–er* thus have a *yod* in their endings; however, since the endings were borrowed, and did not develop historically from Vulgar Latin times, the *–er* conjugation shows no inflected vowel in the stem.

b. The Classical Latin pluperfect indicative (CL *scrīpseram* 'I had written' also built on the perfect stem, retained its pluperfect meaning in older Spanish (*llamara* 'I had called', *bebiera* 'I had drunk'). When the analytic construction (*había llamado, habías bebido*) began seriously to encroach on the territory of the synthetic pluperfect, the latter began to be used as a subjunctive. With the passage of time, it became more important and gained ground to the point where today it is the most common imperfect subjunctive form in Spanish:

> VL clama(ve)ra > Sp. llamara
> VL deb(u)era > Sp. debiera
> VL bibera > Sp. bebiera
> VL dormi(v)era > Sp. durmiera

§200. There was a future subjunctive in Spanish until about 1600. Its uses (except in a few fixed locutions such as *sea lo que fuere*) have been replaced by the present subjunctive (OSp. *quando viniere* = Sp. *cuando venga*). The future subjunctive derived from the Classical future perfect indicative, which was composed of the perfect stem plus the forms of the future of *esse* as the endings:

> VL clama(ve)ro > Sp. llamare
> VL clama(ve)ris > Sp. llamares
> VL deb(u)ero > Sp. debiere
> VL deb(u)eris > Sp. debieres
> VL bibero > Sp. bebiere
> VL biberis > Sp. bebieres
> VL dormi(v)ero > Sp. durmiere
> VL dormi(v)eris > Sp. durmieres

The first person singular ending in Spanish is, of course, analogical with the rest of the conjugation. The etymological outcome, *amaro* (for *amare*) is seen in Berceo and in the *Poema del Cid*.

The Future and Conditional Tenses

§201a. The Vulgar Latin future (§54b), composed of the infinitive followed by the present indicative of *habēre*, having replaced the Classical Latin future, was continued into Spanish:

Vulgar Latin	Spanish
clamare + aio	llamaré
debere + aio	deberé
bibere + aio	beberé
dormire + aio	dormiré

In Old Spanish, there were two variants for the second person plural of *haber; habedes* and *hedes*. It was the latter form that was used in the formation of the future in Old Spanish, and has been carried into modern Spanish as *–éis*.

The analytic nature of the future tense was recognized in Old Spanish, and the two parts could be separated, as in modern European Portuguese, with a pronoun connected to the infinitive:

> darlo e
> traervoslo he
> darmelo hedes

Separating the future formation with pronouns was not rigidly observed in any given Old Spanish text. For example, in the *Poema del Cid*, one sees future forms separated by pronouns as well as non-separated forms such as this one: *dexaré vos las posadas*.

b. *Hacer* and *decir* build their future tenses on the old variant infinitives *far* (modern *har*) and *dir; haré, diré* (§169b).

c. As the two parts of the future formation fused into one word, the new creation began to act phonetically as one word and the unstressed *e* or *i* could fall (§102). In Old Spanish, this phenomenon was more common than today, as shown in these examples:

(arder) ardré	(haber) habremos
(beber) bevrás	(perder) perdrán
(caber) cabrá	(recibir) recibrá
(poder) podré	(saber) sabremos
(querer) querrás	(vivir) vivrán

Sometimes, when a vowel fell, unusual consonant clusters were created, and an additional consonant was inserted in order to make the cluster pronounceable: *m'r* > *mbr* (§149b), *n'r* > *ndr*, *l'r* > *ldr*.

(comer) combré	(tener) tendré
(poner) pondrás	(valer) valdrás
(salir) saldré	(venir) vendrá
(temer) tembremos	

Until the end of the Golden Age (1682), there was an alternate solution to the above. Sometimes the two clashing consonants would merely change place (§151), thus making an easily pronounceable cluster:

(poner) porné	(venir) verná
(tener) terné	

In modern Spanish, it is mostly the commonest verbs which maintain the syncope:

(caber) cabré	(saber) sabrás
(haber) habías	(salir) saldrás
(poder) podrá	(tener) tendrá
(poner) pondremos	(valer) valdremos
(querer) querrán	(venir) vendrán

§202. The development of the conditional tense paralleled that of the future. The endings of the conditional tense derive from the imperfect endings of *haber*: *llamar–ía, deber–ía, beber–ía, dormir–ía, sabría.*

Past Participles

§203a. Of the weak perfect passive participles (§59a), only those of the first and fourth conjugations regularly survived:

Vulgar Latin –are	*Vulgar Latin –ire*
clamátu > llamado	audítu > oído
lavátu > lavado	dormítu > dormido
lucrátu > logrado	ítu > ido
mesurátu > mesurado	partítu > partido
nom(i)nátu > nombrado	servítu > servido
plicátu > llegado	vestítu > vestido

b. The weak perfect participles of the Classical Latin *–ēre* conjugation had *–ētum* endings: *complētum* 'completed', *delētum* 'destroyed', *implētum* 'filled'. However, no weak *–ēre* perfect passive participles were continued into Spanish; these verbs were either lost (*delētum*, for example, no pun intended), or changed to the *–ire* conjugation: CL *complētum* = Sp. *cumplido*, CL *ĭmplētum* = Sp. *henchido*. This phenomenon parallels the loss of the Classical Latin weak *–ēre* perfects. (§192)

c. The weak past participles of the Classical Latin *–ĕre* conjugation ended in *–ūtum*, and although only a few were continued into Old Spanish (for example, *tribuĕre, tribūtum* > OSp. *(a)trevudo; battuĕre, battūtum* > OSp. *batudo*), the *–udo* ending became very contagious and spread analogically to a number of verbs. One reads *metudo, vençudo* in the *Poema del Cid*, and *abatudo, perçebudo, metudo, corrompudo, sabudo, temudo* in the *Libro de Alexandre*; none of these had *–ūtum* endings in Classical Latin. After the thirteenth century, *–udo* began to fade (because a stressed *u* was otherwise unknown in a Spanish verb ending), and all of these verbs were rebuilt using the *–ido* ending.

A few of the CL *–ūtum* passive participles were retained, but as adjectives: CL *acúĕre, acūtum* > Sp. *agudo*; CL *mĭnúĕre, mĭnūtum* > Sp. *menudo*.

§204a. In Vulgar Latin, already a number of Classical Latin strong past participles were made weak, as shown in §60. However, some Classical Latin strong participles were carried into Spanish.

VL apẹrtu > Sp. abierto
VL copẹrtu > Sp. cubierto
VL dụctu > Sp. dicho
VL fáctu > Sp. hecho
VL frịctu > Sp. frito
VL mọrtu (CL mortuum) > Sp. muerto
VL pọsitu > Sp. puesto
VL rụptu > Sp. roto
VL scrịptu > Sp. escrito
VL vịstu (CL vīsum) > Sp. visto

Some strong participles which carried into Old Spanish were later made weak, rebuilt on the infinitive:

CL míssum > OSp. meso / Sp. metido
CL nátum > OSp. nado / Sp. nacido
VL quéstu > OSp. quisto / Sp. querido

A few Old Spanish strong participles were maintained in modern Spanish exclusively as adjectives and nouns, while new formations were created for the participle use in modern Spanish:

VL cọctu > OSp. cocho / Sp. cocido
VL ductu > OSp. ducho / Sp. –ducido
VL tractu > OSp. trecho / Sp. traído

One sees *cocho* in *bizcocho* (lit. 'cooked twice'. The modern *–ducido* is seen only in compounds (*traducido, introducido,* etc.).

Adverbs

§205a. The Vulgar Latin way of deriving adverbs from adjectives with *–mente* (§68) was continued into Spanish:

abierta + mente
lenta + mente
tranquila + mente

b. A number of Classical Latin adverbs not deriving from adjectives were also continued into Spanish:

CL adhūc > Sp. aún	CL quando > Sp. cuando
CL ante > Sp. antes	CL quōmodo > Sp. como
CL cǐrca > Sp. cerca	CL tantum > Sp. tanto
CL iam > Sp. ya	CL magis > Sp. más

The –n of *aún* is analogical with the –n of *en, con, según, sin*. You would expect the –m of *iam* to be maintained as –n (cf. *quem > quien, tam > tan*), but it was lost (contrary to §147). The –s of *antes* is analogical with the –s of *después, detrás, más, menos*. Other examples of the "adverbial *s*" include:

qui sa(be) > quizá (+ s) > quizás
in tunc ce > entonce (+ s) > entonces

c. A number of Classical adverbs were quite short, and prepositions, nouns, or even other adverbs were added to them in Vulgar Latin to give them more emphasis or phonetic substance:

VL ad fǫra > Sp. afuera
VL ad hic > Sp. ahí
VL ad illac > Sp. allá
VL ad pressa > Sp. aprisa
VL ad satis > OSp. asaz
VL de ex pǫst > Sp. después
VL de in ante > Sp. delante
VL de trans > Sp. detrás
VL in tųnc ce > OSp. entonçe
VL ex tųnc ce > OSp. estonçe

Prepositions and Conjunctions

§206a. Most Classical Latin prepositions were continued into Spanish:

CL ad > Sp. a	CL pŏst > Sp. pues
CL ante > Sp. ante	CL pro > Sp. por
CL cĭrca > Sp. cerca	CL secūndum > Sp. según
CL cŭm > Sp. con	CL sĭne > Sp. sin
CL de > Sp. de	CL sŏper > Sp. sobre
CL in > Sp. en	CL trans > Sp. tras
CL ĭnter > Sp. entre	

The development of CL *sĭne* (with short *i*) into Sp. *sin* must be due to analogy with a number of short words which have an –*i*: *mí, ti, sí*. The normal development in Spanish would have been *sen* (compare Ptg. *sem*).

b. A few Romance prepositions are composed of two or more Classical prepositions.

de + ex + pŏst > después
pro + ad > OSp. pora > Sp. para

c. Some Classical prepositions were lost, either because a pair of synonymous prepositions was reduced to only one member for reasons of economy, or, as in the last example below, because a Latin preposition was replaced by one from another source:

ab, de > Sp. de
ex, de > Sp. de
apud, cum > Sp. con
ob, pro > Sp. por
versus, facies (VL facia) > Sp. hacia
tenus, *Arab.* ḥatta > Sp. hasta

§207a. A few important Classical conjunctions remained:

CL ĕt > Sp. y, e
CL nĕc > Sp. ni
CL sī > Sp. si

The development of *et* to OSp. *e* is regular; there was no diphthongization due to the unstressed nature of this conjunction. The modern *y*, however, does present a problem. The following is usually given as the evolution of *y*: the OSp. *e* commonly was found before vowels and would naturally tend to become a *yod* under this circumstance:

OSp. e amigos [yamíɣos] > Sp. y amigos
OSp. e obispos [yoβíspos] > Sp. y obispos
OSp. e uno [yúno] > Sp. y uno

This common case of *e* before vowels (except *i*) is said to have caused *y* to generalize. Before an *i*, however, there was no phonetic reason for the *e* to change its pronunciation, and for this reason modern Spanish maintains *e* before words beginning with [i]: *e hijos, e infantes.*

The development of *nec* to *ni* is obscure, although it could be that it is analogical with *sí.*

b. *Mientras* requires some explanation. *Dum* 'while' and *interim* 'meanwhile' were seen together in popular Latin: *dum ínterim.* With an unexplained change in stressed vowels, from an open *i* to an open *e*, the pair developed to *domientre* in Old Spanish. Since several other Old Spanish words began with the more common *de–* (*debaxo, deantes, detrás, después*), *domientre* became *demientre.* Because there were pairs of words, both with and without *de–* (*demás, más; dende, ende; defuera, fuera*), the form *mientre* was created by analogy. Owing to the related words ending in *–a* (*contra, fuera, nunca*), *mientre* became *mientra.* At this point, the "adverbial *s*" was added, and the modern *mientras* was created.

c. Most Classical Latin conjunctions were lost, however, and were replaced by synonymous conjunctions or others of Romance origin:

CL etsi = Sp. aunque	CL quia = Sp. porque
CL ut = Sp. que	CL ígitur = Sp. por eso
CL sed = Sp. pero	CL cum = Sp. cuando

*   *   *

You now have enough background in Classical and Vulgar Latin, and in historical phonology and morphology of Spanish to allow you to begin a profitable study of the more advanced books and articles on this subject. The BIBLIOGRAPHY is provided to help you find what you need. In any case, if you have digested and understand this much, you are to be congratulated.

Selected Bibliography

THERE IS A very large bibliography in this field. For this reason, we are offering in a first list only the fundamental works in each area. In a second list we have included more detailed studies on many aspects of each area. Nothing has been listed in the area of Lexicography, which is amply treated in Corominas' dictionary.

The difficulty in selecting works for such an appendix as this is well known. At times it may seem incomplete (which it doubtless is), and at others overbearing. Some of the works listed, such as the articles by Malkiel, could be listed in a number of different areas, although we have placed them only in one.

For most books, we have listed the most recent and available editions, but for the sake of perspective, we have also included the date of the first edition.

ABBREVIATIONS

AILC   *Anales del Instituto de lingüística*, Universidad de Cuyo, Mendoza, Argentina.

AJPh   *The American Journal of Philology*, Baltimore.

Archivum   *Archivum*, Revista de la Facultad de Filosofia y Letras de Oviedo.

ArchL   *Archivum Linguisticum*, A Review of Comparative Philology and General Linguistics, Glasgow.

ARSR   *Academia Română. Sectiunea Literară.* = Bulletin de la Section Littéraire de l'Académie Roumaine. Bucarest.

BF   *Boletin de Filología*, Inst. Est. Sup., Montevideo

BH   *Bibliotheca Hispana*, Revista de información y orientación bibliográficas, Madrid.

BRAE   *Boletín de la Real Academia Española*, Madrid.

CSIC   Consejo Superior de Investigaciones Científicas, Madrid.

ELH   *Enciclopedia lingüística Hispánica*, CSIC, Madrid, 1960 (tomo I), 1962 (suplemento al tomo I), 1967 (tomo II). A fundamental work, although heterogeneous.

ForLing	*Forum Linguisticum,* Hamburg.	*RFE*	*Revista de filología española,* Madrid.
Hisp	*Hispania,* American Association of Teachers of Spanish and Portuguese, Los Angeles.	*RFH*	*Revista de filología hispánica,* Buenos Aires.
		RH	*Revue Hispanique,* Paris.
HR	*Hispanic Review,* Philadelphia.	*RLiR*	*Revue de linguistique romane,* Paris-Strasburg.
JHP	*Journal of Hispanic Philology,* Florida State University, Tallahassee.	*RLR*	*Revue des langues romanes,* Montpellier.
		Romania	*Romania,* Paris.
Lg	*Language,* Baltimore.	*RPh*	*Romance Philology,* Berkeley.
LeS	*Lingua e Stile, Quaderni dell'Instituto di Glottologia dell' Università degli Studi di Bologna,* Bologna.	*StL*	*Studia Linguistica,* Revue de Linguistique Générale et Comparée, Lund, Sweden.
Lingua	*Lingua,* Revue Internationale de Linguistique Générale, Haarlem, Holland.	*StN*	*Studia Neophilologica,* Uppsala, Sweden.
MLR	*The Modern Language Review,* Cambridge.	*Thesaurus*	*Thesaurus,* Boletín del Instituto Caro y Cuervo, Bogotá.
NM	*Neuphilologische Mitteilungen,* Helsinki.	*UCPL*	*University of California Publications in Linguistics,* Berkeley and Los Angeles.
NRFH	*Nueva revista de filología hispánica,* Mexico.	*VKR*	*Volkstum und Kultur der Romanen, Sprache, Dichtung, Sitte,* Hamburg.
PIL	*Papers in Linguistics,* Edmonton, Canada.		
PhQ	*Philological Quarterly,* Iowa City.	*VR*	*Vox Romanica,* Annales Helvetici Explorandis Linguis Romanicis, Zürich.
PMLA	*Publications of the Modern Language Association of America,* New York.	*Word*	*Word,* Journal of the International Linguistic Association, New York.
RDTP	*Revista de dialectología y tradiciones populares,* Madrid.	*ZrPh*	*Zeitschrift für romanische Philologie,* Tübingen.

I. VULGAR LATIN

1. Manuals and Anthologies

BATTISTI, C., *Avviamento allo studio del latina volgare* (Bari: Leonardo da Vinci Editore, 1949).

DÍAZ Y DÍAZ, Manuel, *Antología del latín vulgar* (2nd ed., Madrid: Gredos, 1962).

GRANDGENT, Charles H., *Introducción al latín vulgar* (Madrid: CSIC, 1970. 1st ed., 1928). Translation of *Introduction to Vulgar Latin* (Boston, 1907),available in a reprint by Hafner (1962).

HAADSMA, R. A. and Nuchelmans, J., *Précis de latin vulgaire* (2nd ed., Grönigen: Wolters, 1966).

HERMAN, Joseph, *Le Latin vulgaire*, (Paris: PUF, 1967).

MAURER, Theororo H., *Gramática histórica do latim vulgar* (Rio de Janeiro: Livraria Acadêmica, 1959).

MÜLLER, H. F. & TAYLOR, P., *A Crestomathy of Vulgar Latin* (New York, 1932).

ROHLFS, G., *Sermo Vulgaris Latinus, Vulgärtlateinisches Lesebuch* (Halle, 1956; 1st ed. 1951).

VÄÄNÄNEN, Veikko, *Introduction au latin vulgaire* (2nd ed. Paris, 1967). In Spanish, with anthology of texts (Gredos: Madrid, 1975 [reprinted]).

VOSSLER, Karl, *Einführung ins Vulgärlatein* (Munich: Huber, 1958).

2. General and Specific Studies

ANDERSON, James M., "A Study of Syncope in Vulgar Latin," *Word*, 21 (1965), 70-85.

CARNOY, Albert Joseph, *Le Latin d'Espagne d'après les inscriptions* (Hildesheim and New York: Olms, 1971; 1st ed., Louvain, 1902-1903).

COSERIU, Eugenio, *El llamado "latín vulgar" y las primeras diferenciaciones romances* (Montevideo: Universidad, 1954).

GAENG, Paul A., *An Inquiry into Local Variations in Vulgar Latin* (Chapel Hill: University of North Carolina Press, 1968).

HOFFMAN, Johann B., *El latín familiar* (Madrid: CSIC, 1958).

LE COULTRE, J., "La prononciation du latin sous Charlemagne," en *Mélanges Nicole* (Geneva, 1905), 313-34.

LLOYD, Paul, "On the Definition of Vulgar Latin," *NM*, 80 (1979), 110-22.

LÖFSTEDT, Einar, *Late Latin* (Oslo: Aschenoug, 1959).

MOHL, F. G., *Introduction à la chronologie du latin vulgaire* (Geneva: Slatkine Reprints, 1974; 1st ed. 1899).

MOHRMANN, Christine, *Latin vulgaire, latin des chrétiens, latin médiéval* (Paris: Klincksieck, 1955).

MÜLLER, H. F., *A Chronology of Vulgar Latin* (Hildesheim: Verlag Dr. H. A. Gerstenberg, 1970; 1st ed. 1929).

ROBSON, C. A., "L'*Appendix Probi* et la philologie latine," *MA* (1963), 37-64.

SILVA NETO, Serafim da, *Fontes do Latim Vulgar* (3rd ed., Rio de Janeiro: Livraria Acadêmica, 1956; 1st ed., 1946).

——, *História do latim vulgar* (Rio de Janeiro: Livro Técnico, 1977; first ed., 1957).

II. LATIN

BASSOLS DE CLIMENT, M., *Fonética latina*, (Madrid: CSIC, 1973; 1st ed., 1962).

——, *Sintaxis latina*, 2 vols. (Madrid: CSIC, 1966-1967).

DEVOTO G., *Storia della lingua di Roma* (Bologna, 1940).

ERNOUT, A., *Morphologie historique du latin* (3rd ed., Paris: Klincksieck, 1974; 1st ed., 1927).

—— and THOMAS, François, *Syntaxe latine*, (2nd ed., Paris: Klincksieck, 1972; 1st ed., 1951).

FARIA, Ernesto, *Fonética histórica do latim* (2nd ed., Rio de Janeiro: Livraria Acadêmica, 1957).

KENT, Roland G., *The Forms of Latin* (Baltimore: Linguistic Society of America, 1946).

——, *The Sounds of Latin* (New York: Kraus Reprints, 1979; 1st ed. Baltimore, 1932).

LEUMANN, M., *Lateinische Laut- und Formenlehre* (Munich, 1963).

MANIET, Albert, *Phonétique historique du latin* (Paris: Klincksieck, 1975).

MEILLET, Antoine, *Esquisse d'une histoire de la langue latine* (Paris: Klincksieck, 1977; 1st ed., 1928).

NEIDERMANN, M., *Précis de phonétique historique du latin* (3rd ed., Paris, 1953).

NORBERG, D., *Syntaktische Forshungen auf dem Gebiete des Spätlateins und des früheren Mittellateins* (Uppsala, 1943).

——, *Beiträge zur spätlateinischen Syntax* (Uppsala, 1944).

PALMER, Leonard R., *The Latin Language* (London: Faber and Faber, 1968; 1st ed., 1954). Also deals with Vulgar Latin.

PULGRAM, Ernst, *Italic, Latin, Italian: Texts and Commentaries* (Heidelberg: Winter, 1978).

III. GENERAL WORKS IN ROMANCE LINGUISTICS

1. *Classical Textbooks*

BOURCIEZ, Édouard, *Eléments de linguistique romane* (3rd ed., Paris:

Klincksieck, 1967; 1st ed. 1919).

DIEZ, Friedrich, *Grammaire des langues romanes* (Geneva: Slatkine Reprints, 1973). Photographic reproduction of the 3rd ed., 1874-1876. The original German edition was *Grammatik der romanischen Sprachen* (Bonn, 1836-1844), republished in 1980.

GRÖBER, Gustav, *Grundriß der romanischen Philologie*, 2 vols. (Strasbourg: Trübner, 1888-1906).

KÖRTING, G., *Handbuch der romanischen Philologie* (Leipzig, 1896).

MEYER-LÜBKE, Wilhelm, *Grammaire des langues romanes*, 4 vols. (Geneva: Slatkine Reprints, 1974). Reproduction of the original French edition, 1889-1906, itself a translation of *Grammatik der romanischen Sprachwissenschaft* published in Leipzig, 1889-1902.

――, *Introducción al estudio de la lingüística romance* trans. Américo Castro (Madrid: Revista de Filología Española, 1914), a translation of *Einführung in das Studium der romanischen Sprachwissenschaft*. A second corrected edition was published in 1925 with the title: *Introducción a la lingüística románica*.

――, *Diferenciación léxica de las lenguas románicas* (Madrid: CSIC, 1960). A translation of *Die lexicalische Differenzierung der romanische Sprachen* (1954).

MILLARDET, G., *Linguistique et dialectologie romanes: problèmes et méthodes* (Montpellier-Paris, 1923).

2. Modern Manuals

BEC, Pierre, *Manuel pratique de philologie romane*, 2 vols. (Paris: Picard, 1970). The first volume (pp. 187-310) gives philological commentaries about *El poema de mio Cid*.

BOYD-BOWMAN, Peter, *From Latin to Romance in Sound Charts* (3rd ed., Washington: Georgetown University Press, 1980; 1st ed., 1954).

GALMÉS DE FUENTES, A. *Las sibilantes en la Romania* (Madrid: Gredos, 1962).

LAUSBERG, Heinrich, *Lingüística románica*, 2 vols. (Madrid: Gredos, 1986-1988; 1st ed., 1965-1966). Translation of *Romanische Sprachiwissenschaft*, 4 vols. (Berlin, 1956-1957).

WRIGHT, Roger, *Late Latin and Early Romance in Spain and Carolingian France* (Liverpool, Francis Cairns, 1982). Also in Spanish (1989).

3. General Introductions

CAMPROUX, CH., *Les Langues romanes* (Paris: PUF, 1974).

CANFIELD, D. Lincoln, and J. Carey DAWS, *An Introduction to Romance Linguistics* (Carbondale: Southern Illinois University Press, 1975).

ELCOCK, W. D., *The Romance Languages* (2nd ed., London: Faber and Faber, 1975; 1st ed., 1960). See Paul Lloyd's review in *HR*, 46, pp. 241-44, 1978.

KUHN, Alwin., *Die Romanischen Sprachen* (Bern: A. Francke, 1951).

HALL, Robert A., *An External History of the Romance Languages*, (New York: American Elsevier, 1974).

IORDAN, Iorgu, John ORR, and Rebecca POSNER, *Lingüística románica* (Madrid: Alcalá, 1967). Translation and adaptation by Manuel Alvar of the English version published in London in 1937 (itself a translation from the Roumanian). The 2nd English edition was published in Oxford by Blackwell, 1970.

LÜDTKE, Helmut, *Historia del léxico románico* (Madrid: Gredos, 1972)

POSNER, Rebecca, *The Romance Languages* (New York: Anchor Books, 1966).

——, *Consonantal Dissimilation in the Romance Languages* (Oxford: Blackwell, 1961).

ROHLFS, Gerhard, *Romanische Philologie*, 2 vols. (Heidelberg: Winter, 1950-1952).

SAVI-LÓPEZ, Paolo, *Orígenes neolatinos* (Barcelona: Labor 1935; 1st ed. in Italian, 1916).

TAGLIAVINI, C., *Orígenes de las lenguas neolatinas* (Mexico: Fondo de Cultura Económica, 1973). Translation of *Le Origini delle lingue neolatine* (6th ed., Bologna, 1972).

VIDOS, Benedek E., *Manual de lingüística románica* (3rd ed., Madrid: Aguilar, 1973). Translation by F. de B. Moll of the Italian version, *Manuale de linguistica romanica* (1959), which in turn was translated from the Dutch *Handboek tot de Romaanse Taathunde* (1956).

WARTBURG, Walther von, *La fragmentación lingüística de la Romania* (2nd ed., Madrid: Gredos, 1979). Translation of *Die Ausgliederung der romanischen Sprachräume* (1950).

III. GENERAL WORKS ABOUT SPANISH

I. Historical Grammar

GARCÍA DE DIEGO, Vicente, *Gramática histórica española* (2nd ed., Madrid: Gredos, 1970). The first edition was published in Burgos, 1914.

HANSSEN, Friedrich, *Gramática histórica de la lengua castellana* (2nd ed., Buenos Aires: El Ateneo, 1945; 1st ed. Halle, 1913).

LLOYD, Paul, *From Latin to Spanish* (Philadelphia: American Philosophical Society, 1987-). A detailed presentation. Also available in Spanish (1993).

MENÉNDEZ PIDAL, Ramón, *Manual de gramática histórica española* (Madrid:

Espasa Calpe, 1980). The current printing is a photographic reproducción of the 1941 edition. It was originally published in Madrid, 1904, under the title *Manual elemental de gramática histórica española.*

——, *Orígenes del español* (7th ed., Madrid: Espasa-Calpe, 1972; 1st ed. 1926).

METZELTIN, Michael, *Altspanisches Elementarbuch. I. Das Altkastilische* (Heidelberg: Winter, 1979).

PENNY, Ralph, *A History of the Spanish Language* (Cambridge: Cambridge University Press, 1991). A welcome addition. Also available in a Spanish edition (1993).

OTERO, Carlos-Peregrín, *Evolución y revolución en romance*, 2 vols. (Barcelona: Seix Barral, 1971-1976). His new approach answers some old questions.

RESNICK, Melvyn C., *Introducción a la historia de la lengua española* (Washington, D. C.: Georgetown University Press, 1981). A short vademecum of the history of Spanish.

WRIGHT, ROGER, *Early Ibero-Romance* (Newark, DE: Juan de la Cuesta, 1995.

ZAUNER, Adolph, *Altspanisches Elementarbuch* (2nd ed., Heidelberg: Winter, 1921; 1st ed. 1905).

2. History of the Language and General Introductions

ARCELUS ULIBARRENA, Juana Mary, *Introducción a la filología española* (Florence: Valmartina, 1977).

BOLAÑO E LSLA, Amancio, *Manual de historia de la lengua española* (2nd ed., Mexico: Porrúa, 1971; 1st ed. 1959).

CUERVO, R. José, *Disquisiciones sobre filología castellana* prologue and notes by R. Torres Quintero (Bogotá, 1950).

ENTWISTLE, William J., *Las lenguas de España: castellano, catalán, vasco y gallego-portugués* (Madrid: Istmo, 1973; The English edition, *The Spanish Language, together with Portuguese, Catalan, and Basque, was published* in 1936).

LAPESA, Rafael, *Historia de la lengua española* (Madrid: Gredos, 1992, 9th edition; 1st ed., Madrid: Escelicer, 1942). Escelicer had many editions as well.

——, *Einführung in der hispanistische Sprachwissenschaft* (Tübingen: Niemeyer, 1973).

OLIVER ASÍN, Jaime, *Iniciación al estudio de la historia de la lengua española* (3rd ed., Zaragoza, 1939).

POTTIER, Bernard, *Introduction à l'étude de la linguistique de l'espagnol* (2nd ed., Bordeaux, 1978).

QUILIS, A. *Historia de la lengua española I* (Madrid, 1991).

SPAULDING, Robert K., *How Spanish Grew* (Berkeley: University of California Press, 1967). The current edition reproduces the first edition of 1943.

TAVANI, G., *Preistoria e Protostoria delle lingue Ispaniche* (Japadre: L'Aquila, 1968).

TREND, J. B., *The Language and History of Spain* (London, 1953).

3. General Problems

ALONSO, Amado, *Estudios lingüísticos. Temas españoles* (Madrid, Gredos, 1954).

ALONSO, Martín, *Evolución sintáctica del español* (Madrid: Aguilar, 1962).

BADIA I MARGARIT, Antoni, "Por una versión del concepto de «cultismo» en fonética histórica," *Studia Hispanica in Honorem R. Lapesa* (Madrid: Gredos, 1972), 1, 137-52.

BALDINGER, Kurt, *La formación de los dominios lingüísticos en la Península Ibérica* (2nd ed., Madrid: Gredos, 1972; 1st ed. 1963). Translation of *Die Ausgliederung der Sprachräume auf der Pyrenäenhalbinsel* (Berlin, 1958).

BUSTOS TOVAR, J. Jesús de, *Contribución al estudio del cultismo léxico medieval* (Madrid: Anejos del BRAE, 1974).

CASTRO, A., *Glosarios latino-españoles de la Edad Media* (Madrid: RFE, 1936).

CRADDOCK, Jerry, *Latin legacy versus substratum residue. The unstressed "derivational" suffixes in the Romance vernaculars of the Western Mediterranean* (Berkeley, Los Angeles: University of California Press, 1969).

CORRIENTE, F., *A grammatical Sketch of the Spanish Arabic Dialect Bundle* (Madrid: Instituto Hispano-arabe de Cultura, 1977).

GAMILLSCHEG, E., *Romania Germanica*, 3 vols. (Berlin-Leipzig, 1934-1936).

IORDAN, Iorgu, "El lugar del español entre los idiomas romances," *Actas del V Congreso Internacional de Hispanistas* (Bordeaux: Institut d'Études Ibériques, 1977), 49-58.

MENÉNDEZ PIDAL, R., *Cantar de mio Cid. Texto, gramática y vocabulario*, 3 vols. (4th ed, Madrid: Espasa-Calpe, 1964. 1st ed., 1908).

——, "Modo de obrar el substrato lingüístico," *RFH*, 24, (1950) 1-8.

——, *Toponimia prerrománica hispana* (2nd ed., Madrid: Gredos, 1968; 1st ed. 1952).

NEUVONEN, E. K., *Los arabismos del español en el siglo XIII* (Helsinki: Societas Orientalis Fennica, 1941).

SANCHIS GUARNER, M., *Introducción a la historia lingüística de Valencia*

(Valencia, Instituto Alfonso el Magnánimo, 1949).

IV. HISTORICAL PHONETICS

1. General Works

ALONSO, Amado, *De la pronunciación medieval a la moderna en español,* updated by R. Lapesa, 2 vols. (Madrid: Gredos, 1955-1969). Vol I is in a second edition (1976).

ARIZA, MANUEL, *Manual de fonología histórica del español* (Madrid: Síntesis, 1989).

BUSTOS, E. de, *Estudios sobre asimilación y disimilación en el iberorrománico* (Madrid: Anejos de la *RFE*, 1960).

CANFIELD, D. L., *La pronunciación del español en América. Ensayo histórico-descriptivo* (Bogotá: Instituto Caro y Cuervo, 1962).

CUERVO, R. J., "Disquisiciones sobre antigua ortografía y pronunciación castellana," RH, II, 1-69; 5, 237-307, (1895), also in Obras completas, II (Bogotá: Instituto Caro y Cuervo, 1954), 240-476.

DEFERRARI H. A., *The Phonology of Italian, Spanish and French* (Washington, D. C., 1954).

FORD, J. D. M., *The Old Spanish Sibilants* (Boston: Harvard Studies in Philology and Literature, 1900).

FOUCHÉ, Pierre, "Études de Philologie Hispanique," RH, 77, (1929), 1-171.

GAVEL, H., *Essai sur l'évolution de la prononciation du castillan depuis le XIVᵉ siècle* (Paris: Champion, 1920).

GRANDA, G. de, *La estructura silábica y su influencia en la evolución fonética del dominio iberorrománico* (Madrid: Anejos de la *RFE*, 1966).

HARTMAN, Stephen L., *An outline of Spanish historical phonology*, PIL, 7, (1974), 123-92.

IZZO, Herbert, "Pre-Latin Languages and Sound Changes in Romance: The Case of Old Spanish," in *Studies in Romance Linguistics* (Rowley, MA: Newbury House, 1977), pp. 227-53.

KREPINSKY, Maximilian, *Inflexión de las vocales en español* (Madrid: CSIC, 1962).

MACPHERSON, Ian, *Spanish Phonology—Descriptive and Historical* (Manchester: Manchester University Press, 1975)

MALMBERG, B., *Phonétique générale et romane* (The Hague: Mouton, 1971)

MARTINET, André, *Economía de los cambios fonéticos*, (Madrid: Gredos, 1974; 1st ed. in French 1955).

MENÉNDEZ PIDAL, Ramón, *Orígenes del español*, (Madrid: Espasa Calpe, 1950; 1st ed. 1926).

MICHELENA, L., *Fonética histórica vasca* (San Sebastián: Diputación de Guipúzcoa, 1961).

NAVARRO TOMÁS, Tomás, *Manual de pronunciación española* (12th ed., Madrid: CSIC, 1965; 1st ed. Madrid, 1932).

——, *Estudios de fonología española* (Syracuse: Syracuse University Press, 1946).

PENSADO, Carmen, *El orden histórico de los procesos fonológicos*, 1 (Salamanca, 1983).

SCHÜRR, F., "La diptongación ibero-románica," *RDTP*, 7 (1951), 379-90.

STEIGER, A., *Contribución a la fonética del hispano-árabe y de los arabismos en el ibero-románico y el siciliano* (Madrid: Anejos de la RFE, 1932).

TORREBLANCA, Máximo, "Sobre la palatalización de consonantes latinas en español e hispanoromance," *JHP*, 16 (1992 [1993]), 280-327.

——, "Sobre la evolución de sibilantes implosivas en español," *JHP*, 16 (1986 [1987]), 15-73; 223-49.

WRIGHT, Roger, "Linguistic Reasons for Phonetic Archaisms in Romance," in *Papers from the Fourth International Conference on Historical Linguistics*, pp. 331-37, Amsterdam.

2. Specific Studies

ALARCOS LLORACH, Emilio, "Esbozo para una fonología diacrónica del español," *Estudios dedicados a Menéndez Pidal*, 2 (Madrid, CSIC, 1951), 9-39.

——, "Resultados de *g* + *e,i* en la Península," *Archivum* (1954), 330-42.

——, "Quelques précisions sur la diphtongaison espagnole," in *Omagiu lui Iorgu Iordan* (Bucarest: Academia Republicci Populare Romîne, 1958), pp. 1-4.

——, "Efectos de la yod sobre la vocal tónica en español," in *X Congrès International de Linguistique et Philologie Romane* (Strasburg, 1962; Paris: Klincksieck, 1965), pp. 945-50.

——, *Fonología española* (Madrid: Gredos, 1991, 4th ed.; 1st ed. 1950).

ALONSO, Amado, "Substratum, superstratum," *RFH*, 3 (1941), 185-218.

——, "Una ley fonológica del español," *HR*, 13 (1945), 91-101.

——, "Las correspondencias arábigo-españolas en los sistemas de sibilantes," *RFH*, 8 (1946), 12-76.

——, "Trueques de sibilantes en antiguo español," *NRFH*, 1 (1947), 1-12.

——, "Arabe sr > ç, esp. st > ár. ch," *PMLA*, 62 (1947), 325-38. This article was included in *Estudios Lingüísticos. Temas Españoles* (Madrid: Gredos, 1951), pp. 128-50.

——, "Cronología de la igualización c-z en español," *HR*, 19 (1951), 43-61.

——, "Historia del ceceo y del seseo españoles," *Thesaurus*, 7 (1951), 111-200.

ALONSO, Dámaso, "Diptongación castellana y diptongación románica," *ELH*, 1 supl. (1962), 23-45.

⸻, "B - V en la Península Ibérica," *ELH*, 1 supl. (1962), 55-209.

⸻, "Sobre las soluciones peninsulares de los esdrújulos latinos," *ELH*, 1 supl. (1963), 55-59.

BLAYLOCK, Curtis, "The Monophthongization of Latin æ in Spanish," *RPh*, 18 (1964), 16-26.

⸻, "Assimilation of Stops to Preceding Resonants in Ibero-Romance," *RPh*, 19 (1965), 428-34.

⸻, "Latin l-, -ll- in the Hispanic Dialects. Retroflexion and Lenition," *RPh*, 21 (1968), 392-409.

BRÜCH, J., "Die Entwicklung des intervokalen *bl* im Spanischen," *VKR*, 3 (1930), 78-86.

⸻, "L'évolution de l'*l* devant les consonnes en espagnol," *RFE*, 17 (1930), 1-17.

⸻, "Une fois de plus *l* placé devant une consonne," *RFE*, 17 (1930), 414-19.

CASTRO, Américo, "Sobre *tr* y *dr* en español," *RFE*, 7 (1920), 60.

CATALÁN, Diego, "Resultados ápico-palatales y dorso-palatales de -*ll*- y -*nn*-," *RFE*, 38 (1954), 1-44.

⸻, "The End of the Phoneme /z/ in Spanish," *Word*, 13 (1957), 283-322.

⸻, "En torno a la estructura silábica del español de ayer y del español de mañana," in *Homenaje a Harri Meier* (The Hague: Mouton, 1972), 77-110.

CONTINI, G., "Sobre la desaparición de la correlación de sonoridad en castellano," *NRFH*, 5 (1951), 173-82.

CORNU, J., "Études de phonologie espagnole et portugaise. *Grey, ley* et *rey* disyllabes dans Berceo, l'*Apolonio* et l'*Alexandre*," *Romania*, 9 (1886), 71-89.

CORRIENTE, F., Los fonemas /p/, /č/, y /g/ en árabe hispano," *VR*, 37 (1978), 214-18.

CRADDOCK, Jerry, "The Contextual Variants of yod. An Attempt at Systematization," *Festschrift für Jacob Ornstein. Studies in General Linguistics and Sociolinguistics* (Rowley, MA: Newbury House, 1980), pp. 61-68.

DWORKIN, Steven N., "Therapeutic reactions to excessive phonetic erosion. The desdendants of rigidu in Hispano- and Luso-Romance," *RPh*, 27 (1974), 462-72.

⸻, "Derivational Transparency and Sound Change: The Two-Pronged Growth of *ĭdu* in Hispano-Romance," *RPh*, 31 (1978), 605-17.

⸻, "Phonotactic Awkwardness as an Impediment to Sound Change," *ForLing*, 3 (1978), 46-56.

———, "Phonotactic Awkwardness as a cause of lexical blends: the genesis of Sp. cola «tail»," *HR*, 48 (1980), 231-37.

EASTLACK, Ch. L., "The Phonology of 12th century Castilian and its relation to the Phonology of Proto-Romance," *DIL*, 9 (1976), 89124.

FRAGO GARCÍA, J. A., "Nueva contribución a la historia del reajuste fonológico del español moderno," *Cuadernos de Filología*, 2 (Universidad de Valencia, 1979), 53-74.

GARCÍA HERNÁNDEZ, B., "El deslizamiento secuencial de *fui* = *ivi*," *Actas del VI Congreso de Estudios Clásicos*, (Madrid: Gredos, 1983), pp. 331-40.

GONZÁLEZ OLLÉ, F., "La sonorización de las consonantes sordas iniciales en vascuence y en romance y la neutralización de *k-/g-* en español," *Archivum*, 22 (1972), 253-74.

———, "Resultados castellanos de *kw, y ,gw*, latinos. Aspectos fonéticos y fonológicos," *BRAE*, 52 (1972), 285-318.

JORET, C., "Loi des finales en espagnol," *Romania*, 1 (1872), 444-56.

KIDDLE, Lawrence B., "The Chronology of the Spanish Sound Change ʃ > x," *Studies in Honor of Lloyd A. Kasten* (Madison: Hispanic Seminary of Medieval Studies, 1975), pp. 70-71.

LAPESA, Rafael, "La apócope de la vocal en castellano antiguo. Intento de explicación histórica," *Estudios dedicados a Menéndez Pidal*, 2 (Madrid: CSIC, 1952), 185-226.

———, "De nuevo sobre la apócope vocálica en castellano medieval," *NRFH*, 24 (1975), 13-23.

LATHROP, Thomas A. *"Jugar:* Étymologie scabreuse," *Actas del II Congreso Internacional de Historia de la Lengua Española*, I, (Madrid: Pabellón de España, 1992), 1141-44 .

LÁZARO CARRETER, Fernando, "*f* > *h* ¿fenómeno ibérico o romance?, *Actas de la Primera Reunión Toponímica Pirenaica* (Zaragoza, 1949).

LENFEST, Donald, E., "An explanation of the /g/ in *tengo, vengo, pongo, salgo,* and *valgo*," *Hisp*, 61 (1978), 894-904.

———, "*Tengo–Vengo* an Update," *Hisp*, 76 (1993), 634-44)

LLOYD, P. M. and R. D. SCHNITIZER, "A statistical Study of the Structure of the Spanish Syllable," *Linguistics*, 37 (1967), 58-72.

MACPHERSON, Ian R., "Delateralization and Phonetic Change. The Old Spanish Palatals /k/, /tʃ/, [(d)ʒ]," *Studies in Honor of Lloyd A. Kasten* (Madison, 1975), pp. 155-64.

MALKIEL, Yakov, "La f- inicial adventicia en español antiguo," *RLR*, 18 (1955), 161-91.

———, "Towards a unified system of classification of Latin-Spanish vowel correspondences," *RPH*, 16 (1962), 153-62.

———, "The interlocking of narrow sound change, broad phonological pattern, level of transmission, areal configuration and sound symbolism. Diachronic studies in the Hispano-Latin consonant clusters cl-, pl-fl-," *Archivum Linguisticum*, 15 (1963), 144-173; 16 (1964), 1-23.

———, "Sur quelques fausses applications de la Loi de Verner aux faits romans," *Cahiers Ferdinand de Saussure*, 23 (1966), 75-87.

———, "Multiple versus simple causation in linguistic change," *To honor Roman Jakobson*, 2 (The Hague: Mouton, 1967), pp. 1228-46.

———, "The inflectional paradigm as an occasional determinant of sound change," *Directions for historical linguistics. A symposium* (Texas: University of Texas Press, 1968), pp. 216-64.

———, "The five sources of epenthetic /j/ in Western Hispano-Romance: a study in multiple causation," *HR*, 37 (1969), 239-75.

———, "Morphological analogy as a stimulus for sound change," *LeS*, 4 (1969), 305-27.

———, "Derivational transparency as an Occasional Co-Determinant of Sound Change: A New Causal Ingredient in the Distribution of -ç- and -z- in Ancient Hispano-Romance," *RPh*, 25 (1971), 1-52.

———, "Etiological studies in Romance diachronic phonology," *Acta Linguistica Hafniensia*, 14 (1973), 201-42.

———, "In search of penultimate causes of language change: studies in the avoidance of /z/ in Proto-Spanish," *Current Studies in Romance Linguistics* (Washington, DC: Georgetown, 1976), pp. 27-36.

———, "Conflicting prosodic inferences from Ascoli's and Darmesteter's Laws? *RPh*, 28 (1974), 483-520.

———, "The Fluctuation Intensity of a Sound Law: Some Vicissitudes of ě and ŏ in Spanish," *RPh*, 34 (1980), 48-63.

———, "From Falling to Rising Diphthongs. The Case of Old Spanish io > éu," *RPh*, 29 (1975), 435-500.

MARTINET, André, "The unvoicing of Old Spanish sibilants," *RPh*, 5 (1952), 133-156.

MEIER, H., "Español *piar, piada*," Verba, 6 (1979), 25-28.

MEYER-LÜBKE, Wilhelm, "La evolución de *c* latina delante de *e* e *i* en la Península Ibérica," *FRE*, 8 (1921), 225-51.

———, "La sonorización de las sordas intervocálicas latinas en español," *RFE*, 11 (1924), 1-32.

MILLARDET, G., "Sur le traitement de *a*-yod en vieil espagnol," *Romania*, 41 (1912), 247-59.

MONTGOMERY, T., "La apócope en español antiguo y la *i* final latina," *Studia hispanica in honorem R. Lapesa*, 2 (Madrid: Gredos, 1975), 351-62.

MOURIN, L., "À propos de l'évolution du x latin dans la Péninsule Ibérique," *Mélanges de linguistique et de littérature à la mémoire de István Frank*, (Sarrbrücken: Universität des Saarlandes, 1957), pp. 472-79.

NARO, A. J., "On f > h in Castilian and Western Romance," *ZrPh*, 89 (1972), 1-13.

NAVARRO, T., "The Old Aspirated h in Spain and the Spanish of America," *Word*, 5 (1949), 166-69.

NELSON, D. E., "Syncopation in *El Libro de Alexandre*," *PMLA*, 87 (1972), 1023-38.

PENNY, Ralph, "The Convergence of b, v and -p- in the Peninsula: A Reapprisal," *Medieval Hispanic Studies Presented to Rita Hamilton* (London: Tamesis, 1976), pp. 149-59.

———, "The Re-Emergence of /f/ as a Phoneme in Castilian," *ZrPh*, 88 (1972), 463-82.

———, "Secondary Consonant Groups in Castilian," *JHP*, 7 (1983) 135-40.

PIETSCHE, K., "Zur spanischen Grammatik 1. Vom auslautenden unbetonten y," *ZrPh*, 34 (1910), 641-50; 35 (1911), 167-79.

QUILIS, R. J., "Para la cronología de la fricativa velar sorda," *RFE*, 46 (1963), 445-449.

RINI, Joel, "Metathesis of YOD and the Palatalization of Latin Medial k'l, g'l, t'l' k's, ssj, sj,; ky, ult in Hispano- and Luso-Romance," in *Linguistic Studies in medieval Spanish*, eds. Ray Harris-Northall and Thomas D. Cravens, Hispanic Seminary for Medieval Studies, University of Wisconsin, Madison (1991), 109-33.

———, "The Diffusion of -ee- > -e- in Ibero-Romance Romance Infinitives: creer, leer, veer, preveer, proveer, seer, poseer," *NM* 92 (1991), 95-103.

———, "A New Perspective on the Origin of le for les," *JHP*, 12 (1988), 209-19.

———, "Excessive Analogical Change as an Impetus for Lexical Locc: Old Spanish connusco, convusco," *RF* 102 (1990), 58-64.

———, "The Redundant Indirect Object Construcions in Spanish: A New Perspective," *RPh* 45 (1991), 269-86.

———, "On the Evolution of Spanish cigüeña and the Blending of Multiple Variants," forthcoming in *HR*.

———, "On the Evolution of Spanish cigüeña and the Blending of

———, "Syntactic and Pragmatic Factors in the Morphological Reduction of Latin HABEO > Spanish he," Forthcoming in *Neophilologus* (1995).

SÖLL, L., "Der Zusammenfall von b und v und die Variation der stimmhafte Verschlusslaute im Iberoromanischen," *Beiträge zur romanischen Philologie*, 3 (1964), 380-98.

SPAULDING, Robert K., and Patt, Beatrice, "Data for the Chronology of 'theta' and 'jota' ", *HR*, 16 (1948), 50-60.

TILANDER, Gunnar, "L'Évolution du x latin dans la Péninsule Ibérique," *Romania*, 84 (1963), 79-87.

TOVAR, A., "La sonorización y caída de las intervocálicas y los estratos indoeuropeos en Hispania," *BRAE*, 28 (1948), 265-80.

——, "Sobre la cronología de la sonorización y la caída de intervocálicas en la Romania Occidental," *Homenaje a Fritz Krüger* (Mendoza: *AILC*, 1, 1952), pp. 9-15.

WAGNER, M. L., "Etimologías españolas y arábigo hispánicas," *RFE*, 21 (1934), 225-47.

WRIGHT, Roger, "Pretonic Diphtongization in Old Castilian," *VR*, 35 (1976), 133-43.

ZAUNER, A., "Español pujar y soso," *RFE*, 16 (1929), 154-60.

V. MORPHOLGY AND SYNTAX

AEBISCHER, P., *Matériaux médiévaux pour l'étude du suffixe d'origine germanique -ING dans les langues de la Péninsule Ibérique* (Zaragoza: Instituto de Estudios Pirenaicos, 1949).

ALEMANY BOLUFER, J., Tratado de la formación de palabras en la lengua castellana. La derivación y composición. Estudio de los sufijos y prefijos empleados en una y otra (Madrid: Victoriano Suárez, 1920).

ALVAR, Manuel and Bernard POTTIER, *Morfología histórica del español* (Madrid, 1987).

ALGEO, James E., "The concessive conjunction in medieval Spanish and Portuguese; its function and development," *RPh*, 26 (1973), 532-45.

ARKINS, Dorothy M., "A reexamination of the Hispanic Radical Changing Verbs," *Estudios dedicados a Menéndez Pidal*, 5 (Madrid: CSIC, 1954), pp. 39-65.

BADÍA, A., Los complementos pronominalo-adverbiales derivados de *ibi* e *inde* en la Península Ibérica (Madrid: Anejos de la *RFE*, 1947).

BLAYLOCK, Curtis, "The -udo participles in Old Spanish," *Homenaje a Antonio Tovar* (Madrid: Gredos, 1972), pp. 75-79.

——, "Los pretéritos fuertes en -sk- del español medieval," *Studia Hispanica in Honorem R. Lapesa*, 3 (Madrid: Gredos, 197S), 92-96.

BONFANTE, G., "The Latin and Romance Weak Perfect," *Lg*, 17 (1941), 201-11.

BOUZEL, Jean, "Orígenes del empleo de *estar*," *Estudios dedicados a Menéndez Pidal*, 4 (Madrid: CSIC, 1953), 37-58.

CRABB, Daniel M., *A comparative Study of Word Order in Old Spanish and Old French Prose Works*, (Washington D.C.: The Catholic University of America Press, 1955).

DARDEL, Robert de, *Le parfait fort en roman commun* (Geneva, 1958).

————, *Recherches sur le genre roman des substantifs de la troisième déclinaison* (Geneva, Droz, 1965).

D'OVIDIO, F., "I riflessi romanzi di *viginti, triginta, quadraginta, quinquaginta, sexaginta, setp(u)aginta, oct(u)aginta, nonaginta, novaginta*," *ZrPh*, 7 (1884), 82-106.

DWORKIN, Steven N., *Etymology and Derivational Morphology-The Genesis of Old Spanish Denominational Adjectives in -ido* (Tübingen: Niemeyer, 1985)

ENGLAND, John, " 'Dixo Rachel e Vidas': Subject-Verb Agreement in Old Spanish," *MLR*, 71 (1976), 812-26.

ESPINOSA, Aurelio M., Estudios sobre el español de Nuevo Méjico (Buenos Aires: Biblioteca de dialectología hispanoamericana 1, 1930; 2, 1946). Reworking and notes by Amado Alonso y Ángel Rosenblat.

GARCÍA ANTEZANA, Jorge, "Aspectos morfológicos y sintácticos de los verbos "ser" y "estar" en el Libro de Buen Amor," *Actas del I Congreso Internacional sobre El Arcipreste de Hita* (Barcelona, 1973), pp. 237-47.

GASSNER, Armin, *Das altspanischen Verbum* (Halle, 1897).

GEORGES, E. S., "Past-participial nouns: their development from Latin to Romance," *RPh*, 21 (1968), 368-91.

GONZÁLEZ-OLLÉ, F., *Los sufijos diminutivos en el castellano medieval*, (Madrid: Anejos de la *RFE*, 1962).

HAKAMIES, Reino, *Étude sur l'origine et l'évolution du diminutif latin et sa survie dans les langues romanes* (Helsinki: Annales Academiae Scientiarum Fennicae, 1951).

HALL, Robert A., Jr., "Spanish Inflection," *Studies in Linguistics*, 2 (1945), 24-36.

HARRIS, Martin, "The history of the conditional complex from Latin to Spanish; some structural considerations," *ArchL* (1971), 25-33.

HUTTER, H. S., *The development of the function word system from vulgar latin to modern Spanish (Descriptive studies in Spanish grammar)*, (Urbana, 1954).

JENSEN, Frede and LATHROP, Thomas A., *The Syntax of the Old Spanish Subjunctive* (The Hague: Mouton, 1973)

KAHANE, Henry and Renée, "The augmentative feminine in the Romance Languages," *RPh*, 2 (1948-1949), 135 and following.

KURYŁOWICZ, J., "La Conjugaison en *-ir* de l'espagnol," in *Omagiu lui Alexandru Rosetti la 10 de ani* (Bucarest: ARSR, 1965), pp. 357-60.

LAPESA, Rafael, "Los casos latinos: restos sintácticos y sustitutos en español," *BRAE*, 44 (1964), p. 57.

————, "Sobre el artículo ante persona en castellano antiguo," *Sprache und Geschichte. Festschrift für Harri Meier zum 65 Geburtstag*, (Munich, 1971), pp. 277-96.

LATHROP, Thomas A.: See: Frede JENSEN.

LEVY J. F., "Tendential transfer of Old Spanish *hedo* < *fœdu* to the family of *heder* < *fœtere*," *RPh*, 27 (1973), 204-10.

MALER, Bertil, *Synonymes romans de l'interrogatif* QUALIS, *Studia Romanica Holmensia* (1949).

MALKIEL, Yakov, "The suffix *-ago-* in astur-leonese and galician dialects," *Lg*, 19 (1943), 256-58.

——, "The etymology of Sp. *ceneño*," *Studia Philologica*, 45 (1944), 37-49.

——, "The etymology of hispanic *que(i)xar, quejarse*," *Lg*, 21 (1945), 142-83.

——, The derivation of hispanic *fealdad(e), fieldad(e) and fialdad(e)* (Berkeley, Los Angeles: University of California Publications in Linguistics, 1945).

——, "Old Spanish *nadi(e), otri(e)*," *HR*, 13 (1945), 204-30.

——, "Probleme des spanischen Adjektiv-abstraktums," *Neuphilologische Mitteilungen*, 46 (1945), 171-91; 47 (1946), 13-45.

——, "The etymology of hispanic *vel(l)ido* and *melindre*," *Lg*, 22 (1946), 284-316.

——, "The Romance Word-Family of Latin AMBAGO," *Word*, 3 (1947), 59-72.

——, Three Hispanic word studies: Latin *macula* in Ibero-Romance, Old Portuguese *trigar*, Hispanic *lo(u)çano* (Berkeley: University of California Publications in Linguistics, 1947).

——, "The Latin base of the Spanish suffix *-eño*," *AJPh*, 65 (1948), 372-81.

——, Hispanic *alguien* and related formations. A stuy of the stratification of the romance lexicon in the Iberian Peninsula (Berkeley, Los Angeles: UCPL, 1948).

——, "La etimología de *cansino*," *NRPH*, 2 (1948), 186-94.

——, "The etymology of Spanish *maraña*," *BH*, 50 (1948),147-71.

——, "The etymology of Hispanic *restolho, rostoll*" RPh, 1 (1948), 209-34.

——, "Studies in the Hispanic infix *-eg-*," *Lg*, 25 (1949), 139-65.

——, "The contrast *tomáis, - tomávades: queréis - queríades* in Classical Spanish," *HR*, 17 (1949), 159-65.

——, "Los derivados hispánicos de *tepidus*," *Romania*, 74 (1952), 145-76.

——, "Ancient Hispanic *vera(s)* and *mentira(s)*," *RPh*, 6 (1952), 121-72.

——, "Studies in Hispano-Latin homonymics. *Pessulus, pactus, pectus, despectus, suspectus, fistula* in Ibero-Romance," *Lg*, 28 (1952), 299-338.

——, "*Apretar, pr(i)eto, perto*. Historia de un cruce hispanolatino," *Thesaurus*, 9 (1953), 1-135.

——, "A cluster of four homophones in Ibero Romance," *HR*, 21 (1953), 20-36.

212   THE EVOLUTION OF SPANISH

————, *Studies in the reconstruction of Hispano-Latin word families UCPL*, 11 (Berkeley, Los Angeles, 1954).

————, "En torno a la etimología y evolución de `cansar', `canso', `cansancio'" *NRFH*, 9 (1955), 225-76.

————, "Antiguo español y gallego-portugués *troçir*," *NRFH*, 10 (1956), 385-95.

————, "Los interfijos hispánicos, problema de lingüística histórica y estructural," *Miscelánea homenaje a André Martinet*, 2 (La Laguna, 1958), pp. 107-99.

————, "Old Spanish *judezno, morezno, pecadezno*," *PhQ*, 37 (1958), 95-99.

————, "Toward a reconsideration of the Old Spanish Imperfect in -*ía*, -*íe*," *HR*, 27 (1959), 435-81.

————, "Paradigmatic resistance to sound change. The Old Spanish preterite forms *vide, vido*, against the background of the recession of primary -*d*-," *Lg*, 36 (1960), 281-346.

————, "Diphthongization, Monophthongization, Metaphony. Studies in their Interaction in the Paradigm of the Old Spanish -*ir* Verbs," *Lg*, 42 (1965), 430-472.

————, "Le nivellement morphologique comme point de départ d'une «loi phonétique». La monophtongaison occasionnelle de *ie* et *ue* en ancien espagnol," in *Mélanges Frappier*, 2 (Geneva: Droz, 1970), 701-35.

————, "Sound change rooted in morphological conditions: the case of Old Spanish /sk/ changing to /θk/," *RPh*, 23 (1970), 188-200.

————, "The rise of nominal augments in Romance," *RPh*, 26 (1973), 306-34.

————, "New problems in Romance interfixation I: The velar insert in the present tense (with an excursus on -*zer*, -*zir* verbs)," *RPh*, 27 (1974), 304-55.

————, "Multiconditioned sound change and the impact of morphology on phonology," *Lg*, 52 (1976), 757-78.

————, "The interlocking of etymology and historical grammar (exemplified with the analysis of Spanish *desleir*)," in *Current Progress in Historical Linguistics* (Amsterdam: North Holland, 1976), pp. 285-312.

————, "Contacts between *blasphemare* and *æstimare* (with an excursus on the etymology of Hispanic *tomar*)," *RPh*, 30 (1977), 102-17.

————, "Problems in the diachronic differenciation of near homophones," *Lg*, 55 (1979), 1-36.

————, "Points of Abutment of Morphology on Phonology: The Case of Ancient Spanish *esti(e)do* `stood'", *RPh*, 34 (1980), 206-09.

MANCZAK, Witold, "Espagnol classique `tomáis', `queréis', `mais', `tomávades', `queríades'," *Kwartalnik neofilologiszny*, 23 (1976), 1-2.

MARTÍNEZ, F. A., De algunos casos de prefijación en español antiguo," *B.A.*, col. 8 (1958).

MENDELOFF, Henry, *The Evolution of the Conditional Sentence Contrary to Fact in Old Spanish* (Washington, D.C.: Catholic University Press, 1960).

MENÉNDEZ, Pidal, Ramón, "Sufijos átonos en español medieval," *Bausteine zur romanischen Philologie. Festgabe für A. Mussafia* (Halle: Niemeyer, 1905), pp. 386-400.

MONTGOMERY, Thomas, "On the development of Spanish *y* from *et*," *Romance Notes*, 8 (1966), 137-42.

——, "On the verb system of *Biblia Escurialense 6*," *HR*, 36 (1967), 129-40.

——, "Complementarity of stem vowels in the Spanish second and third conjugations," *RPh*, 29 (1976), 281-96.

NEIRA MARTINEZ, J., "Las alternancias acentuales de los verbos en *-iar*," *Archivum*, 23 (1973), 135-47.

NELSON, D. E., "The domain of the O.Sp. *-er* and *-ir* verbs: a clue to the provenience of the *Alexandre*," *RPh*, 26 (1973), 265-305.

PATTISON, David G., "The Latin Suffix *-aticu* in Early Old Spanish," *VR*, 32 (1973), 60-65.

——, *Early Spanish Suffixes* (Oxford: Blackwell, 1975).

PENNY, Ralph, "Verb-Class as a Determiner of Stem-Vowel in the Historical Morphology of Spanish Verbs," *RLiR*, 36 (1972), 343-59.

PÉREZ TORAL, M., *Sintaxis histórica funcional del español* (Madrid, 1992).

POSNER, Rebecca, "Romance imperfect and conditional endings: a further contribution," *StN*, 37 (1965), 3-10.

RAMSDEN, H., Weak-pronoun position in the early romance languages (Manchester: Manchester University Press, 1963).

RINI, Joel, *Motives for Linguistic Change in the Formation of the Spanish Object Pronouns* (Newark, Delaware: Juan de la Cuesta, 1992).

ROSSI, Teresa María, "Formas de futuro en un romanceamiento bíblico del s. XIII," *ZFR*, 91 (1975), 386-402.

STAAFF, Erik., *Les pronoms abrégés en espagnol* (Uppsala, 1906).

TOGEBY, KNUD, "Les désinences de l'imparfait (et du parfait) dans les langues romanes," *StN*, 36 (1964), 3-8.

——, "L'Apophonie des verbes espagnols et portugais en *-ir*," *RPh*, 26 (1973), 256-64.

WAGNER, M. L., "Iberoromanische Suffixstudien," *ZrPh*, 44 (1944), 321-37.

WALSH, John K., "The hispano-oriental derivational suffix *-i*," *RPh*, 25 (1971), 159-72.

VI. MANUALS OF DIALECTOLOGY

As a fundamental bibliography of dialectology, you can use: ALVAR, M., *Dialectología española* (Madrid: CSIC, 1962).

ALVAR, Manuel, *El dialecto aragonés* (Madrid: Gredos, 1953).
——, *El dialecto riojano* (Madrid: Gredos, 1976).
GARCÍA DE DIEGO, Vicente, *Manual de dialectología española* (2nd ed., Madrid: Cultura Hispánica, 1959).
LOPE BLANCH, Juan M., *El español de América* (Madrid: Alcalá, 1968).
MENÉNDEZ, PIDAL, Ramón., *El dialecto leonés* (Oviedo: Instituto de Estudios Asturianos, 1961; 1st ed., 1906, *Revista de Archivos, Bibliotecas y Museos*).
STAAFF, ERIK, *Étude sur l'ancien dialecte léonais*, (Uppsala: Almqvist & Wiksell, 1907).
ZAMORA VICENTE, A., *Dialectología española* (Madrid: Gredos, 1967.

VI. ETYMOLOGICAL DICTIONARIES

COROMINAS, J., *Breve diccionario etimológico de la lengua castellana* (Madrid: Gredos, 1961). It is now in the fifth printing of the third edition (1990).
——, *Diccionario crítico etimológico de la lengua castellana* (Bern, 1954, 4 volumes).
—— and J. A. PASCUAL, *Diccionario crítico-etimológico castellano e hispánico* (Madrid: Gredos, 1991, 6 volumes).
GARCÍA DE DIEGO, Vicente, *Diccionario etimológico español e hispánico* (Madrid: SAETA, 1955).
MEYER-LÜBKE, Wilhelm, *Romanisches etymologisches Wörterbuch* (Heidelberg: Winter, 1972; 1st ed. 1911).

VIII. LINGUISTIC COMMENTARIES AND TEXTS

ALARCOS LLORACH, E., C. HERNÁNDEZ, F. MARCOS MARÍN, *Comentarios lingüísticos de textos*, I (Valladolid: Universidad de Valladolid, 1979).
ALVAR, M., *et al.*, *El comentario de textos*, 4. *La poesía medieval* (Madrid: Castalia, 1983).
ARIZA VIGUERA, M., J. GARRIDO MEDINA, G. TORRES NEBRERA, *Comentario lingüístico y literario de textos españoles* (Madrid: Alhambra, 1981).
MARCOS MARÍN, F., *El comentario lingüístico* (Madrid: Cátedra, 1977).
——, *Comentarios de lengua española* (Madrid: Alhambra, 1983).

IX. ANTHOLOGIES AND TEXTS

ALVAR, M., *Textos hispánicos dialectales*, 2 vols. (Madrid: CSIC, 1960).
GIFFORD, D. J., and F. W. HODCROFT, *Textos lingüísticos del medioeoo español* (Oxford, 1959).
GONZÁLEZ-OLLÉ, F., *Lengua y literatura españolas medievales. Textos y*

glosarios (Barcelona: Ariel, 1993, 2nd edition).

MENÉNDEZ PIDAL, Ramón, *Crestomatía del español medieval*, 2 tomos (Madrid, 1965-1966) (finished and revised by Rafael Lapesa y M. Soledad de Andrés).

X. BIBLIOGRAPHIES

BIALIK HUBERMAN, Gisela, *Mil obras de lingüística española e hispano-americana: Un ensayo de síntesis crítica* (Madrid: Playor, 1973).

CATALÁN, Diego, *Lingüística Ibero-Románica* (Madrid: Gredos, 1974). A history of Hispanic linguistics which can be used profitably as a bibiography.

FOULCHÉ-DELBOSC, R., y Barrau-Dihigo, L., *Manuel de l'Hispanisant*, 2 vols. (New York, 1920-1925).

ROHLFS, G., *Manual de filología hispánica* (Bogotá: Caro y Cuervo, 1957).

SERÍS, Homero, *Bibliografía de la lingüística española* (Bogotá: Caro y Cuervo, 1964). More than 7500 articles. Very detailed and useful indices.

WOODBRIDGE, Hensley C., and Paul R. OLSON, *A Tentative Bibliography of Hispanic Linguistics* (Urbana, 1952).

In addition to the above, certain journals regularly publish bibliographies, particularly *PMLA* and *Zeitschrift für Romanische Philologie. The Year's Work in Modern Language Studies* published by The Modern Humanities Research Association is also useful. The latest edition of Lapesa's *Historia de la lengua* has an extensive bibliography as well. Particular mention is due the *Bibliographie lingustique de l'année*, published by Walter de Gruyter in The Hague.

Finally, there is an on-line bibliography of Hispanic Linguistics compiled by Milton Azevedo, Jerry R. Craddock, and Charles B. Faulhaber of the University of California, Berkeley. This is the best, most up-to-date way possible of maintaining a bibliography. Information about using it can be obtained by getting in touch with Jerry Craddock at the Department of Spanish and Portuguese of that University.

Word Index

All Spanish examples seen in the text are listed below with the exception of verb forms and nouns listed in conjugation and declension models, unless there is something otherwise noteworthy about these examples.

Numbers following the listings refer to sections, and not pages. An italicized n following a section number refers to the footnote corresponding to that section

NOTE: Spanish alphabetization now matches English alphabetization rules except that ñ entries follow n entries.

rey 95d, 140b, 152d
rezo 126c
ribera 88, 124a
riega 171b
rienda 98, 102, 151b
río 128b
risueño 109
robar 91
roble 102, 149a
roer 129a
rogar 130b
rojo 132d
romance 68
roto 60, 85, 204
royo 137b
rueda 113, 125a
ruido 113
rumor 95a

S

sábana 102
sábado 156b
saber 51a, 124a, 169b
saco 132a
sacudir 51b
saeta 132c
sagrado 126a
sal [salir] 95b, 186b
sal [salt] 95ab
sale 95b
saldré 150c
salgo 177b
salido 60
salud 95a
salvaje 157b
sangre 82, 102, 149a
santiguar 151c
santo 15e
saña 32
sauce 145
sauco 128b
se [i. o. pron.] 43, 168d

sé [saber] 182
sé [ser] 186d
sea 138a, 185a
seca 132a
sed 95a, 119a, 125a
seda 4, 80a, 125a
seis 148a
segar 126a
seguir 13b, 169c
según 206a
segundo 167
seguro 89, 126a, 160a
seis 166a
seiscientos 166d
sembrar 119a, 149b
senda 98, 150b
sendero 99a
sendos 142bn
sentido 60
sentir 169c, 175b
seña 28b, 140b
señero 142bn
señor 140a
señora 153a
sepa 109, 124b
séptimo 167
ser 129a, 169b
serie 154
serpiente 29a
servil 16
servir 169c, 175b
sesenta 166c
seso 119a
setecientos 166d
setenta 166c
sexto 167
si 207a
sí [yes] 147a
si [pron] 43
siella [OSp] 81bii
siempre 148a, 164, 171b
siendo 188

virtud 95a
visto 60, 204
vivir 128a, 169c
vo [OSp.] 179, 180b
vos [OSp] 168a
vosotros 41, 168a
voy 180b
voz 126c
vuestra merced 168a
vuestro 165b

Y

y 207a
ya 118a, 164, 205b
yace 118a
yacer 118a, 168d
Yagüe 118a
yazgo 187c
yegua 81a
yente [OSp.] 117cn
yerma 102
yermo 81a
yerno 117, 151b
yo 156a, 168

General Index

Numbers following entries refer to sections.

Glossary—Spanish–English

There are doubtless many Spanish words that you are not familiar with in the text (**ábrego, lirón**). We include this glossary so you won't have to use your dictionary to learn what these less common words mean. Old Spanish words are also defined (**caloña, orebze**).

abeja bee
abogado lawyer
aborrecer to hate
ábrego south-west wind
abrigo overcoat
abuelo grandfather
aburrir to bore
Adán Adam
adormecer to make sleepy
agudo sharp
agüero omen
águila eagle
aguzar to sharpen
ajeno someone else's
ajo garlic
alimaña pest
aliviar to relieve
alma soul
altiplanicie high plateau
amanecer to break day
amenaza menace
apaciguar to pacify
araña spider
árbol tree
arce maple
arder to burn
argüir to argue
arrojar to throw

arroyo stream
artejo knuckle
asa handle
asaz quite (O.Sp.)
azufre sulphur

barbecho fallow,
barrer to sweep
bastón cane
basura garbage
Belén Bethlehem
beodo drunk
berza cabbage
beso kiss
bizcocho biscuit
bledo blite
boca mouth
boda wedding
bondad goodness
buey ox
buitre vulture

cabalgar to ride a horse
cabezo summit
cabildo chapter house
cabo corporal, cape (geog.)
cabra goat
cadena chain

cadera hip
caldero cauldron
caldo broth
callar to remain silent
caloña untruth (O.Sp.)
candado padlock
caña cane
capellán chaplain
caramillo pipe (mus.)
cárcel jail
carecer to lack
caridad charity
caudal abundance
cavar to dig
cebo animal feed
cebolla onion
cedo soon (O.Sp.)
ceja eyebrow
ceñir to gird
cepo trap, pillory
cercar to surround
cereza cherry
certidumbre certainty
césped lawn
chinche bug
ciego blind
ciervo deer
cigüena stork
cincho belt
cirio wax candle
clave key (to test)
cocer to boil
codicia greed
codo elbow
cojo lame
col cabbage
colgar to hang
collazo farmhand
complacer to please
comulgar to take communion
concebir to conceive
concha shell

conde count
condestable constable
conejo rabbit
consejo advice
conviene it is suitable
copa drinking glass
coraza cuirass
corlar to put gold varish on
corona crown
correa strap
cortés courteous
corteza bark (of tree)
coto (hunting) preserve
coz horse's kick
crecer to grow
crudo raw
cruz cross
cuajo clotting
cuchara spoon
cuchillo knife
cuelga it hangs
cuello neck
cuerno horn
cuero leather
cuervo crow
cueva cave
cuévano basket
cuidar to take care
cumbre summit
cuna cradle
cuña wedge
cupe I fit in [past]
cursi pretentious

dañar to damage
daño damage
dedo finger
deducir to deduce
delgado thin
despecho spite
deuda debt
diezmo tithe

diluir to dilute
disminuir to diminish
doblar to fold
ducho expert
dueño owner
dureza hardness
duro hard

echar to throw
eje crux
embellecer to beautify
embestir to attack
emblanquecer to make white
encía gum (in mouth)
encina Holm oak tree
ende there (O.Sp.)
engendrar to engender
enjambre swarm of bees
enjuto dry
envejecer to grow old
era threshing room floor
erguir to erect
escudo shield
espalda shoulder
espárrago asparagus
espejo mirror
espiga ear (bot.)
espítiru spirit
esponja sponge
esposo husband
estaño tin
estiércol manure
estío summer
estrecho narrow
estrella star

fe faith
feligrés parishioner
fiel faithful
fiero fierce
fleco fringe, bangs
fragua forge

fregar to wash dishes
freno brake
frente forehead
fresno ash tree
frito fried
fuelle bellows
fuera outside

galgo greyhound
gallo rooster
gato cat
gestiones measures
gota drop (of water)
gozo joy
grado degree
graso fatty
grey flock
griego Greek
gruñir to grunt

haba lima bean
hada fairy
harén harem
hastío boredom
haz bundle (**fasce**), face (**facie**)
helar to freeze
hembra female of the species
henchir to fill
herir to wound
hervir to boil
hiedra ivy
hielo ice
hierro iron
hígado liver
higo fig
hilo thread
hiniesta genista
hinojo knee
hito bull's eye
hocino trowel
hogaño this year
hogar home

hoja leaf
holgar to rest
holgazán loafer
hongo mushroom
hormazo heap of stones
hormiga ant
hornazo Easter cake
hostal pension hotel
hoya ditch
hoz scythe (**falce**), ravine
hube I had (**haber**)
huebos necessary (O.Sp.)
huérfano orphan
hueso bone
huir to flee
humildad humility
humo smoke

infante,-a prince(ss)
ingle groin

jabón soap
jamás never, ever
jeringa syringe
jibia cuttle fish
judío Jew(ish)
juez judge
jugo juice
junto together
jura [someone] swears
juzgar to judge

labrar to work metals, carve, cut, plow
lago lake
landre glandular tumor
latir to beat (as a heart)
laude tombstone
leal loyal
lecho cot
lechuga lettuce
lego lay (not ecclesiastic)

legumbre vegetable
lejía bleach
lenteja lentil
leño friewood
leudo leavened
lenzuelo rustic tarpaulin
librar to free
lid combat
lidiar to fight
liebre hare
linde boundary
lirón dormouse
liviano slight
llaga wound
llama flame
llano plain
llave key
llorar to cry
loa [someone] praises
loar to praise
lobo wolf
lograr to succeed
lomo back (of animal)
luce it shines
lucir to shine
lumbrar to illuminate

macho male of species
madeja skein
madera wood
madrugar to get up early
madurar to ripen
magro meager
mancha spot
manga sleeve
mansedumbre meekness
margen margin
mariachi Mexican musician
mármol marble
martillo hammer
mascar to chew

Matusalén Methusaleh
maza mace
mecer to rock
menudo small
meollo marrow
merecer to deserve
mermar to decrease
mezclar to mix
miel honey
milagro miracle
moneda coin
monte mount(ain)
montés wild
moro Moor
mosca fly
muchedumbre crowd
mudar to change
mudo mute
muela molar
muelle pier
muro wall
muslo thigh

negrecer to make black
nido nest
niebla fog
nieta granddaughter
nodrir to nourish
nombrar to name
novio fiancé
nublar to cloud over
nuera daughter-in-law
nuez walnut
ñu wildebeest

obedecer to obey
obstruir to obstruct
oca goose
oloroso sweet smelling
orebze (O.Sp.) goldsmith
oreja ear
osar to dare

oso bear
oscurecer to become dark
otero knoll
otoño autumn
ove O.Sp. for **hube**

pacer to graze
padecer to suffer
paja straw
palo stick
paño cloth
pared wall
pastor shepherd
paz peace
pecar to sin
pecho bosom
peine comb
pelliza pelisse
pelo hair
pera pear
perdiz partridge
perecer to perish
pescar to fish
pez fish
pezuña cloven foot
piel skin, fur
piélago high sea
pierna leg
piezgo wineskin
pino pine tree
piñón pine nut
plazo time limit
podre pus
popa stern (of ship)
portazgo toll
posar to alight (as a bird)
poyo stone bench
pozo well (water, etc.)
prado meadow
pregón public announcement
presto prompt

prisión prison
probar to prove
provecho benefit
puebla it populates
puente bridge
punto point
puño fist
pureza purity
quebrar to break

quepo I fit in [present]
queso cheese

rábano radish
rabia rabies
rabo tail
ramo branch
raudo swift
recejo suspicion
recio vigorous
recobrar to recover
red net
redondo round
regir to govern
reír to laugh
reja grating
revés wrong side (of cloth)
rey king
rezo I pray
ribera bank of river
riega (someone) waters
rienda rein
risueño smiling
roble oak tree
roer ro gnaw
rogar to beg
roto broken
royo red
rueda wheel
ruido noise

sábana sheet
saco bag
saeta arrow
sagrado sacred
sal salt
salud health
sangre blood
santiguar(se) to cross oneself
sauco elder (bush)
seco dry
seda silk
segar to reap
según according to
sello stamp
sembrar to sow
senda path
sendos one each
seno bosom
seña signal
señero unique
servil servile
seso brain
iglo century
so under (O.Sp.)
soberbia pride (sin)
sol sun
soldar to solder
sollar to blow
sonar to sound
sope O.Sp. for **supe**
sospecha suspicion
soto grove
subir to go up
sucio dirty
sudar to sweat
sueldo salary
suegra mother-in-law
sueño dream, sleep
sufrir to suffer
superficie surface
suso above (O.Sp.)

tabla plank
techo roof
teja tile**tejo** disk
tejón badger
tela cloth
temblar to tremble
temer to fear
teñir to dye
tesoro treasure
tibio tepid
tierno tender
tierra earth
tijera scissors
tildar to put an accent on
tinieblas darkness
tizón half-burned stick
topo mole
tórax thorax
torcer to twist
toro bull
torre tower
tórtola turtle dove
tos cough
tose [someone] coughs
traidor traitor
trapo rag
través bias (cloth)
trébol clover

tribu tribe
trigo wheat
troncho stalk
trucha trout
turbio muddy, cloudy
uña fingernail
vacío empty

vado ford (of a river)
vajilla dishes
val valley
vecino neighbor
veda (someone) prohibits
vega fertile plain
vello soft body hair
venga [someone] avenges
vergüenza shame
veta vein
vid grapevine
vil vile
viña vineyard
viuda widow

yacer to lie (in death)
yegua mare
yermo barren land
yerno son-in-law